Afro Central Americans in New York City

UNIVERSITY PRESS OF FLORIDA

Florida A&M University, Tallahassee
Florida Atlantic University, Boca Raton
Florida Gulf Coast University, Ft. Myers
Florida International University, Miami
Florida State University, Tallahassee
New College of Florida, Sarasota
University of Central Florida, Orlando
University of Florida, Gainesville
University of North Florida, Jacksonville
University of South Florida, Tampa
University of West Florida, Pensacola

Afro Central Americans
in New York City

Garifuna Tales of Transnational Movements in Racialized Space

Sarah England

University Press of Florida

Gainesville · Tallahassee · Tampa · Boca Raton

Pensacola · Orlando · Miami · Jacksonville · Ft. Myers · Sarasota

Publication of this paperback edition made possible by a Sustaining the Humanities through the American Rescue Plan grant from the National Endowment for the Humanities.

First cloth printing, 2006
First paperback printing, 2023

28 27 26 25 24 23   6 5 4 3 2 1

A record of cataloging-in-publication data is available from
the Library of Congress.
ISBN 978-0-8130-2988-7 (cloth)
ISBN 978-0-8130-8014-7 (pbk.)

The University Press of Florida is the scholarly publishing agency for the State University System of Florida, comprising Florida A&M University, Florida Atlantic University, Florida Gulf Coast University, Florida International University, Florida State University, New College of Florida, University of Central Florida, University of Florida, University of North Florida, University of South Florida, and University of West Florida.

University Press of Florida
2046 NE Waldo Road
Suite 2100
Gainesville, FL 32609
http://upress.ufl.edu

For Lombardo Lacayo, a true *hijo del pueblo*. May he rest in peace.

Contents

Illustrations

Tables

Preface

The two main theoretical subjects of this book, transnational migration and ethnic social movements, have become very popular in the social sciences in the time since this research was conducted. Both processes are seen as ways that nation-states and nationalisms are being challenged and reworked politically and ideologically through redefinitions of citizenship, human rights, and national belonging. They have been celebrated as ways some of the more marginalized peoples in the world have become agents in international relations—by traveling across borders, forming international organizations, and creating new transnational identities and arenas of political action. Yet this agency is still uneven and in many ways constrained by the international division of labor and the ideological constructions of race and nationalism.

In this book I examine these two aspects of transnationalism in my attempt to unravel the story of one such people, the Garifuna, who are involved in both types of movements—transnational migration and transnational grassroots organizing. The Garifuna are an Afro Indigenous people born out of the mixture of Africans and Caribs on the island of St. Vincent, exiled to Central America, and turned transnational migrants to the United States since the 1940s. They are thus members of three diasporas—the African diaspora, the Garifuna diaspora, and the Central American diaspora. They are simultaneously black, indigenous, and Latino; Honduran, Belizean, Guatemalan, Nicaraguan, and North American; part of Central America and part of the Caribbean. As an ethnic group they share a common language, history, and culture that unites them across national borders. Yet they also find themselves in many different nation-states with different ideologies and systems of race, class, and gender that structure those societies and the place of Garifuna in them in multiple ways. Like many other immigrant groups in the United States and ethnic groups in Latin America, the Garifuna are engaged in struggles for rights to full political, economic, and social participation in the countries where they reside. In Central America, this struggle is particularly acute where Garifuna villages and agricultural lands are threatened by the encroachment of agribusiness and tourism and where blackness has made Garifuna the objects of overt and covert forms of discrimination. In response, Garifuna have created a number of organizations in both Central America and the United States with the purpose of trying to bring economic, political, and social empowerment to Garifuna communities.

This book explores the ways in which the experiences of transnational migration affect the social movements of the Garifuna in both Central America and New York City. I do this through a detailed discussion of the family relations, community dynamics, economic practices, history, and grassroots organizing of one particular Garifuna transnational community with members traveling between and living in Limón, Honduras, and New York City. I tell the story of how Limón became a center of Garifuna organizing in the 1990s when some members of the community challenged the practices of a Honduran *terrateniente* (large landowner) and the National Agrarian Institute though the formation of an agricultural cooperative and ethnic social movement called El Movimiento Negro Iseri Lidawamari (Black Movement New Dawn). Though the cooperative was mainly manned by local Limoneños, its scope of action and alliances were both national (with other Garifuna organizations, indigenous organizations, and some sections of the Honduran state) and transnational (with Limoneño hometown associations in New York, pan-indigenous, and pan–Afro Latino organizations throughout the Americas). I show how Limoneños in both Honduras and New York participated in these movements but also had different ideas about how they should be carried out and what their goals should be. I argue that this difference of opinion partially stems from the fact that they are negotiating several different race and class systems simultaneously, such that their ideas about upward mobility, community development, and racial/ethnic identity are more complex than if they were taking place in one national context. This ethnography of Limón–New York thus provides a window through which to examine the microdynamics of transnational migration—what propels it, what sustains it, how cultural ideologies and social structures are transnationalized—and the ways the macrodynamics of the global system—the international division of labor, ideologies and practices of international aid organizations and NGOs, and the politics of racial, ethnic, and national identities—play themselves out in shaping the experiences and social action of Garifuna in the United States and Central America.

Acknowledgments

As is always the case, this book would not have been possible without the help and support of many people. Most important, I would like to thank the many Limoneños who let me into their homes; shared their experiences, opinions, and family histories with me; tolerated my questions; and allowed me to get a glimpse into their world. Without their cooperation, insight, and hospitality I could not have collected the rich amount of information that I did. Thanks especially to Johnny, Janeth, Yoya, and Delca, who gave me a place to stay and many a delicious meal. Bernardo Guerrero was absolutely pivotal for this project as he carried me all over Honduras and New York City, introducing me to family, friends, and organizations. It was with him that I experienced everything from fishing in the sea in a dugout canoe, making cassava bread, and dancing *punta* at a wake to negotiating the New York City subway and organizing a hometown association event in a South Bronx social club. His dedication to the struggle of the Garifuna was a source of inspiration, and he continues to act always with the community in mind, establishing libraries, organizing young people, and educating people like myself about the Garifuna and their situation. Lombardo Lacayo and Teofilo Lacayo were also invaluable as sources of information on Garifuna history and were, as are so many people anthropologists encounter, extremely insightful, able to clearly articulate their own philosophies of life and struggle and reflect those of others. I spent many hours talking with them, sharing ideas and perspectives about the Garifuna, Honduras, the United States and the world. Celso Castro was also a great support in New York City, providing contacts and analysis, and, just as important, letting me see the green grass of New Jersey every once in awhile, a welcome break from the concrete of the Bronx. I would also like to thank Domingo Martinez, Elda Martinez, Guillermo Manaiza, Tito and Tita Valentin, and Felicia Lacayo, who not only carried me to meeting after meeting of different organizations but were also there to just chat, relax, and provide companionship. Horacio Martinez of OFRANEH, Celio Alvarez Casildo of ODECO, and Walter Krochmal of FEDOHNY were also invaluable in giving me access to the documents and resources of their offices and insight into the inner workings of Garifuna organizations.

Inspiration and guidance for this project came from the faculty and students at UC Davis, where the camaraderie, intellectual stimulation, and mutual support made the many years of research and writing that went into this project a wonderful experience. I benefited immensely from the support and guidance of all three of my dissertation committee members, who were always pushing me to explore new avenues of thinking about race, social movements, and migration and to connect social theory to social activism. Charlie Hale guided me in the formulation of this project and continued to give me advice and support even from a distance. Carol Smith and Luis Guarnizo were always there to read drafts, provide contacts, give advice, and work through difficult issues. I also benefited from advice and classes with Roger Rouse, Suzanna Sawyer, Stefano Varese, and Philippe Bourgois. Many friends and colleagues also read portions of the manuscript and served as sounding boards for ideas and difficult issues. I benefited from the comments and ideas of Mimi Saunders, Jennifer Bickham-Mendez, Circe Sturm, Kathy Dill, Shannon Speed, Holly Ober, and Alex Greene, who struggled alongside me with their research and writing. A special thanks to Mark Anderson, who helped me clarify many issues about race and identity in Honduras and who has always been willing to share ideas, insights, and data from his own research. Pierre Beaucage, who did research in Limón in the 1960s, also helped me immensely by providing me with publications and data from that research. His work provided much-needed historical background and microlevel analysis of the community.

Another key to the completion of this book was the financial support I received from the Research Institute for the Study of Man, the Inter-American Foundation, the Social Science Research Council, and the University of California Regents Dissertation Writing Fellowship. I want to thank the people at these institutions for recognizing the merit of this project, having the confidence in me to carry it out successfully, and helping me achieve that both financially and logistically. The Inter-American Foundation was especially helpful, not only financially but also through the many seminars they organized in which fellows were able to think through and test the waters of their thinking with others.

Finally, I want to thank my parents for grooming me for this project from my first trip to Mexico at age 12 and for all the Latin American films they made me watch while they were students at UT Austin. Thanks to Maria for introducing me to Latin America, Spanish, and a love of talking to people. And thanks to my father, Nelson, for his careful readings of this manuscript, his editorial advice, and the many hours he spent discussing social theory with me. I also want to thank my husband for supporting me throughout this project with babysitting time and understanding when I needed to disappear for hours to meet a deadline. Thanks to Randy, who spent some of his first year in the field and who gave me an excuse to initiate many a conversation. I hope that this book will provide him with a permanent link to Honduras and Limón.

Abbreviations

AGROINVASA	Agroindustrial Vallecito, SA
BENIC	Belizean National Indigenous Peoples Council
CABO	Central American Black Organization
CAHDEA	Consejo Asesor Hondureño para el Desarrollo de las Etnias Autóctonas
CODEH	Comité para los Derechos Humanos de Honduras
CONPAH	Confederación de Pueblos Autóctonos de Honduras
FEDOHNY	Federación de Organizaciones Hondureños de Nueva York
FHIS	Fondo Hondureño de Inversion Social
IIRIRA	Illegal Immigration Reform and Immigrant Responsibility Act
ILO	International Labour Organization
INA	Instituto Nacional Agrario
INS	Immigration and Naturalization Service
IRCA	Immigration Reform and Control Act
OAA	Organization of Africans in the Americas
ODECO	Organización de Desarrollo Etnico Comunitario
OFRANEH	Organización Fraternal Negra Hondureña
ONEGUA	Organización Negra de Guatemala
UNCUGA	Unificación Cultural Garifuna

1

Transnational Movements, Racialized Space

Don Miguel is a man in his fifties who lives with his family on the tenth floor of a housing project in the South Bronx. He first arrived in New York from his native Honduras in the 1970s. For eight years he lived in an apartment with fellow Hondurans in Central Harlem and worked several jobs in order to save enough money to bring his wife and four children to join him. Today, after more than twenty years in New York City, Don Miguel works as a doorman in one of the apartment buildings of a wealthier New York neighborhood. His wife, like many women from Honduras, also works in one of these apartment buildings as a home attendant, taking care of the elderly and the infirm. Both are able to work their full twelve-hour shifts now because all four of their children, having been brought to the United States at an age young enough to go through the U.S. educational system, are now in college and are supporting themselves with jobs, though they all still live at home. The three-bedroom project apartment also occasionally houses aunts, cousins, and other relatives newly arrived from Honduras until they are able to find employment and get oriented to the city.

As Don Miguel walks to the subway station to travel to work, his physical appearance would indicate to many that he is an African American rather than Central American. If he speaks to anyone on the way, however, his Spanish accent might identify him as an Afro Dominican or Afro Puerto Rican or maybe even an Afro Honduran, if the listener is tuned in enough to variations in accent. If he is walking and talking with someone else from his natal village, however, a passerby might believe that he is from Africa. This is because he will most likely be speaking in Garifuna, the language that was created by his ancestors over 400 years ago on the island of St. Vincent when African maroons mixed with Island Carib to form the ethnic group to which Don Miguel belongs: the Garifuna (also known as the Black Carib). In 1797, the British exiled the Garifuna from St. Vincent to the Caribbean coast of Central America, where the survivors of the passage established villages along the coasts of Belize, Guatemala, Honduras, and Nicaragua. There they fished, grew cassava, worked on banana plantations, and used their skill as sailors to trade up and down the coast, living an existence that was culturally and socially tied more to the Caribbean than to the interior until the Central American states began to push for national economic and social integration in the 1950s. In the 1940s, Garifuna men began working as U.S. merchant marines, eventually settling in port cities of the U.S. south as well as San Francisco and New York City. Women began to migrate in the 1960s to work as nannies and home attendants, often bringing children and other family members with them. Over the decades, immigration has increased to the point that it has become an integral part of Garifuna society, serving as a rite of passage for many and an economic necessity for most, linking cities such as New York and Los Angeles with villages in Honduras, Belize, and Guatemala through kinship ties, economic transactions, and community organizations (map 1.1). It was in one of these coastal Central American villages—Limón, Honduras—that Miguel, his wife, and his four children were born.

Though Don Miguel has lived in New York City for over twenty years, he and his wife are currently using all of their savings to build a house in Limón. Indeed, Don Miguel tries to travel back to his village at least once a year to visit relatives, see about his property there, and participate in family and community rituals. He will take with him one huge suitcase filled with clothes, electronics, shoes, and other gifts for his relatives and will return with beans, cheese, cassava bread, medicinal herbs, and other items that will sustain his culinary connection to Honduras for another year. While he is there he might go fishing in one of the mahogany dugout canoes that many Garifuna men still fish in; he might attend a ninth-night wake complete with rum-drinking, drumming, and *punta* dancing; and he might consult a *buyei* (shaman) about a sickness or bad dream he has had. His wife might join a group of women making *ereba* (cassava bread) from the cassava root that they have grown in their gardens upriver from the village; she might join a *parranda* dance group that travels from house to house during the Christmas season, singing and dancing; or she might spend the days making coconut oil, cassava starch, and other food items that she will take back to New York. On the other hand, they might spend their time watching Cinemax from the satellite dish they have set up on their house, hire local women to do chores for them while they go to the beach, and stock up on American food items at the city supermarket for their largely New York–raised children.

As they approach retirement age, Don Miguel and his wife look forward to finally moving back to Limón for good to live in their new house, a house he could never have afforded to build or buy in the United States, where they will mainly get by on their retirement and Social Security checks and perhaps the income from a small business such as a restaurant or store. He, like many other Garifuna transmigrants that I talked to, told me that though he had to work hard in New York, endure cold winters, live in impoverished neighborhoods,

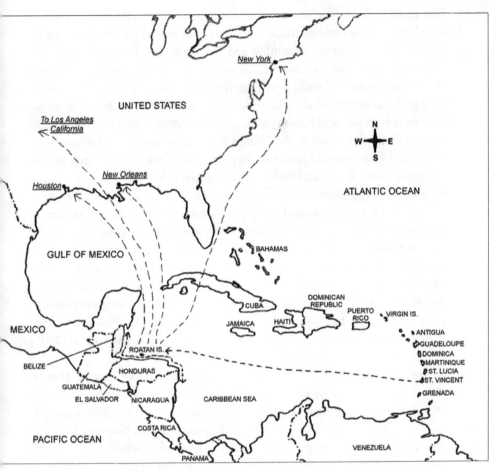

Map 1.1. Routes of Garifuna exile and migration.

and deal with North American racism, it was well worth it to escape the poverty of Honduras and achieve the material success professionals from his village cannot always attain. Though it was achieved in New York, this material success can only manifest itself in the context of Honduras, where the salary and retirement pay of the New York working poor translate into a decent middle-class lifestyle. In spite of the opportunities the United States has afforded him, therefore, Don Miguel still has his eye on returning to Honduras, where he will be surrounded by people for whom his title of "Don" has meaning and where his status is not that of perpetual foreigner but rather that of an *hijo del pueblo* (native son).

In many ways Don Miguel's story and the social processes it illustrates are typical of migration patterns of recent decades. He is a member of what scholars have come to refer to as "transnational communities"—communities in which social processes are embedded in and carried out in two national contexts simultaneously, in this case Honduras and New York City. Like many other immigrant groups, Garifuna mainly migrate for economic reasons: to support family back home and build a nest egg for their eventual return. However, as they get jobs, form families, raise children, attend educational institutions, accrue work histories, and become increasingly integrated into the fabric of U.S. society, their connection to the United States grows deeper and deeper such that if and when they do return to their country of origin, they often do not make any more of a clean break with U.S. society than they did with family back home in the village when they first left. The end result is that individuals and families become as rooted socially and economically in New York City as they are in Honduras. For first-generation immigrants, this connection to the United States tends to remain on the level of economic and social ties, while their national loyalties and sense of cultural identity tend to remain rooted in Honduras. This is manifested in continued interest and participation in Honduran politics, the creation of hometown associations that support development efforts, and their continued primary identification as Honduran rather than American—a set of social processes that Glick Schiller and Fouron (2001) call "long-distance nationalism."

But in the case of the Garifuna, there is an extra piece of the story. Though they continue to identify more with Honduras (or Belize, Guatemala, or Nicaragua) than with the United States, this long-distance nationalism is complicated by the fact that within Central American countries, Garifuna have historically been seen as marginal to national cultures and societies, a nice folkloric sideshow at best, a dangerous primitive contamination at worst. In Honduras, for example, "blackness," in contrast to "indigenismo,[1] has only recently been recognized as an integral part of the mestizo national identity, and Garifuna are largely ignored in narratives of the history, construction, and functioning of the nation-state. As in most societies, marginalization from the ideological mainstream coincides with a set of social practices and policies that largely exclude Garifuna communities from the political and economic power of the state and national society. Currently this is manifested primarily through the increasing expropriation of Garifuna land due to the expansion of agribusiness, cattle ranching, and, most recently, tourism into the North Coast,[2] where Garifuna villages are located. This latest development push on the part of the state has left entire villages virtually landless, dependent on neighboring cities for employment in a poorly remunerated service sector and on remittances sent by relatives in the United States. Though these are familiar processes throughout Central America that affect mestizo peasants as well as indigenous peoples and Garifuna alike, incursions into Garifuna municipalities of the coast are often justified by state officials and developers not only by the neoliberal logic of free market expansion, but also by the logic of race.

Though Garifuna have a long history of active involvement in the economy through the production of bananas, plantation labor, shipping, North Coast industries, services, teaching, and nursing, there is a dominant stereotype in Honduras of Garifuna as only fun-loving blacks who only dance *punta*, drink *guaro*, and make babies, a stereotype that has been used to justify their general exclusion from economic development plans of the state except as service workers and tourist attractions. In response, Garifuna have formed a number of grassroots social movements to combat this sort of racism and the economic onslaught on their communities. These social movements are largely based on economic issues such as the recovery of Garifuna lands, establishment of Garifuna businesses, and other forms of economic development in Garifuna communities, but they are also about combating racial and cultural discrimination through the implementation of bilingual education, recognition of Honduras as a multicultural nation, and respect for Garifuna history and cultural difference from the mestizo mainstream. Consequently, these social movements not only pose a challenge to the dominant development narratives of the state that support foreign investment in large-scale capitalist enterprises, they also challenge Honduran narratives of nation that presume the necessary homogeneity of cultural and national identity and downplay ethnic diversity. Garifuna throughout the diaspora (in other parts of Central America and the United States) have joined these social movements either by supporting them directly through fund-raising activities or indirectly through coalitions. They have also formed a host of other organizations to address issues specific to their locality. Consequently, while most Garifuna enact their daily lives vis-à-vis a particular bilocal transnational community (such as New York–Honduras or Belize–Los Angeles), grassroots organizing has come to join Garifuna in a more multi-national organizing effort.

As I discovered during my fieldwork period, Garifuna grassroots organizing occurs at many different levels—from very local village associations, to pan-national Garifuna organizations—and in alliance with many other ethnic/racial groups—indigenous peoples, Afro Latinos, Latinos, African Americans, and so forth. Though the general goals of all of these organizations are broadly shared—namely, the economic and social empowerment of the Garifuna people—the strategies that they have devised vary considerably depending on the particular group's analysis of the causes of socioeconomic marginalization and how best to address it.

My main argument in this book is that this diversity of opinion stems from the transnationalization of race, class, and gender that has greatly complicated the way Garifuna are positioned vis-à-vis these systems of inequality in two national contexts. Because they move back and forth between the race and class systems of the United States and Honduras, Garifuna experience and analyze marginalization in ways that are complicated by the strategies they use to negotiate these two systems. This has led to the emergence of disparate discourses and strategies of organizing within the Garifuna transnational community that belie any simple understanding of ethnic social movements as arising from a homogeneous experience of racial discrimination and ethnic identity. The principal concern of this book, then, is to explore how these Garifuna transnational social movements are informed and shaped by the experience of negotiating the multiple structures and ideologies of race, class, and nationalism their members encounter in the United States and Central America.

I do this in two ways: 1) through an in-depth analysis of the way family and community processes are carried out in one particular transnational community to provide the context for understanding how Garifuna experience and perceive of the larger structures of inequality in which they are embedded, and 2) through an analysis of the organizing strategies and ideologies of particular Garifuna grassroots organizations, especially in terms of how they mobilize collective identities. Bringing these two social phenomena together —transnational migration and social movements—allows for a greater understanding of how peoples around the world are participating in and shaped by the processes of globalization in a multiplicity of ways.

TRANSNATIONAL MOVEMENTS

Though I am dealing with a community that spans several national borders, this book is still in many ways a classic anthropological study in that one of my main goals is to give a detailed description and analysis of the basic social structures, cultural ideologies, and workings of one particular community. When I use the word community, however, I am not simply referring to the inhabitants of one physical location, but rather, I am referring to the people that constitute a community through a shared sense of belonging, continual interaction, and commitment to its perpetuation. The community that is the focus of this study exists in two primary locations—Limón and New York City—separated by several thousand miles, but connected into one social space through kinship networks, community organizations, economic transactions, and a host of other social processes that serve as the glue that holds it together. Much of this book is taken up in explaining the microdynamics of these social processes as they are carried out in both Limón and New York City, such as the history of Garifuna migration to New York City; the economic, residential, and racial integration of Garifuna into the South Bronx and Harlem; the history of Limón in the context of Honduran development efforts; the inner workings of Garifuna kinship networks and economic transactions; the dynamics of class mobility; and the history and politics of Limoneño community organizations. In all of this I also pay close attention to the various ideologies, worldviews, and cultural systems through which these processes are experienced, interpreted, and ultimately perpetuated.

I do this detailed description of how the transnational community operates, however, not merely to document the fact of transnationalism. A copious anthropological and sociological literature already exists that argues that unilinear models of immigration that assume that immigrants eventually assimilate and cut off all ties to the home country are no longer tenable in a world where many migrants continue to participate in the social, cultural, political, and economic life of their home countries through kinship networks, remittances, political organizing, and other means. Rather than assimilate and forget the home country, social life for many transmigrant populations is "embedded in networks of relationships that connect them simultaneously to the [cultural contexts and societies of] two different nation-states" (Basch, Glick Schiller, and Szanton Blanc 1994, 7; see also Georges 1990; Glick Schiller and Fouron 2001; Guarnizo 1994; Kearney and Nagengast 1989; Kyle 2000; Levitt 2001; Mahler 1998; Miles 2004; Popkin 1999; Rouse 1991, 1992; Guarnizo and Smith 1998; Smith 2005). In this sense, the Garifuna are not unique but are rather another example of "transnationalism as usual." What is unique is that the "cultural bifocality" Garifuna experience in this transnational space is not just one of dual class positions (Rouse 1992), national identities (Glick Schiller and Fouron 2001), or gender relations (Grasmuck and Pessar 1991; Mahler 1999) but is also of racial/ethnic identities between the United States and Central America and even within the United States and Central America. Indeed, Garifuna occupy an ideological border zone between four racial/ethnic identities—black, indigenous, Latino, and Garifuna—expressed differently in each of the nation-states within which they live. This is of crucial importance because this multiplicity of racial/ethnic identities influences the ways they are integrated into the various race, class, and gender hierarchies of these countries. It structures job opportunities, residential patterns, and educational possibilities, all of which contribute to the shaping of their daily lives. And even more interestingly, it also serves as a way that Garifuna often negotiate their positions in these structures. In Honduras, for example, Garifuna are considered to be both black and indigenous, both of which are minority identities but with somewhat different implications vis-à-vis the national imaginary. In New York City, Garifuna negotiate between being Latino immigrants, American blacks, and Afro Latinos, all of which again carry different implications for how they are viewed by the larger society, how they fit into the ethnic mosaic of New York, and how they envision their future in the United States. Garifuna activists shift in and among these identities in their claims to the "roots and routes" of Garifuna past, present, and future and in the alliances they build with other ethnic organizations. The Garifuna experience as it relates to issues of identity is even more complex than that of many other transnational groups and could more accurately be termed "multifocal" rather than bifocal.

My goal in detailing the daily life of negotiating race, nationalism, class, and gender in the transnational community is to provide the context, the lived experience out of which Garifuna consciousness and grassroots activism are formed. Following the Gramscian tradition, I understand consciousness to be the level of awareness of structural systems of inequality and the hegemonic premises upon which they are based as well as the perception of one's place within those ideological and structural systems, all of which emerge from the practical experiences of daily life (Gramsci 1971). Activism, then, is the process of forming collective identities around those particular manifestations of consciousness and attempting to mobilize that collectivity around certain strategies for empowerment. It is not enough to understand the structures of inequality actors face and how they shape their material conditions of life; it is also necessary to explore how they understand those structures and their relationships to them. That is, I seek to understand how Garifuna are situated in the racialized and gendered international division of labor by looking at macrostructural processes of the global economy, demographic movements, residential shifts, and so forth *as well as* how individual Garifuna view that location and how that understanding contributes to their proposed solutions for empowerment.

The second and equally important focus of this book is on the dynamics of grassroots organizing within the Limoneño and larger Garifuna community. My analysis draws much inspiration from new social movements literature, which has placed a great deal of emphasis on theories of power that recognize the significant role identity plays in structuring hierarchies and shaping resistance. For example, the pioneering work of Escobar and Alvarez (1992) demonstrates that what makes the Latin American social movements of the 1990s "new" is that they foreground collective identities other than class in their struggles for empowerment. Rather than envisioning a singular national subject (the mestizo male worker, for example) who will take over state power and build a new society (which was the main image of the struggles up until the 1990s in Central America), current social movements in Latin America are more interested in broadening the definition of citizenship and rights to include those that are based on cultural, racial, ethnic, class, and gender differences and particularities. This new way of "doing politics" has pushed social scientists away from analyses based primarily on the material relations of power that enable and constrain resource mobilization and towards a consideration of the way collective identities are constituted through people's self-understanding of race, class, gender, and culture. Drawing on Foucauldian analysis, they argue that social movements are both economic struggles and struggles over meaning and representation. They recognize that discourse and representation have as much capacity to construct and discipline subjects as do the management of capital and coercion. But they also recognize that the subordinated are able to appropriate and rearticulate those discourses and representations in their own efforts to empower themselves. Thus, the framework they propose for the analysis of social movements includes an examination of the practices of everyday life that shape cultural meaning and practical consciousness; the hegemonic premises that justify systems of inequality; the ways that meaning, representation, consciousness, and identity are mobilized for collective action against inequality; and how that action is both enabled and constrained by socioeconomic macrostructures (Escobar and Alvarez 1992, 71).

Using the new social movements literature as a basic framework for analysis, my main argument is that the types of collective identities and political strategies that emerge among Garifuna grassroots organizations are intimately related to the ways that individual Garifuna experience and envision their place in the international division of labor, the racial and gender hierarchies of two national contexts, and the global arena of human rights activism. The forms of consciousness that arise in this context are not unitary, however, but rather are contradictory; that is, different sectors of Garifuna society contest or accept them at different times and are critical of some hegemonic premises and not of others. This is because the structures and ideologies of power Garifuna encounter in the transnational community are multiple and multivalent, emerging from the complex intersections of global, transnational, national, and local processes.

I want to stress that this multifocality of daily experience, consciousness, and activism is not only experienced by transmigrants—that is, Garifuna who actually migrate back and forth between Honduras and the United States—but also by those who do not move. Most sites in the world today are what Appadurai (1996) calls translocalities—spaces through which images, goods, and peoples flow, connected through networks of kinship, labor, and leisure that are both local and nonlocal. In this way people are able, with or without moving, to imagine ways of being that are not merely local. In the case of Limón, for example, even before the advent of transnational migration, Garifuna villages were being shaped by the activities of multinational fruit companies that brought North American capital, West Indian labor, and Anglo ideologies of race. In the 1950s, development programs of the state, inspired and often financed by U.S. Cold War politics, brought ideologies of modernity, upward mobility, and development that responded both to local and nonlocal realities. And today the Internet, transnational television channels such as Univision, and other forms of communication enable new forms of imagined community even for those who have never left Honduras. Thus, while this book is mainly about the Limoneño transnational community (which includes transmigrants and nonmigrants), other actors also appear such as functionaries of the state, international NGOs, transnational capitalists, and academics such as myself who have contributed to the circuits of ideological and material relations Limoneños interact with. My goal in doing this is to show the importance of global financial markets, global discourses of race and rights, global political power plays, and global social movements in shaping local phenomenon as well as the creative ways that people such as the Garifuna mobilize these forces to their own ends.

RACIALIZED SPACE

As much of this book is concerned with understanding how Garifuna negotiate collective identities based on race, ethnicity, and nationalism, it is important to clarify what these terms mean and how I will be using them. As many scholars have pointed out, though these three terms have different histories and connotations, they are heavily imbricated in one another and are often conflated by scholars, by government institutions, and in popular usage. This stems from the fact that all three have largely served the same purpose of attempting to draw boundaries around populations based on phenotypic and cultural traits that are presumed to be primordial and immutable and are used to distribute rights in strategically unequal ways.

Race is a concept that is said to have emerged in Europe some time before the 1500s and the beginning of colonization. Though different scholars point to somewhat different origins of the concept of race, all agree that it was a European invention used to distinguish different classes of animals and then people based on putatively biological traits (Banton 1977; Smedley 1999; Stolcke 1991). By the 1800s, after 300 years of colonization and the emergence of Linnaean classification and Darwinian theory, race had become solidified as a biological concept that assumed that the world's human population can be divided into discrete categories of interbreeding populations whose physical and mental characteristics are determined by their biological makeup.

Beginning in the first half of the 1900s, scholars such as Ruth Benedict (1943) and Ashley Montagu (1964) began to question the scientific validity of the concept of race, arguing that the world's population exhibits continuous differences rather than discrete categories and that mental and physical characteristics are as much adaptations and learned traits as they are biological. Thus, they advocated the use of the term "ethnic group" instead of "race" to refer to populations with distinct histories, cultures, and languages. Though race has since been largely discredited by anthropologists, sociologists, and geneticists as having no biological reality (see Back and Solomos 2000; Marks 2002; and Smedley 1999 for review of this literature), it is still a powerful ideology that continues to organize society structurally and ideologically in the Americas (Omi and Winant 1994). This can be seen in the fact that even when the term "ethnic group" is used, it still often carries racial connotations because different ethnic groups are assumed to simply be subsets of larger racial groups. In other words, to belong to an ethnic group is also to have a racial identity that is assumed to correspond to that ethnic group. For example, the Garifuna consider themselves to be a distinct ethnic group because of their history, language, and culture. But they also consider themselves to fall within the larger racial category of black. To be ethnically Garifuna, then, automatically implies a racial identity as well. (They could also claim to be racially indigenous; however, as I will argue in Chapter 6, they use this element of their identity more as a way to make claims to their status as a "people" rather than as a strictly racial identity.)

Nationalism is another category that has been widely discussed. It has been shown that despite its connection to an artificial or imagined political community (Anderson 1983), it also has often carried racial connotations (Balibar 1991; Gilroy 1993b; Williams 1989). In the search to create a unified and primordial identity, racial identities have been conflated with national identities, often obscuring or erasing the presence and contribution of racial minorities (Gilroy 1993b; Tsuda 2003; Williams 1991). Rather than seeing national identity as simply a matter of citizenship, place of birth, or acquired culture, some tend to conflate it with one racialized group (for example, in the case of the Japanese) and/or with ethnicity (in the case of "hyphenated Americans"). Thus, even national identities, which are theoretically based on a political relationship to a particular nation-state, often have racial connotations.

Peoples such as the Garifuna pose an interesting challenge to these different ideologies because they straddle many different racial and national categories. As Clara Rodriguez (2000) has argued, Latinos in general have challenged the race-based thinking of the United States, and it has become more common for people to understand that Latinos can be of any race and of many nationalities. Changes on U.S. census categories in 2000, where "Hispanic" is no longer listed as one of the major racial categories, but rather as a cultural category that encompasses peoples of many different races and nationalities, demonstrates that it is now more commonly understood that being ethnically Latino does not guarantee a "brown" racial identity. There is no simple correspondence between being Dominican, for example, and being of a particular race because Dominicans can be black, white, and anything in-between. Similarly, Central Americans can be mestizo, indigenous, black, and any mixture thereof. Some people who are classified by the U.S. census as ethnically Latino, may actually identify more with others of their racial group (black, indigenous, white) than as Latino. As these complexities come more and more to the fore of public awareness in the United States, other assumptions about race and ethnicity are also being rethought and reworked, in a process that detaches them more and more from each other and from their biological connotations.

And yet despite the growing recognition that race, ethnicity, and nationalism are historically and culturally specific categories that do not have a biological basis, the terms are still widely used and often conflated. During my fieldwork period, I often heard Garifuna use the terms imprecisely and interchangeably, referring to themselves variously as an ethnic group, as a race, and as a nation. In some ways I wish to maintain this ambiguity because it reveals a great deal about how racial, ethnic, and national identities are mobilized in different moments to both include and exclude others in the formation of a notion of peoplehood. This will come out mainly in the chapters in which I discuss how Garifuna activists use the terms. In my own analysis, I will use the terms in the following manner: "race" or "racial" refers to ideological constructions of peoplehood or assumptions about character that refer to biological/phenotypical traits; "ethnic group" or "ethnicity" refers to a group of people with a distinct culture and history who are minorities within the nation-state; and "nationality" refers to notions of belonging to a particular nation-state or nation (understood as a politicized ethnic group), irregardless of place of residence or citizenship.

MAPPING THE NATIONAL/ETHNIC/RACIAL LANDSCAPE

So far, I have suggested that for the Garifuna the nation-state of origin is not the only context for their history, identity, community, or political activism. Through transnational migration and the experience of diaspora, Garifuna have created forms of community that in many ways allow them to transcend national contexts. At the same time there are also circumstances that *vary* by national context, circumstances that have a significant impact on the forms identity, power relations, and social movements take. Therefore, it is important here to give a brief introduction to those national contexts. Because my research is concerned primarily with Honduran Garifuna, I will concentrate on the particular place of Garifuna in Honduras and New York City.

Garifuna home communities are located in Belize, Guatemala, Honduras, and Nicaragua. (For discussions of the situation of Garifuna in Belize and Los Angeles, see Macklin 1985, Miller 1993, and Wright 1995; for Nicaragua, see Davidson 1980 and Perry 1990; and for Guatemala, see Gonzalez 1969). Honduras has by far the largest population with approximately 100,000[3] in forty-three villages and the principal cities, followed by Belize with a population of 12,000–20,000 in six villages and Belize City[4], Guatemala with a population of 16,700 in Livingston and Puerto Barrios[5], and Nicaragua with a population of only 1,500 in three villages.[6] Considering that most of these figures are already over a decade old and that Garifuna do not exhibit lower-than-average fertility rates for Central Americans, I would estimate the total Central American Garifuna population to be around 200,000. The main areas of settlement in the United States are New York City, Los Angeles, and New Orleans. Estimates for these populations are extremely difficult to obtain because the Immigration and Naturalization Service (INS) and the U.S. census count Garifuna by their nation-state of origin, not their ethnicity. The *Los Angeles Times* (O'Conner 1998) gives a figure of 25,000 for that city and 100,000 for the entire United States. It would be safe to say that there are probably 100,000–200,000 in the United States, or roughly the same amount as are in Central America. Considering that many Garifuna are probably not counted throughout the diaspora due to their mobility and/or because they are "mixed," I would estimate the total population of Garifuna at around 400,000.

Whatever the actual figures are, the reality is that the Garifuna constitute a small minority of the population in all the nation-states within which they reside. They are also considered to be a minority group in the sense that they are racially and/or culturally distinct from the national society. This minority status (both numerical and ethnic) has implications for their relationship with their national societies and other ethnic groups. Here I want to briefly explore their history in relation to Honduran society as a way to provide a general backdrop for understanding their location in the racial/ethnic landscape of that country.

According to 1998 population estimates, the majority of the Honduran population is ladino.[7] Anyone who is not classified as ladino is considered to be an ethnic minority. Out of a population of over 6 million people, only 10 percent of Hondurans are classified as ethnic minorities, among them six indigenous groups (Tolupanes, Tawakas, Pech, Miskitu, Chorti, and Lencas), Garifuna, and the English-speaking black creoles (*Negros de habla inglesa*).[8] While Garifuna are the largest of the ethnic groups in Honduras, until the 1990s it was difficult to find them even mentioned in Honduran history books.[9] In fact, a perusal of most historical texts of Honduras written before the 1990s will generate the same story line: a noble but primitive indigenous population and a smattering of African slaves suffered under the oppression of Spanish colonial rule, which was replaced by the modern nation-state, under whose tutelage the ladino arose as the new national subject through the "natural" miscegenation and acculturation of the population, erasing all of the racial and cultural differences that had separated and exploited the population under the colonial system. Consequently, the ethnic groups that represent racial and cultural heterogeneity are seen as a very small minority, insignificant to "national" history beyond the colonial period. The fact that histories of Honduras present racial heterogeneity as a nonissue is a reflection of the way Honduran nationalism has been constructed through the ideological erasure of cultural and racial difference, a topic to which I will return in more depth in Chapter 6. For now it is important to recognize that racial and cultural diversity has characterized Honduras from colonial times to today, shaping the character and politics of the nation, and forming much of the backdrop of current social movements.

When the Garifuna arrived in Honduras in 1797, the colonial society they encountered was one in which racial and cultural distinctions formed the backbone of the social and economic hierarchy. They were used to determine the economic niche, legal status, and potential marriage partners of the population. After 100 years of the rapid decline of the indigenous population due to slaving, disease, and dislocation, the Crown established laws meant to "preserve" the dwindling labor pool by separating indigenous peoples from the Spanish population in relatively autonomous settlements called *pueblos de indios*. Though they were forced to pay tribute to Spanish landowners (*hacendados*) through the cultivation of cacao and indigo and later in cash, royal decrees gave them a certain degree of social and political autonomy. They prohibited the settlement of nonindigenous peoples in their communities (except for priests), allowing for indigenous leaders (*caciques*) to serve as middlemen between the *pueblos* and colonial administrators. This facilitated the perpetuation of "traditional" religious *cofradías* and assured indigenous peoples access to a certain amount of communal land for subsistence agriculture (MacLeod 1973; Rivas 1993). This accounts for the survival of some of the Honduran indigenous groups in western Honduras such as the Chorti and the Lenca, who remain as distinct groups. Today they are greatly impoverished because many communities are still in relations of debt servitude to large landowners (Rivas 1993)

Indigenous peoples in the regions of the North Coast and the Mosquitia (eastern Honduras), areas the Spanish considered to be less desirable for settlement, managed to survive as distinct groups to a larger degree than other areas of Honduras. For example, the seminomadic tribes of eastern Honduras, the Pech, also known as the Paya, and the Tawaka fled deep into the lowland tropical basin of the Mosquitia into areas little traversed by the agents of Spanish colonial society (except, of course, for missionaries). There they were largely able to escape the tribute and debt peonage systems of colonial society and survive by shifting cultivation, hunting, and trading with the Miskitu for manufactured goods (MacLeod 1973; Newson 1986; Rivas 1993). The Miskitu, who were strengthened through an alliance with the British, were also able to remain relatively independent from Spanish colonial society, surviving by a combination of shifting cultivation, turtle hunting, and trade with the British (Helms 1971; Nietschmann 1973; Rivas 1993). In central Honduras, the Tolupanes (also known as the Jicaques or Xicaques), who were originally from the coastal region, fled into the mountains of Yoro, where they lived in fortressed communities, descending only occasionally to minimize relations of debt servitude with tobacco and coffee farmers (Chapman 1992; Rivas 1993). These four groups also live in extreme poverty, battling cattle ranchers, lumber companies, and the state to maintain the little bit of land they have left (Chavez Borjas 1984; Cruz Sandoval 1984; Herlihy and Leake 1990).

While the colonial system was largely predicated on the ideal of racial segregation, with each group occupying its economic and political niche based on assumptions of inherent racial capabilities (Barahona 1991; MacLeod 1973), the exigencies of the colonial economy led to the uprooting and dislocation of much of the population as they sought wage labor in the mines of the interior, on the plantations of the Pacific coast, and in urban areas. Here indigenous peoples and poor "whites" (Spanish *peninsulares* or their American-born offspring, known as *criollos*) met with freed blacks (descendants of African slaves brought as early as 1540 to replace the indigenous peoples in the mines of the interior) and formed a myriad of racial *castas* (castes) out of all the possible mixtures of the three "pure races." This added *mulatos* (black mixed with white), *zambos* (black mixed with indigenous), mestizos (indigenous mixed with white) and ladinos (at that time a term used to refer to anyone of any race mixture that had acculturated to Spanish culture and language) to the three "pure" racial categories of *indígena, blanco,* and *negro.*

Spanish *peninsulares* and *criollos* monopolized the two main sources of wealth and power—land and public office—because they served as merchants, public administrators, and *hacendados.* The indigenous population lived in relatively autonomous rural communities and freed blacks and *castas* were excluded from both indigenous communities and from opportunities to own land and serve as public administrators. Because they were in the anomalous position of being "free" (from slavery and tribute) and yet not the social or political equals of the *criollos* or *peninsulares,* the *castas* served as a ready supply of cheap and mobile labor (that is, not tied to a particular community or hacienda; MacLeod 1973). Many were hired as plantation managers, as muleteers transporting goods, as traders, as cowboys herding cattle, and in other middleman positions. Others settled on *tierra ociosa* (unoccupied land), rented land from indigenous communities, or took over indigenous lands. The *castas* gained a reputation as a rootless and shiftless population, living on the margins of both the Spanish and indigenous worlds, necessary to the colonial economy yet always under suspicion and thereby excluded from power (Barahona 1991, 214).

By the time that the Garifuna arrived in 1797, this mixed population of *castas* represented around 60 percent of the population, mainly concentrated in the south-central regions of the country. The indigenous peoples were mainly present in the eastern region of the Mosquitia and western regions of Copan, La Paz, Santa Barbara, Ocotepeque, Lempira, and Intibucá (Newson 1986, 335). Newson (1986) argues that though the indigenous population had gone through a period of natural increase in the 1700s, it was offset by the processes of *mestizaje* (miscegenation) and acculturation. Thus, in the 1800s the Indian population again declined, this time due not to mortality, but rather in terms of racial and cultural classification.[10] Meanwhile, the freed blacks had integrated into the ladino population to the point that while they were known as a racial presence in departments such as Olancho, they were not considered to be a distinct ethnic group. What the Garifuna found in the 1800s was a society divided between a northeastern region that was sparsely populated by indigenous peoples and a few Spanish forts and ports, and a southwestern region that was more densely populated by Spanish towns, *pueblos de indios,* and ladino settlements (Adams 1975). The Garifuna found space to establish themselves along the Caribbean coast, in between and around ports, reaching as far east as the Mosquitia and, eventually, as far west as Belize.

In the 1840s, the racial/ethnic landscape of Honduras was again made more complex by the arrival of English-speaking blacks and whites from the Cayman Islands (Isleños). The Cayman islanders settled on the Bay Islands (off the Caribbean coast), which at the time were under British control (Davidson 1974). In 1860, the British gave Honduras sovereignty over the Bay Islands, but it was not until the middle of the 1900s that the islands began to be "hispanicized" through the assimilationist policies of the state and ladino migration to the islands. Consequently, Isleños continue to speak English and consider themselves to be racially and culturally distinct from ladinos (Davidson 1974). In the early part of the 1900s, the population of English-speaking blacks (*Negros de habla inglesa*) was increased by the West Indian labor the multinational fruit companies, which had established themselves on the Caribbean coast, imported. As foreign blacks, this group was vulnerable to the immigration policies of the Honduran state and was protected only by the Anglo fruit companies. During the 1930s world depression when the production of bananas declined, many of the West Indian workers were repatriated. Some, however, settled in the port towns of Tela, Puerto Cortés, and La Ceiba, and a few settled as farmers and ranchers around Garifuna villages. Today they constitute a small minority and are generally classified within the group of *Negros de habla inglesa*.

A final group of people who are rarely mentioned but who are also important to the history and current politics of Honduras are the Palestinian and Lebanese Arabs who began to arrive in Honduras in the early 1900s, attracted by entrepreneurial opportunities in the banana enclave. They began as small merchants in the North Coast cities and have since become some of the wealthiest capitalists in the country, dominating the agribusiness and industrial sectors of the North Coast, and more recently moving into the realm of political power (Euraque 1996a; Gonzalez 1992). Both they and white Isleños (who now dominate the Bay Island tourist industry) are excluded from the list of ethnic groups in Honduras, though they are considered to be racially and culturally distinct from the ladino population. (This reveals a great deal about how the definition of "ethnic" in Honduras is not merely about racial and cultural difference but also about class.)

Within this racial/ethnic landscape, the Garifuna have held a rather anomalous position. On the one hand, they have mainly resided in rural villages along the Caribbean coast where, like indigenous peoples, they have had a subsistence economy based on shifting cultivation, fishing, and hunting. They also speak an indigenous language (Garifuna)[11] and have domestic structures and religious and other socioeconomic practices that distinguish them from the Hispanic/ladino population. Unlike other Afro-Hondurans, the Garifuna have been classified as an indigenous group at least since the 1860s, when they were listed in indigenous legislation under the name *morenos* along with other so-called *indios selváticos* (jungle Indians) of the North Coast (Alvarado Garcia 1958, 19–20). On the other hand, Garifuna men have long been engaged in cross-border migratory wage labor such as in logging camps in Belize and Nicaragua, in the banana plantations and ports of Honduras, and as merchant marines, where they have learned English and have come to identify with the Afro Caribbean culture region. This affinity with blackness, orientation towards the Caribbean, and involvement in wage labor abroad differentiates Garifuna from the model of the primordialized and isolated Indian. Thus, Garifuna inhabit geographical and ideological border zones between Central America and the Caribbean, Hispanic and West Indian, indigenous and black. They are a people with many of the cultural and social structural features of the Afro Caribbean, they are located in a Hispanic country, and they are fighting for rights to land and cultural autonomy alongside Honduran indigenous peoples.

The Garifuna also occupy a border zone in the racial/ethnic landscape of New York City. Arriving as a part of the wave of Latin American and Caribbean immigrants whose numbers increased after the abolition of country quotas in 1965, Garifuna pioneers to New York City predated the massive wave of Central American ladino migration by three decades. Consequently, though the Garifuna represent a small percentage of the population in Honduras, they make up a majority of the population of Hondurans in New York City (in contrast to Los Angeles and New Orleans, where Honduran ladinos outnumber Garifuna). In New York City, Honduran Garifuna have mainly settled in Central Harlem and the South Bronx, neighborhoods that are generally characterized as African American, West Indian, and Hispanic Caribbean (that is, Dominicans and Puerto Ricans). This is in contrast to Belizean Garifuna, who tend to concentrate in West Indian–dominated neighborhoods in Brooklyn, and Honduran ladinos, who tend to settle in Hispanic parts of Brooklyn, Queens, and Long Island (Reichman 2004). Not only do Honduran Garifuna live in the same neighborhoods as many Caribbean peoples but they have also been integrated into the labor market in a similar fashion as superintendents, home attendants, nurses, domestics, and workers in other service occupations (Foner 2001; Kasinitz 1992; Sutton and Chaney 1987). In contrast, Honduran ladinos tend to work in construction, landscaping, and food service, more like Salvadorans (Mahler 1995), Guatemalans (Hamilton and Chinchilla 2001), and Mexicans (Smith 2005).

Though Honduras was the fifth highest source country for immigration to the Bronx in 1990 and the sixth highest in 2000 (New York City Department of City Planning 1992b, 2000), Garifuna have until recently been virtually invisible. In part this is due to the fact that they are not concentrated in any one neighborhood but live scattered within several community districts of the South Bronx, Harlem, and northern Brooklyn, perhaps dominating a particular building but not an entire neighborhood. Another reason for their invisibility lies in their relatively small numbers and their cultural and physical similarity to other Afro Caribbean peoples (West Indian, Hispanic) and African Americans. While Honduran ladinos are often mistaken for Salvadorans, Honduran Garifuna are mistaken for African Americans or West Indians if they are speaking English, for black Dominicans if they are speaking Spanish, or even for Africans if they are speaking Garifuna.

The positioning of the Garifuna vis-à-vis other Hondurans and other Afro Hispanic peoples has significant implications for the forms their sociocultural structures, sense of identity, and social movements take. As will become apparent throughout this book the complexity of the Garifuna situation is due not only to their transnationalism but also to the cultural and racial border zone they occupy between Hispanic Central America and the Afro Caribbean.

DOING ETHNOGRAPHY IN A TRANSNATIONAL COMMUNITY: INSERTION INTO THE FIELD

The metaphor of traveling has become important in anthropological literature of late as a way to explore what many see as a new phase of world history characterized by an unprecedented degree of movement—be it by transmigrants, tourists, businessmen, international aid organization workers, or researchers (Clifford 1997). With people go ideas, preconceptions, ideologies, and other mental phenomenon that shape their experiences and encounters with others. This is not only true of the subjects of anthropological study but also of the researchers themselves, whose preconceptions, academic theories, and racial/ethnic, class, and gender identities not only shape the projects they formulate before going to the field but also the ethnographic encounter itself and the particular interpretation that ultimately becomes the ethnography (Behar 1993; Marcus 1998). At this point, then, I want to give some background about how this project developed and through what experiences, theoretical lenses, and preconceptions I held as a white American female academic.

My first experiences with Garifuna came during a weekend trip to Livingston, Guatemala, in 1990 during a Kakchikel Maya language course I was attending in the highland town of Antigua. What sparked my initial interest was the fascinating mix of English Caribbean, Central American mestizo, indigenous Mayan, and expatriate European culture that permeates this relatively small town. "Postmodern" conceptions of "hybridity," "border zones" (Anzaldua 1987), "third spaces" (Bhabha 1990), and so forth were all the rage in academia at the time, and I seemed to have found such a place, a true border zone between Spanish Central America and the Caribbean, indigenous and black, crosscut by the constant movement of transmigrants and tourists. And yet, just as many scholars have discovered, most of the Garifuna that I talked to saw nothing postmodern about this. For them this is the normal existence of a people trying to participate in the global economy of consumption and production, living out the results of colonialism that had created an Afro Indigenous peoples and then landed them in Hispanic Central America. Like other ethnic peoples in Latin America, the Garifuna that I encountered were politicized and active in identity-based social movements, struggling for "ethnic" human rights, land, bilingual education, and other means of living a dignified life in their coastal villages. This involved making claims to land based on ancestral occupation, using much the same language of peoplehood that I had heard among the Kakchikel language teachers. But it occurred to me that this could not be the "usual" social movement of indigenous peoples struggling for rights to land because the Garifuna are not just indigenous but are also of the African diaspora. At the same time, as I was to hear again and again, they are also not "just black" but are also indigenous and Hispanic. The question that arose for me was what this complexity of identity and positionalities might mean for political consciousness and activism. What does it mean for a transnational community with a decided affinity towards "blackness" to be claiming primordial rights to territory in Central America? What does it mean to be Afro Indigenous in a ladino state? What does it mean to be Afro Hispanic in New York? How might Garifuna in Central America and the United States be negotiating these identities and positionalities in their political struggles?

Through contact with a Garifuna activist in Texas, I found out about a grassroots cooperative that had been formed in 1990 in the Garifuna village of Limón, Honduras, by a group of Limoneños concerned with the growing trend of landlessness in Garifuna villages, as well as with the effects of racial and cultural discrimination nationally. This cooperative, called *El Movimiento Negro Iseri Lidawamari* (Black Movement New Dawn), had reclaimed a 10,000–hectare area of land within the municipality of Limón called Vallecito that is on the border of an enormous African palm plantation that at the time was owned by a group of military officers. In a climate of political reform after a decade of military rule, these Garifuna were able to garner enough international and national support to occupy the land with no military backlash.

Map 1.2. Selected Garifuna settlements in Central America. Garifuna villages are under-lined.

They planned to set up an agricultural cooperative; build a school that would educate Garifuna children in farming, the Garifuna language, and history; and set up a political base for a pan-Garifuna social movement. Equipped with theoretical frameworks for viewing the relationship between ethnicity and nation-building, grassroots organizations and development, and the nego-tiation of identities in social movements, I set out to look at the history and political activities of this cooperative mainly in terms of what it could reveal about the relationship of the Garifuna as an ethnic group to the Honduran nation-state.

I first arrived to in Limón to conduct field work with Iseri Lidawamari in the summer of 1993. Limón is located in the eastern Department of Colón, one of the largest but also most sparsely populated departments in Honduras (map 1.2). The village of Limón itself is the *cabacera* (municipal seat)[12] of the municipality of Limón, and constitutes the largest of the Garifuna villages in

Honduras, with a population of around 4,000.[13] Though the majority of those who live in the village of Limón are Garifuna, there is also a substantial population of ladinos who have been migrating into the municipality ever since it was the site of United Fruit Company plantations in the 1930s. Today probably three-fourths of the population of the municipality of Limón is ladino, mainly residing in *aldeas* and *caseríos* (hamlets) scattered throughout the municipality. At the time of my field work, Limón had potable water but no electricity (with the exception of gas-powered generators run only on special occasions) and was still relatively distant from any major urban centers, as it is located at the end of the coastal "highway." (Trujillo and Tocoa, where there are banks, shops, telephones, and so forth, are both about a two-hour bus ride from Limón). Consequently tourism had not yet become very popular (despite the gorgeous beach) and most Garifuna regard Limón to be a relatively "traditional" Garifuna village. However, like their neighbors to the west, many Limoneño households have very little land on which to cultivate and rely mainly on remittances from relatives abroad for their survival. Indeed, during the period of time I conducted research (1993–1997), approximately 53 percent of Limoneños[14] were currently residing living outside of Limón, working in the United States and in different locations in Central America. Most of them send money back to family in Limón.

Within a week of my arrival in Limón, I met with Lombardo Lacayo, Teofilo Lacayo, and Bernardo Guerrero, the primary leaders of Iseri Lidawamari. The sudden appearance of a gringa in Limón, a town literally at the end of the road with few amenities for visitors, did not seem to be a surprise to anyone. In fact, I discovered that through contacts with the Dutch embassy, Iseri Lidawamari had actually come to be well known in some European nongovernmental organization (NGO) circles such that the arrival of gringos looking for Lombardo was not a rare occurrence. Thus I was welcomed as another *"compañera de lucha"* (companion in struggle), took the four-hour hike down the beach and through the forest to Vallecito (the location of the cooperative), and began participating in village meetings, seminars, and conferences with other members of Iseri Lidawamari.

Much of my time was spent in Limón, where I lived with an older woman and three of her grown children. There I participated in the daily round of activities as best I could, though as many anthropologists have learned, urban skills such as driving and using a computer do not at all prepare one for the skills needed in a rural community. I was able to lend a hand in grating cassava, carrying firewood, washing clothes, babysitting, and other gender-appropriate activities, through which I learned a great deal about the routines of daily life for women. As a gringa who could drive, I was also recruited to drive the old Toyota four-wheel drive down the rutted and muddy road to Vallecito, where we chopped weeds, planted cassava, and built fishing nets for the cooperative.

My residence in Limón was constantly punctuated, however, by traveling in and out of the village, in order to follow the organizational activities of Iseri Lidawamari. What I found in 1993 was a great flurry of organizational activity among indigenous peoples and blacks in Honduras that had been stimulated by the 1992 anti-quincentenary campaign. Just about every week there was a seminar or conference or workshop going on somewhere in one of the Garifuna communities or in the cities discussing issues of land rights, human rights abuses, bilingual education, and the reformation of the Honduran constitution regarding ethnic peoples. These events were generally organized by one of the national-level ethnic organizations such as the Consejo Asesor Hondureño para el Desarrollo de las Etnias Autóctonas (CAHDEA) (Honduran Counsel for the Development of Autocthonous Peoples; CAHDEA), by a national-level Garifuna organization such as La Organización Fraternal Negra Hondureña (OFRANEH) (Fraternal Black Honduran Organization; OFRANEH), by the Honduran human rights organization Comité para los Derechos Humanos de Honduras (CODEH) (Committee for Human Rights in Honduras; CODEH), or by the United Nations and other international organizations. The underlying theme of these meetings was often a critique of the homogenizing, top-down discourses of Honduran nationalism and of national development plans, both of which had long excluded indigenous and black communities as important actors or beneficiaries. Though the administration of President Leonardo Callejas (1990–1993) had recently implemented an economic reform package with all the accouterments of neoliberalism that was raising the cost of living and reversing the few gains peasants had made with the 1974 agrarian reform, there was simultaneously a political *apertura* (opening) and pressure for democratic reform. Most significantly, there was a sense that the time had come for the voices of indigenous peoples and blacks to be heard, backed by international support and a growing sympathy for identity-based issues. As I heard one Garifuna man say when he was confronted by the military police in Limón, "Do you think these are still the times of Columbus? I've read the Constitution, I know my rights."

After six months of participating in this circuit of political activism, I realized that this social movement could not be understood as a merely "local" or even "national" phenomenon. Aside from the obvious participation of international NGOs, that negotiated between ethnic groups and the state, and in many ways shaped the discourses within which rights were being articulated, there was also a large number of Garifuna transmigrants participating in these organizations. Indeed, in the 1993 national elections, Lombardo Lacayo, one of the founders of Iseri Lidawamari, ran for mayor of Limón as the Liberal Party candidate and was supported by money raised by Limoneño hometown associations in New York. As I talked to those transmigrants who returned for the elections, for Christmas, for Easter Holy Week, and for other village events, I became fascinated by the bifocal lens that being a transmigrant appeared to entail. Here were men and women who were returning to Limón as successful *"hijos del pueblo"* (children of the village), having built nice houses, bought cars, and gained much respect in the community through their participation in the hometown associations that had brought potable water and other amenities to Limón. Yet in New York City, these same people were living in the South Bronx and Harlem, working as janitors, maids, and home attendants. From the lens of a white American who grew up in Texas, these social geographies and employment niches conjured up images not of success stories, but of the working poor living in the infrastructurally peripheralized inner city. Evidently the complexity of Garifuna society and political activism was more than an issue of "hybrid" racial/ethnic identities and culture. It also involved the "bifocality" (Rouse 1992) of living in two localities with class structures articulated in distinct ways with race, ethnicity, and gender. Clearly, in order to understand the socioeconomic and cultural context out of which Garifuna political consciousness and activism arises, I would have to gain an in-depth understanding of the community as a whole and its articulation with the class structures, racial/ethnic ideologies, and nation-states of both Honduras and the United States.

Consequently, in the summer of 1995, I went to New York City, equipped this time with the theoretical lenses for viewing transnational migration and globalization. Finding Limoneños in New York was not difficult, as I had already met many of them on their return trips to Limón and many of them had already seen me on one of the many videos of village events that circulate throughout the Limoneño community in New York. I had originally planned to focus on Limoneño hometown associations and their involvement in development projects back home. What I found, however, was that the same flurry of organizational activity that I had seen in Honduras around identity-based social movements was being replicated in New York, though in ways particular to the New York reality. As I expected, every Garifuna village had its hometown associations (Limoneños had the record with six different organizations), but I also found Garifuna participating in pan-Garifuna organizations that unite all Honduran Garifuna; others that unite Garifuna of Honduras, Belize, and

Guatemala; pan-Honduran organizations that unite Garifuna and ladinos; Hispanic immigrant organizations; and Afro Hispanic organizations. These organizations formulate a politics much broader than those of hometown associations, challenging many categories of racial and national belonging that the Garifuna had formerly been inscribed into, and generating creative alliances.

During my year in New York City, the president of OFRANEH and the mayors of Limón and Aguan (a neighboring Garifuna village) visited the city to try to *"concientizar"* (raise the consciousness of) the transmigrants about the issue of Garifuna land loss, which has been especially acute since the declaration of tourism as the new national development plan of Honduras, and to garner their participation in Garifuna social movements. While these meetings were widely attended and most voiced solidarity with the cause, I also began to detect a split within the community over the issues of the meaning of development, how it should be implemented, and how closely it should be associated with ethnic identity and "ethnic rights." The community was also divided about what that ethnic identity should be. Through these meetings and through household surveys and interviews, I was gaining a clearer understanding of the complex ways that discourses of development, ethnicity, and community solidarity were being articulated in these different organizations and how these revealed the functioning of class, ethnicity, and kinship in transnational space.

Living in New York City was perhaps as revelatory to me about the bifocality of the Garifuna and their perceptions of the United States as it was about my own perceptions of New York City and specifically Harlem and the Bronx that I had absorbed through the U.S. media. Philippe Bourgois (1995), who lived in and conducted research in East Harlem, has written about his field experience as one of living in and doing ethnography in apartheid. Manhattan is especially striking in this regard. Merely by crossing the street at East 96th Street, one goes from one of the wealthiest neighborhoods in the United States (the Upper East Side) to one of the poorest (Spanish Harlem). Each time I rode the #2 subway line from 42nd Street (Grand Central Terminal) up to the Bronx, this racial and class apartheid was obvious. At 42nd Street, the train is crowded with people of all colors and classes; by 96th Street, most whites have exited the train; from 102nd Street to 145th Street, most people getting on and off the train are black; and after entering the Bronx at 3rd Avenue, the passengers are primarily Hispanic and black with a sprinkling of whites going all the way to the most northern stops where there are still a few Italian neighborhoods (in which Italian residents are fast being outnumbered by West Indians). For one year I traveled this route, getting off at 125th Street right in the heart of Harlem, passing the African glove vendors, the Jamaican record stores, and the department stores on my way to my apartment on 122nd Street. At other times, I stayed on to travel into the Bronx, getting off at 3rd Avenue to go to Vamos a La Peña del Bronx or at East Tremont for a hometown association meeting or interview or on Grand Concourse to go to the office of the Federation of Honduran Organizations of New York (FEDOHNY). In many ways, these neighborhoods conform to the images one sees in the media of burned-out buildings, graffiti, derelict 20–story projects with broken elevators, streets littered with trash, and so on—images of the "peripheralized areas of the core" (Koptiuch 1997). Yet what was surprising to me is that though Garifuna are aware that they are living in a peripheralized inner-city area, they rarely seem to leave these neighborhoods. There they can shop on 3rd Avenue in the Everything Under $10 stores, attend Hostos College, hold festivals and soccer tournaments in St. Mary's and Crotona Parks, and buy their plantains and cassava in one of the many Dominican *bodegas*.

What I found, then, was that among the Garifuna in New York, and especially in the Bronx, I was mainly in a milieu that is something of a replica of the Dominican Republic—culturally Hispanic, but racially a spectrum from white to black and everything in between. As a consequence of this and other factors, being a white American in the midst of Garifuna ethnic mobilization was less of an issue than I had feared it would be. Though Garifuna do not exactly have the "Anglo affinity" that others have noted among Central American Atlantic coast residents (Gordon 1998; Hale 1994b; Howe 1998), they also do not generally exhibit extreme feelings of resentment towards white Americans, even after living in the "racial apartheid" of New York City for many years. Within Garifuna social movements, much more emphasis is placed on the racism and discrimination that they face vis-à-vis Honduran ladinos, who they refer to as *chumagü* in Garifuna. This distrust of ladino Hondurans even came out prominently in the context of New York City–based organizations. Whites (as in white Americans or gringos in general) were not usually identified as the collective enemy of the Garifuna cause, though most Garifuna I knew in New York had at least one story of discrimination by an American white.

There is one more aspect to my fieldwork period that had a profound impact on both the field work as a personal experience and on the ways that I came to live and perceive the transnational community. During my fieldwork period in New York, I was pregnant with my first child, which gave me great insight into the ways that Garifuna women experience childbirth in the United States and the strategies they use for getting state aid. The fact that as a poor graduate student I was eligible for Medicaid and WIC (federal food aid to Women, Infants, and Children) just like the women I lived with helped bridge some of the gaps that inevitably exist between being a white American woman living among black immigrant women. And finally, when I returned to Limón in the summer of 1996 for a final six months of research, I had my four-month old son in tow, creating a very different research experience than I had had on previous trips. This time I was much less mobile, unable to take off for meetings at the drop of a hat or participate in organizational activities with the freedom that I had had before. I found myself spending much more time "stuck" in the family compound worrying about feeding time and naps. And yet in the end, this also proved to be an invaluable experience because it provided the opportunity to spend more time talking with women about childrearing, differences between Limón and New York, relationships with husbands, and relationships with children. In addition, I was actually living out the limitations that are placed on women in the realm of political activism when they have children. While being a gringa was still an axis of difference, being a mother was something I could now more fully share.

ORGANIZATION OF THE BOOK

This book is an example of what Marcus (1998) calls multisited ethnography—ethnography that considers how social processes are carried out and constructed in and through multiple sites. This emphasis on spatial multiplicity in research and writing, like the traveling metaphor, has gone far in discrediting former images of bounded communities and social processes. In writing about the Garifuna, this is a necessary and essential step because, as I will argue in the next chapter, movement and mobility are for them not merely signs of a "postmodern condition" but are rather hallmarks of the formation and historical development of their society. For 200 years, they have traveled across national borders in search of work, to sustain family connections, and to fulfill ritual obligations. Migration to the United States does not so much represent a break with a "traditional way of life" but rather a continuation of practices that had have already been long established. I try to convey this sense of movement as a normal state of affairs in my writing strategy by moving back and forth between Honduras and New York City in each chapter, showing how kinship, class, community organizing, and racial/ethnic identities are lived and negotiated through both sites simultaneously. I do not privilege either New York or Honduras as the beginning of the transmigration process but rather treat both places with equal analytical weight. In addition, I consider how both migrants and nonmigrants participate in these transnational social formations, further emphasizing the point that despite the geographical dispersion of Limoneños, there is a certain continuity of cultural ideologies and social systems throughout the transnational community. At the same time, I pay attention to the specific ways that these cultural principles and social systems are refracted through different labor markets, racial formations, and nationalist ideologies in two national contexts. This paints a complex picture of the transnational community as a space where members imagine themselves and act as one community, but where there is also social differentiation based on nation-state of residence, legal status, gender, class, and so forth.

After this general introduction, the next chapter traces the history of the Garifuna from their "ethnogenesis" on St. Vincent, to their exile to Central America, and later migration to the United States. I show that while Garifuna migration has a cultural logic specific to Garifuna history and society, the paths and possibilities of this migration have been affected by a historically shifting racialized and gendered division of labor (both national and transnational) that in many ways determines what jobs are available for whom and where. Since the 1600s, colonial administrators, state functionaries, and multinational employers have at various historical moments discursively constructed Garifuna men and women as free blacks illegitimately usurping the lands of indigenous peoples (a construction that was used to justify their exile from St. Vincent), as "native" blacks who are "good labor" (thereby giving them access to jobs with the multinational fruit companies while discouraging entrepreneurship), and as Hispanic immigrants in the United States (shaping the job niches and residential conditions they find in New York City). I explain how it is a combination of these macrostructral forces and Garifuna cultural orientations that has led to specific patterns of migration that differentiate them in some important ways from other Central Americans.

The next two chapters describe in detail the ways that the transnational community operates on a daily basis, underscoring the complexities of kinship and class in the construction of unity and diversity within the community. Chapter 3 focuses specifically on kinship, households, and community networks. I argue that the kinship system and domestic structure of "matrifocality" is one of the main organizing principles of the transnational community because it shapes the character of transnational households, patterns of remittances and investments, and community-level rituals of solidarity. At the same time, however, this principle of matrifocality is articulated with the gendered division of labor and other conditions in Honduras and New York City, creating a different set of resources, obligations, opportunities, and constraints for Garifuna men and women in the two different locations. I continue this argument as it applies to class in Chapter 4 through an analysis of the socioeconomic conditions and class dynamics of the Limoneño transnational community. I argue that while Limón–New York City can be seen as one social space linked by the transnational practices of Limoneños, each locale (Limón and New York City) must also be analyzed as a "translocality" or "place" that has a particular history and conditions shaped by the intersection of global political-economic structures and ideologies with local cultures, labor market conditions, and ethnic immigrant compositions. I use demographic data and household surveys to show that the same differences in opportunities between Honduras and the United States that drive the transnational migration circuit also create multiple class positions that Garifuna occupy vis-à-vis two national societies and one another. I use in-depth interviews and life histories to further analyze how Garifuna transmigrants, return migrants, and nonmigrants perceive of their place within the international division of labor, and how this is related to their analysis of whether migration ultimately leads to upward mobility or simply double exploitation.

In Chapter 5, I continue the discussion of how Garifuna perceive of the race and class dynamics of transnational migration through a detailed discussion of the history of two different Limoneño grassroots organizations and their strategies for community development. I show that the discourses and strategies they use to mobilize Limoneños to action emerge from both the practical experiences of economic exploitation and racial discrimination, and from a "long conversation" with discourses of development, modernity, and progress emanating from the state, international aid agencies, and NGOs. Again, using in-depth interviews with activists, teachers, and other representatives of the community, I explore the very different ways that Garifuna understand the meaning of community development and how best to carry it out.

In the final ethnographic chapter, I move away from an analysis of Limoneño organizations in particular to consider identity politics in the broader context of the Garifuna "nation in diaspora." I show that the practical experience of not quite fitting in to the hegemonic racial, ethnic, and national categories of black, indigenous, Hispanic, Honduran, and American—neither in Honduras nor in New York City—leads Garifuna to question and challenge the ways they have been inscribed into these categories. I describe how Garifuna negotiate between these different identities in a context within which each identity is ideologically linked to a certain set of rights vis-à-vis the state and the international arena.

This supports many current arguments that racial/ethnic identities are fluid, shows that the forms that they take are in many ways constrained by societal ideologies and expectations associated with particular identities.

This book is, then, both an attempt to understand the complexities of transnational migration and how it is linked to ethnic social movements in the Americas today. Though the Garifuna are a small population relative to others on the world stage, their experiences and struggles can teach us a great deal about how race and ethnicity matter in the construction of inequality and resistance to it.

2

From Indigenous Blacks to Hispanic Immigrants

A History of Garifuna Movement and Labor Migration from the 1600s to the 1990s

Don Raul and I are in his restaurant talking about his experiences in the United States. The fine cutlery and dinnerware that he brought from New York City contrast sharply with the rough construction of the wooden building. Now a return migrant, Don Raul spent the better part of his youth in the United States. He first went to New Orleans in 1956, where he worked as a cook. Eventually he became disillusioned by the official racial segregation of the U.S. south and headed for New York City in 1963. There he was able to obtain U.S. residency and a job working as the superintendent of a primarily Jewish apartment building in the South Bronx. He returned to Limón in 1990, bought a piece of land, and opened a restaurant. When asked why he migrated, he says:

> It was poverty that obligated me to leave. There was food, more than now—but it was a question of progress, of money, there was less money. Limoneños cultivated a lot, more than now. The poverty was a question of clothes, of houses—it was very difficult in those times. That was one of the reasons I left the village in those times, to better myself. I eventually sponsored all of my brothers and sisters. It is a way to break the chain of poverty—to migrate.

This was the kind of explanation I was to hear over and over in my interviews with transmigrants of Don Raul's generation. U.S.-bound migration was talked about as a duty to family members, as a means of economic upward mobility, and often as a masculine adventure to see the world. It was not talked about as a question of extreme economic deprivation, landlessness, and political violence, the kinds of narratives I was used to reading about for other Central American migrants to the United States, especially Salvadorans, Nicaraguans, and Guatemalans. This led me to see that there was something different about Garifuna migration, something that was not fully captured by the political and economic frameworks that dominate the literature on Central American migration (Burns

1993; Hagan 1994; Hamilton and Chinchilla 1991; Mahler 1995; Repak 1995; Stepick 1993; Wellmeier 1998). Indeed, Garifuna migration is more like that of Mexicans and West Indians, who began migrating to the United States early in the 1900s in response to direct recruitment by that government (the *bracero* program in the case of Mexicans and as merchant marines in the case of West Indians and Garifuna). This was the foundation for the chains of migration that would eventually snowball into a much larger phenomenon in the 1980s. In many ways, patterns of Garifuna migration seem to more closely resemble those of the West Indians (Kasinitz 1992; Levine 1987; Palmer 1990; Patterson 1987; Richardson 1992) and Mexicans (Chavez 1998; Kearney and Stuart 1981; Massey, Alarcon, Burand, and Gonzalez 1990; Mines 1981)—always present, always economically motivated, but not driven by crisis.

In contrast, larger patterns of Central American migration to the United States have been understood as a response to economic crisis and political turmoil that began in the 1970s and intensified in the 1980s. Before 1970, there was already a great deal of internal migration within Central America, as well as some professional and elite migration to the United States, but it was not until the 1980s that the number of Central American immigrants from all socioeconomic sectors rose dramatically. Focusing on this later and larger population, analytical frameworks for understanding Central American migration generally center on the dislocation of peasants, high unemployment rates, and the sharply unequal distribution of land and wealth created by capitalist penetration beginning in the 1960s that led to economic crisis and, in some countries, armed revolution and political repression in the 1970s and 1980s (Hamilton and Chinchilla 1991). In combination with these push factors, the 1980s witnessed changes in the U.S. economy that opened up more and more low-paying service sector and agricultural jobs to Central American immigrants with or without legal documentation (Sanderson 1985; Sassen-Koob 1985). Central American migration has generally been understood as a result of the restructuring of the international division of labor, the increasing absolute poverty in Central America, and political turmoil. These factors are understood to have led to the massive migration of peoples to the United States in search of better economic opportunities and political asylum.

Though patterns of Garifuna U.S.-bound migration have been impacted by these global economic changes and the political turmoil of the 1980s, these changes cannot be seen as the direct cause of Garifuna migration. That migration was established as an integral part of the social fabric well before that decade. Indeed, internal, seasonal, and transnational labor migration has been a part of Garifuna society and culture throughout Garifuna history. Many have argued that the very structure of Garifuna society is built around the extended absences of men that began with the trading patterns of the Caribs on St. Vincent, continued through the era of seasonal internal migration in Central America in the 1800s and early 1900s, and has been translated into transnational migration since the 1950s (Beaucage 1970; Gonzalez 1988; Helms 1981; Kerns 1983). Studies show that for most of Garifuna history, labor migration was not motivated by absolute poverty but was rather used as a means of obtaining industrial goods to supplement an otherwise adequate subsistence economy. Since the 1980s, however, neoliberal economic reform in Central American countries has produced an increasingly uneven distribution of land, high unemployment, and a higher cost of living, leading to the increasing dependence of many Central American households on foreign remittances. So while economic trends in the 1970s and 1980s did not initiate Garifuna migration to the United States, they have affected current patterns, opening up some opportunities and closing off others.

In this chapter, I review the history of Garifuna movement and migration from the 1600s to the beginning of the second millennium using ethnohistorical and ethnographic works and my own research data with Limoneños. Unlike many scholars of migration, I do not begin with an account of the nation of origin; instead, I begin with the origins of the Garifuna as a people. While I recognize that national context is important, I do not privilege it because in many ways Honduras is merely one of multiple sites Garifuna have passed through in their history of displacement, exile, and migration. Indeed, though there are specific studies of communities from each of the four Central American nations in which Garifuna villages are located, the picture that is drawn of Garifuna patterns of migration is strikingly similar for all four. This is due to three factors. First, employment opportunities on the Caribbean coast of all four countries since the 1800s have not only been similar but often have actually been provided by the same multinational companies. Second, the Caribbean coast of Central America has been subject to structurally similar agrarian reform and national development laws that have impacted Garifuna communities in parallel ways. Third, despite the fact that Garifuna are citizens of different nations, the cultural orientations and domestic structures through which their migration operates are consistent throughout the diaspora and are more akin to patterns found among Afro Caribbean peoples (Black West Indians) than among Hispanic populations. To understand the patterns of Garifuna movement and migration, it is necessary to go back to the beginning of Garifuna history on St. Vincent and move toward the present, seeing their society as a whole rather than merely as a number of subchapters of national histories.

This is not to say that national context is unimportant, however. Nation-building projects (both economic and cultural) have impacted Garifuna communities in some distinct ways, and migration destinations do vary for the Central American nations. For example, while Honduran Garifuna find themselves within a "Hispanic ladino nation," Belizean Garifuna find themselves within a "Black West Indian nation." Also, while Honduran Garifuna mainly migrate to New York City, Belizean Garifuna are more abundant in Los Angeles. I will discuss the role these differences play in the politics of diaspora in later chapters. For now, I will focus on the history of the Garifuna as a whole up to the 1950s and then use my own research data to show the particular context of Honduran Garifuna migration to New York City from 1950 to the 1990s (for studies of Belizeans in Los Angeles, see Macklin 1985 and Miller 1993).

OF HOMELANDS AND EXILES: BEGINNINGS ON ST. VINCENT

Ethnohistorical and ethnographic accounts of the Garifuna unanimously portray them as a people for whom male mobility and labor migration have been integral elements of their culture from the moment of their "ethnogenesis" on St. Vincent in the 1600s.[1] This orientation is attributed both to the social structure and economic activities inherited from the Island Carib and the exigencies of the colonial economy and later exile. Even before the arrival of Europeans or Africans to the Caribbean, Carib men traveled throughout the Caribbean to engage in trading, raiding, and warfare. The long absences of men were facilitated by a social organization that created villages centered on women's networks and labor. This was achieved through the practice of matrilocal postmarital residence; grooms went to live in the villages of their wives. This created strong networks of female kin because mothers, daughters, and sisters were not separated and could engage in collective forms of labor and childcare. The sexual division of labor also placed the responsibility for growing food on the women, who lived more permanently in the village and were more able to tend their plots. Primary food production and childrearing were carried out by female kin, who formed the core of the village, while men moved around for warfare, trading, and fishing and to visit wives in other villages (Helms 1981).

When Europeans began to settle on the Caribbean islands in the early 1600s, the Caribs engaged the Spanish, Dutch, French, and British in both trade and warfare for over 100 years. The Caribs used two strategies in their attempts to prevent further colonization of the Lesser Antilees: allying themselves with a European force whose aim was to prevent the colonization of an island by another national group and organizing large-scale raids on European settlements, during which time they often captured African slaves. By 1660, however, the Caribs had been weakened and an agreement was signed that the islands of Dominica and St. Vincent would be declared "reserves" where Caribs could live unmolested by Europeans, who would then go about the business of colonizing the surrounding islands (Wilson 1993, 1997).

Though part of the agreement was that the Caribs would no longer raid European settlements or harbor runaway slaves, they clearly continued to do so (Beaucage 1970, 41). As early as 1612, European writers noted the appearance of a large number of Africans among the Carib war and trading parties (Wilson 1993, 1997). This population of Africans was progressively augmented by the wreck of one or several slave ships (for which several dates are given—1635, 1675, 1742) and by the integration of African maroons from neighboring islands. By 1700, British and French documents began to refer to the "Black Caribs" as a separate group from the "Red Caribs," claiming that the former had come to dominate the latter, causing a split and hostilities between the two groups (Beaucage 1970, 43; Kerns 1983, 22).

Whether or not the Black and Red Caribs came to form two separate groups and, if they did, the nature of the relations between them is highly contested. In a critical analysis of European colonial discourse of indigenous and African groups in early Caribbean history, Hulme and Whitehead (1992) argue that the narrative of the Black and Red Caribs as distinct ethnic groups stems from European notions that race constituted inherently distinct essences marked by color. Europeans assumed that dispositions, cultural practices, and political alignments could be demarcated by phenotypes. In colonial documents, the Black Caribs came to carry the trope of degenerate and dangerous blacks (fed at the time by colonial fears of slave rebellion), while the Red Caribs came to represent the docile, victimized indigenous population (Anderson 1997). According to Hulme and Whitehead, this demarcation was convenient for French and British colonists, who used it as a way to justify policies of expansion into Carib territory on St. Vincent as "saving" the Red Carib from Black Carib domination.

This narrative of racial distinction is constantly interrupted, however, by accounts that portray the two groups as allies and/or as one phenotypically diverse but culturally unitary group, blurring the presumed racial and therefore political boundary between them. Whether or not they were a distinct group at this point in history, most ethnohistorians agree that the people who came to be referred to as the Black Caribs during the 1700s had the same basic social structure as that described for the Island Carib, established themselves politically and economically on the island, and continued to acquire trade goods through exchange with Europeans (Beaucage 1970; Gullick 1976; Helms 1981; Kerns 1983; Taylor 1951). Throughout the 1600s and 1700s, French and British colonists settled on the leeward side of St. Vincent with their African slaves and were involved in cash cropping (of sugarcane, cacao, coffee, indigo, cotton, and so forth) and cattle raising. Black Caribs were mainly concentrated on the windward side of the island, where they protected their territory from European settlement. During this period, women sold agricultural products in local markets to these colonists, both men and women traded natural resources for manufactured goods, and Black Caribs were introduced to Catholicism and the French and English languages. Accounts claim that some chiefs produced cotton and tobacco with plantations and even slaves and that many of the men hired themselves out to transport sugar by canoe from the shore to British cargo ships. Thus, the accumulation of goods through raiding and warfare was replaced by economic exchange in the form of trade, wage labor, and cash cropping. Beaucage (1970) argues that this entrance into the money economy did not fundamentally alter Black Carib economic values or the division of labor because wage labor and cash cropping were mainly done in order to buy manufactured goods, not to survive, and employed a sexual division of labor that was consistent with past practices (that is, women in agriculture, men in wage labor and trade).

As the century progressed, the British became more interested in the island for the production of sugarcane and in obtaining Carib lands to do so. In 1763, St. Vincent was ceded to the British through the Treaty of Paris, effectively ending official Carib control of the island and beginning the process of encroachment on Carib lands by St. Vincent planters (Gonzalez 1988). British documents speak of failed attempts to convince the Black Caribs to sell their lands and lament the "underuse" of these lands for swidden instead of for intensive agricultural production (Kerns 1983, 26). This encroachment on Carib lands led to tensions and warfare in 1772, in 1779, and again in 1795 when the Caribs (Black and Red), under the leadership of a Black Carib chief, Chatoyer (Satuye), sided with the French to fight the British. The Carib-French alliance was defeated in 1796, the French were sent to the island of Guadelupe, and about 5,000 Black Caribs were rounded up and exiled to Central America. The Red Caribs found among them were separated from the Black and remained on St. Vincent.

Gonzalez (1988) argues that British documents speak of wanting to remove the Black Caribs from St. Vincent even before 1772, which proves that the presence of politically and economically autonomous free blacks on the island was seen as a nuisance and a danger even before there was open warfare. The fact that the Black and Red Caribs were separated also reveals the discourse of racial distinction the British used to claim that the Black Caribs were usurping the land from the gentle Red Caribs, who they promoted as the legitimate owners of the land. As Mark Anderson argues:

> It is clear that in the end Europeans did not simply use a distinction of "Black" and "Red" Caribs as a justification for the conquest of St. Vincent, but also employed these categories to make sense of the complex racial and cultural dynamics among the residents of the island. Emerging victorious in 1796, the British carried that understanding to its logical conclusion, classifying the Caribs according to color and "sending the yellow (lighter-skinned) people back to St. Vincent" to live on reserves and the Blacks to permanent exile in Central America. In this sense the "origins" of the people known today as the Garifuna should not only be traced to a process of racial-cultural interchange in the 17th century but also to the racial segregation of so-called and so-determined Black Caribs at the moment of deportation. (Anderson 1997, 27)

From this account, it is obvious that from the beginning of its history, Garifuna society was shaped by the combination of preexisting Carib and African socioeconomic structures and cultural forms and the racial and economic logics of European colonialism. European discursive constructions of the Garifuna as illegitimate usurpers of indigenous lands reveal how racial discourses are mobilized in the service of different economic and political projects, in this case to justify colonial domination and the expansion of a global mercantile capitalism in the Caribbean. These discursive and material relations of power ultimately led to the exile of the Garifuna from their place of "ethnogenesis" and insertion into yet another location of the colonial economic and cultural power struggle.

A New Homeland: Central America

In 1797, after an arduous journey from St. Vincent that reduced the number of the survivors of the Carib wars by half, about 2,000 Garifuna were left on the island of Roatan off the North Coast of Honduras. After a short period, they made their way to the mainland at Trujillo, then a Spanish fort and small town. At the time of their arrival, the Caribbean coast of Central America was relatively unpopulated because of the decimation of the indigenous population by slaving, disease, dislocation, and warfare and the fact that most Spaniards and ladinos did not want to settle in what they considered to be an area made inhospitable (and unprofitable at the time) by the tropical climate, distance from the main population centers of the Central American colonial provinces, and the presence of "jungle Indians" and pirates (Floyd 1967; Naylor 1986; Newson 1986). Most Spanish settlement was on the Pacific side and the interior, where there were indigenous peoples to put on *encomiendas,* cultivate indigo and cacao, and collect tribute from. The Spanish found the seminomadic indigenous peoples of the coast and the east to be unwilling to settle in permanent villages to engage in these economic pursuits; they tended to flee to the mountains instead. The Spanish were mostly interested in the alluvial gold deposits they exploited through Indian and African slave labor and the establishment of Spanish ports along the coast to allow for the transport of cacao, indigo, and other goods to Spanish settlements in the Caribbean and to Europe (MacLeod 1973; Newson 1986). The lack of Spanish settlement in the area made these ports vulnerable to attack by British and Dutch pirates, necessitating the erection of forts to defend them and stake a claim to the territory for the Spanish Crown. Thus, while Honduran histories often present the Caribbean coast of Central America as a frontier zone on the margins of the Spanish colonies that were relatively unimportant to the formation of the national society and national events, it was actually already a center of racial and cultural diversity and exchange, transnational commerce, and international political maneuvering.

British presence on the Caribbean coast of Central America began in the 1600s with a few settlements in the Mosquitia, the Bay Islands, the San Andres Islands, and Belize. These British, known as buccaneers and baymen, established a few sugar plantations in Central America for which African slaves were imported from the Caribbean, but the plantations were not very successful (Floyd 1967). Most economic activity revolved around trade with the indigenous population for such goods as sarsaparilla, sea turtle shells and meat, and other marine and forest products in exchange for rum, guns, and other European manufactured products. Other activities included logging of precious woods, contraband trading with ladino settlements of the interior, and raiding Spanish ports and ships. Throughout the period, British interest in the area was more focused on controlling trade than in colonizing, and they depended greatly on alliances with the indigenous population (Floyd 1967; MacLeod 1973; Naylor 1986).

The most important alliance the Anglos made with Indians in the area Garifuna were to settle in was with the Miskitu of the Mosquito Coast (La Mosquitia), an area that spans eastern Honduras and northwestern Nicaragua. Miskitu men served as middlemen between the indigenous peoples of the interior (Paya, Sumu, Rama, and Tawaka) who collected forest products and the buccaneers who provided European manufactured goods. In 1687, the British cemented this relationship more formally by declaring the Mosquitia a kingdom with whom the British Crown was in alliance. During the next 200 years, the Miskitu expanded their territory of influence, making claims as far north as Trujillo, Honduras, and as far south as San Juan del Norte, Costa Rica. This alliance created a loyalty to the British, and Miskitu often joined them in raiding Spanish settlements and forts (Floyd 1967; Hale 1994b; Naylor 1986).

Though the Spanish had only a weak presence in the area, they consistently claimed prior sovereignty over the Mosquitia and the Bay of Honduras, alleging that the Mosquito Kingdom was a farcical strategy on the part of the British to take advantage of "naive and savage" Indians for their own political purposes. After more than a century of attacks and counterattacks on Atlantic Coast settlements and forts, the British agreed in 1787 to give up any claims to the Bay of Honduras in exchange for grants of logging concessions to British entrepreneurs by the Spanish Crown and the right to maintain settlements in Belize. Yet the continued isolation of the coast from the centers of Spanish power, the lack of Spanish settlement, continued British interest in trading and logging, and the refusal of the Miskitu to give up their claim as an autonomous kingdom maintained the Atlantic coast as a zone of Anglo-Spanish conflict well into the 1800s. It was not until 1860 that the British relinquished all rights over the Bay Islands and the Mosquito Shore to Honduras in exchange for solidification of their control over Belize as a British colony.

It is within this political and cultural milieu that the Garifuna entered the scene in 1797, just twenty-four years before Central American independence. Trujillo had already existed as a Spanish fort for two centuries and had considerable settlement around it. Some Garifuna stayed near Trujillo, where they established themselves as agriculturists and fishermen who provided goods for the local markets. Others moved east toward the Mosquitia, where they settled villages within the boundaries of the Miskitu Kingdom, reaching as far south as Bluefields, Nicaragua, while others went west to southern Belize, arriving as early as 1802 to work in the British logging camps there. All along the coast they encountered isolated and largely uninhabited stretches of beach, where they established villages generally at the mouths of rivers. Here they were able to take advantage of marine, riparian, and forest resources, and they were able to reproduce to a large degree the economic activities and division of labor they had on St. Vincent (Beaucage 1970; Davidson 1976). Women continued as the main cultivators of cassava and other ground foods, and men contributed the initial labor of clearing the plot and helped with harvests. Plots were located away from the village, accessible by travel upriver or down the coast by canoe.

Though cultivation was mainly for subsistence, women in villages located near ports produced agricultural goods and raised animals (pigs and chickens) for sale to markets at key times of the year, such as Christmas, when they wanted to buy manufactured goods. Women could also be hired to do laundry and cook for travelers, seasonal workers, and the military (Miller 1993).

Even at this early date, British and American travelers to Central America noted that Garifuna men were often absent from the villages. They traveled up and down the coast, where they engaged in wage labor such as transporting goods for hire between Belize and Honduras (which the Crown and later the Honduran state considered to be smuggling) and working in the British mahogany logging camps of the Mosquitia and Belize and on sugar plantations— employment niches opened by labor shortages created by the end of the slave trade in 1807 (Bolland 1977). Garifuna used wages earned in these enterprises to buy European manufactured goods (such as cloth, cutlery, soap, and metal tools), which they carried back to the villages. The time men spent in the villages was dedicated to fishing, building houses, and making canoes, the implements to make cassava bread, and fishing nets. In the late 1800s, many men invested their cash earnings in the cultivation of coconuts (to be made into copra) to sell to the North American and European schooners that traveled along the coast. Men and women also grew bananas in small-scale enterprises (*poquitero*) to sell to these schooners (Charles 1890; Gonzalez 1988; Kerns 1983). Coconuts were particularly popular because their cultivation is compatible with migratory wage labor; it required an initial input of labor and capital but after that only light maintenance, which could be done by relatives or the migrants when they visited home. Most households relied on a combination of the subsistence cultivation of women, the migratory wage labor of men, and some cash cropping by men and women. The general picture Beaucage and others draw of Garifuna in the 1800s is one of a people who were primarily self- sufficient in terms of basic needs but who had developed a taste for consumer goods that was most quickly met by male migratory wage labor.

THE CONSTRUCTION OF GARIFUNA MEN AS "GOOD LABOR"

The 1800s is often presented as a second golden era in Garifuna history (the first being the period of autonomy on St. Vincent)—a period of the expansion of the Garifuna population and reconstruction of their society after the disruptive effects of exile, a time when the Garifuna were once again able to maintain relative political and cultural autonomy while at the same time taking advantage of opportunities for wage labor and small enterprises such as the *po-*

quitero. Despite the jealously guarded isolation of Garifuna villages (attributed to a lingering fear of loss of autonomy after their experience on St. Vincent), the presence of Garifuna on the Caribbean coast and the mobility of Garifuna men brought them into contact with a wide variety of groups—Spanish, British, North Americans, indigenous people, and even Black Haitians fleeing the Haitian revolution who had settled around Trujillo. After the independence of the Central American nations from Spain in 1821, many European and American travelers became interested in Central America because of its natural resources and as a possible interoceanic route. In their evaluations of the resource and human potential of Central America, these writers generally depicted the Garifuna as an almost cosmopolitan group that was already privy to the "civilized manner" of wage labor and consumption of European manufactured goods, as people who were widely traveled, were familiar with a wide variety of European languages, and were (at least nominally) Catholic. The conclusion most of these writers drew was that the Garifuna showed promise for "progress towards civilization" as a good population of "industrious and ingenious" laborers and consumers (Anderson 1997; Gonzalez 1988).

This portrayal of the Garifuna is interesting given the predominance of colonial and postcolonial discourses of race in the Americas in which blackness was generally equated with a lack of civilization, racial impurity, degenerate character, and lack of industry (Gilroy 1993a; Wade 1993). These are the same images and discourses French and British writers used to describe the "Black Caribs" on St. Vincent to discredit their claims to St. Vincent as a homeland. Blackness was contrasted with the nobility and passivity of the Red Caribs, whose nativeness justified their need for Europeans to "protect" them from the Black Carib. This discourse reappears in Central America in discussions between Spanish and Anglos about the Miskitus, who had also mixed with Africans (brought as slaves by the British). Mary Helms (1977) shows how Spanish authors condemned the Miskitu as hostile savages and British lackeys, emphasizing their African features and "degenerate" character and attacking the legitimacy of the Miskitu Kingdom. The British, on the other hand, emphasized an Indian heritage, drawing a clear distinction between impure Miskitus who had mixed with Africans (called *zambos*) and pure Miskitus with whom the British claimed to be allied and whose nativeness legitimized the Miskitu Kingdom's claims over its territory. Although these writers argue about the extent of African heritage among the Miskitu, they share a common racial logic that equates blackness with degeneracy and portrays miscegenation or "hybridization" as a form of further debasement of the "blood" of "pure" Indians (Anderson 1997; Helms 1977; Olien 1985).

There is, however, another logic at work here—the economic logic of "productivity." Though Anglo writers generally portrayed the Indians as noble and passive, the fact that they wanted to stay far from European settlements and were not easily convinced to engage in wage labor led the Anglos to conclude that they had yet to discover a "love of money" and therefore would not constitute a reliable workforce. It was in this respect that the Garifuna differed from Indians in the minds of Anglos. Mark Anderson argues that representations of the Garifuna by Anglo authors of the 1800s are striking in that they consistently recognize the phenotypical blackness of the Garifuna yet at same time point out their "exceptional" character as a strong and healthy race of good laborers. "For foreigners such as [Thomas] Young [a British envoy], the willing participation of the Garifuna in the expanding wage economy translates into a positive evaluation of their inner character, rendering them superior to other non-white populations on the Atlantic coast despite their visible 'blackness'" (1997, 30). The British viewed Garifuna positively as a people who had already accepted a money economy that had expanded their notion of needs beyond the realm of subsistence. Thus, as laborers and consumers they were useful to the Anglo entrepreneur, along with the other abundant local resources.[2]

Consequently, in 1899, when the United Fruit Company, the Standard Fruit Company (formerly Vacarro Brothers), and the Cuyamel Fruit Company (which had been buying bananas from *poquitero* growers) began to receive land concessions from Central American nations to cultivate bananas, Garifuna men were among the laborers they preferred. Ladinos from the interior of Honduras and Guatemala and from El Salvador began migrating to the North Coast of Honduras to work on the plantations as well. Despite the protests of the Honduran government, the banana companies also began importing Black West Indians in 1912, citing labor shortages and the better physical suitability of blacks (including the Garifuna) for hard labor in the tropical climate, as opposed to ladinos, who they said succumbed easily to the heat and tropical diseases; and indigenous peoples, who had the reputation of generally avoiding wage labor (Argueta 1992; Echeverri-Gent 1992; see also Bourgois 1989 and Purcell 1993 for black labor on the banana plantations of Costa Rica and Conniff 1985 for black labor on the Panama Canal). Black West Indians were also preferred because they spoke English and were otherwise "anglicized." They were often given the preferable jobs of working on the railroads, in port cities, and as crew heads. This labor pool included some Garifuna who either immigrated from Belize or had spent time in Belize in the British mahogany camps, where they learned English.

In the 1920s, this racial diversity became an issue of national debate, especially about the races that were considered undesirable. Black West Indians especially bore the brunt of an incipient racialized nationalist discourse expressed by both ladino plantation workers with whom they competed for jobs and the Honduran elite, which was balking at the imperialistic power of the fruit companies. Both sectors argued that blacks were not only a threat to employment opportunities for "Honduran" (ladino) workers but also were a threat to the "blood" of the nation and to the image of Honduras in the world community of nations. This resulted in strikes led by ladino-dominated unions that demanded the repatriation of West Indian workers and restrictions on further immigration of blacks, Arabs, and "coolies" that were often stated in explicitly racist language (Argueta 1992; Echeverri-Gent 1992; Euraque 1998; Posas 1981b). This put the Garifuna in the paradoxical situation of being ideologically and culturally positioned between the "native ladino" and the "foreign black." In company records and other state documents, for example, they are listed neither as "*hondureños*" (which implied ladino) nor as "*negros*" (which implied West Indians) but rather as "*morenos*," racially black but not foreign (Anderson 2000).

In any case, Garifuna ethnicity became a form of cultural capital, a way for Garifuna to distinguish themselves from indigenous peoples, ladinos, and even other blacks through their reputation as good "native" workers (Beaucage 1989; Coehlo 1995; Gonzalez 1988). While Garifuna men may have actively promoted this unique ethnicity to gain jobs preferable to planting, weeding, harvesting, and so forth on the plantations, they were certainly still constrained by a racial order that placed most of them beyond the pale of the Anglo employees and ladino elite. They were hired in positions that would have made the accumulation of wealth difficult, positions that enabled them to maintain their valued positions as "good labor" but did not enable them to engage in capitalist entrepreneurship.

As a result of the presence of the fruit companies, then, from 1900 to 1930 the population of the North Coast grew with the influx of ladino and black workers, European and North American managers and capitalists, and even Palestinian, Lebanese, and Chinese immigrants attracted by entrepreneurial opportunities in the enclave economy. The port towns of Puerto Cortez, Tela, La Ceiba, Trujillo, and Puerto Castilla in Honduras; Puerto Barrios, Guatemala; Belize City, Belize; and Bluefields, Nicaragua grew in size and importance in their respective national economies. Garifuna men became employees of the fruit companies as plantation harvesters, railroad mechanics, port stevedores, and service employees for the managers and other occupations in the banana enclaves (carpenters, metalsmiths, and so forth). Fruit company employment was compatible with labor migration patterns Garifuna men had already established. They worked on the plantations and in the ports for eight to ten months of the year and returned home at key periods in the agricultural cycle and for holidays. Cash cropping declined in importance for Garifuna during this period due to the drop in the price of copra on the world market and the impossibility of competing with the multinational fruit companies in banana cultivation (Beaucage 1970). Other opportunities opened up, however, and in the 1920s some Garifuna in Honduras were raising cattle to sell for meat to plantation workers, though they did not eat much of it themselves (they preferred fish). In 1935, the Standard Fruit Company opened a vegetable-oil factory in La Ceiba that bought *corozo* (cohune palm nuts) collected mainly by women. These cash-generating activities were compatible with male migration and female subsistence practices, supplementing these forms of livelihood.

In the 1930s, banana production experienced a slump due to the world recession and the spread of the banana disease *sigatoka*. The United Fruit Company reduced its scope of operations, pulling out of Colón and the Mosquitia as well as southern Belize. Men from these areas now had to migrate to the western departments of Honduras (Atlántida, Yoro, and Cortez) and to Guatemala to find employment in port cities and plantations. Some ladino and West Indian workers settled on the land left vacant by the departure of the fruit companies, establishing *aldeas* (hamlets) near Garifuna villages and engaging in agriculture and cattle ranching.

SHIFTING DESTINATIONS OF MIGRATION: INTERNAL AND ABROAD

In the 1940s, Garifuna men found a new, more lucrative occupation as merchant marines. This employment niche opened up due to the decrease in North American manpower during World War II, which led shipping companies to recruit merchant marines from the ports of Central America and the West Indies. Though it meant longer periods away from their villages and families, many Garifuna men chose this work because it paid better than plantation labor and they were able to have the company regularly send a portion of their check to family members in the villages. In addition, merchant marines continued to receive checks upon retirement, which meant the possibility of living out old age in relative luxury in Central America. Some of these men joined the National Maritime Union, headquartered in New York City, then a center of the shipping industry. Membership in the union afforded merchant marines higher wages, benefits, and U.S. residency, but it also meant that members had to visit the headquarters in order to change companies, put papers in order, and so forth. Some Garifuna men set up a residential base in New York City, forming the pioneer population of Garifuna migrants to the city.

Employment in the merchant marine and migration to the United States became increasingly popular in the 1950s as a result of another decline in employment opportunities in the banana enclaves. In 1954, Honduran North Coast banana-plantation workers and laborers in the small factories of San Pedro Sula, La Ceiba, and Tegucigalpa joined in a general strike that lasted for three months.[3] It finally ended in a settlement that included the legalization of unionization, institution of benefits, and permanent employment (as opposed to seasonal contract labor). Despite the fact that these were victories for labor, within a year the fruit companies switched to more mechanized forms of production and reduced their labor forces by half (Dunkerly 1988; Euraque 1996b; Posas and del Cid 1983). For Garifuna men, these changes in plantation labor made employment with the fruit companies less appealing. In order to receive benefits they had to become permanent and regular employees, which would have interfered with their preference for flexible seasonal labor that allowed them vacations of several months to return to their villages. Some men brought their families to live with them in the *campos* (plantation camps), but by the latter part of the 1960s, plantation labor had become much less popular and more Garifuna began going to major cities to work in the service industry and factories. Others opted to find work in the fishing industry of the Bay Islands. Still others went to the United States.

Data collected by Canadian anthropologist Pierre Beaucage in Limón in 1963 demonstrates that while destinations of male labor migrants were changing due to shifting opportunities, migration as a socioeconomic feature of Garifuna society remained constant.[4] Beaucage interviewed fifty-nine Garifuna men to elicit information about their migration histories and those of their fathers and children (see Table 2.1). Of the fifty-nine interviewees, fifty-three were or had been labor migrants, beginning their migration careers at an average age of eighteen and spending an average of fifteen years outside their villages. If the median age of the interviewees is fifty and the median age of first migration is seventeen, then this sample essentially represents migration from the 1930s to 1963. The vast majority of this generation of men had migrated to work for the multinational fruit companies on the plantations and in the port cities. The most popular occupation listed was *finquero* or *yardero* (plantation worker), the second most popular was *muellero* (stevedore), and the rest were cooks, tailors, mechanics, brakemen, carpenters, servants, day laborers, and others. Most of the fathers of the interviewees (a group that would include those who had migrated before the 1930s) had migrated to Belize or Nicaragua to work in logging and/or gone to the ports and plantations of the fruit companies. None of the fathers were listed as migrating to the cities of the Honduran interior or to the United States. In contrast, none of the children of the men interviewed

Table 2.1. Migration Destinations for Three Generations of Garifuna Men in a
Population Interviewed by Pierre Beaucage, 1930s–1960s

Destination	Father of Interviewee	Interviewee	Children of Interviewee
Total Incidents of Migration	28	92	40
Logging Camps			
Belize	10	5	0
Nicaragua	1	0	0
Total logging	11	5	0
Fruit Plantations			
Tela	4	14	0
Puerto Castilla	3	15	0
La Ceiba	2	24	5
Plantations	4	19	2
Shipping	4	4	2
Total Fruit Companies	17	76	9
Honduran Cities			
San Pedro Sula	0	6	10
Tegucigalpa	0	2	7
Total Honduran cities	0	8	17
United States	0	3	14

Source: Migration surveys of Pierre Beaucage, 1963.

(whose sex was not specified in this study) were involved in logging and only a
few were engaged in plantation labor. The majority had migrated to Honduran
cities and to the United States (the city was either unspecified or was listed as
New York City). This sample is one illustration of the progressive shift in the
destinations of Garifuna male migrants away from the logging camps and plantations of the Central American Caribbean coast to the cities of the interior and
the United States.

Though women were largely excluded from Beaucage's survey,[5] other ethnographic data points to the increasing migration of Garifuna women during
this period. Coehlo, who conducted field work in the late 1940s, mentions
that Honduran women had migrated to Central American cities and ports as
domestics, cooks, and nurses (Coehlo 1995, 110). Gonzalez reports that while
few of the labor migrants she surveyed in Livingston, Guatemala, in 1956 were

women, nearly half of the labor migrants she surveyed were women by 1975. Interestingly, the United States was a more common destination for women at that time than it was for men, who were still working mainly in Central America (Gonzalez 1987, 152–153). This is because more women in the United States (both white and African American) were entering the labor market, which created a demand for women to work as domestics and in child care that was largely filled by women from the Caribbean, Mexico, and Central America (Enloe 1989; Foner 1986; Hondagneu-Sotelo 1994a; Repak 1995; Sassen-Koob 1984; Watkins-Owens 2001).

Kerns (1983) and Miller (1993) also document increased labor migration among Belizean Garifuna women in the 1970s, who worked on plantations packing bananas and in towns and cities as shop clerks, domestics, teachers, and nurses. Both argue that while there was no cultural resistance in Garifuna society to women taking jobs, women were greatly disadvantaged in the labor market; they found more temporary jobs and earned up to one-third less than men in comparable positions. Many women preferred to stay in their villages, where they could engage in multiple occupations (doing stints of wage labor, selling bread, cultivating, and so forth) and where they paid no rent, had no child care costs, and had plenty of female relatives to help out. Alternatively, a growing number of women chose to migrate to the United States, where the growing demand for domestic labor and home health care was a more lucrative option than working in the Central American labor market.

The shifting destinations of migration reveal more than changes in Garifuna work patterns; they also reveal the changing relation of Garifuna to the national societies within which they resided. Logging and plantation labor were predominantly located on the Caribbean coast in areas culturally dominated by English-speaking blacks, Anglos, and indigenous peoples, groups that were removed from the centers of Hispanic society. The 1950s marks the beginning of greater integration into and identification with the national societies of residence as more Garifuna sought jobs outside of the plantation enclave, moved to the capital cities, attended urban schools, and even began to attend national universities to be trained as teachers, doctors, and nurses (Beaucage 1989). In Belize especially, Garifuna became known as proficient teachers and many now hold government posts (Kerns 1983; Miller 1993). By the 1970s, ethnographers were already referring to Garifuna villages as "nurseries and nursing homes," implying that the majority of the male working-age population (and increasingly the female working-age population) was away from the village, either for many years or seasonally. They left behind a population of primarily elderly men and women and young children that engaged in some agriculture and fishing but primarily relied on money earned outside the village (Beaucage 1970; Gonzalez 1988; Instituto de Investigaciones Económicos y Sociales 1965; Kerns 1983).

While Garifuna villages fit the characteristics of rural communities with access to land and marine resources, they were highly proletarianized. In Honduras, the origins of this *patron asalariado* (pattern of wage labor) cannot be explained simply as a function of a lack of access to land. It must also be understood as a result of certain Garifuna economic practices and cultural orientations that were not conducive to the development of large-scale commercial agriculture as an alternative mode of generating cash. One of these factors was the dominance of customary pricing in the local markets. In a system of customary pricing, the prices do not respond to supply and demand but rather stay the same based on customs. Everyone agrees on the "normal price." Anyone who goes above that price is socially stigmatized. This reduces incentives for capital inputs, as prices cannot be raised to cover the cost of inputs. Exchange between village members was largely based on reciprocity, and the prevailing sentiment among Garifuna was that any hint of profit maximization and accumulation of wealth was morally suspect by the community. Another disincentive is that at the time of Beaucage's field work, Garifuna did not consider land to be a commodity and therefore it did not serve as a form of capital or stored wealth. Rights to land stemmed only from the act of clearing it for cultivation; however, this sense of ownership lasted only as long as the crops did. As a result, land was a free resource, and few Garifuna sought to accumulate it through private ownership. In addition, even if Garifuna wanted to engage in cash cropping, there were no suitable markets for the main agricultural products they grew because they were not part of the ladino diet (for more detailed explanation, see Beaucage 1970).

In the 1970s, this situation changed as more ladinos began moving into the North Coast municipalities, looking for land to claim for small-scale farming, ranches, and agroindustry. This forced Garifuna to begin the process of legalizing their plots of land as individual owners to avoid its expropriation by the Instituto Nacional Agrario (INA). It has also encouraged Garifuna to give their land a "social function"—a criteria the INA uses to determine whether land is being used or not. Since fallowing and mixed-crop swidden agriculture are often not considered to fulfill this criteria, many Garifuna have lost land that had belonged to their families for generations through customary recognition of use rights. This situation has been exacerbated in the last few decades by increasing economic difficulties that have encouraged some Garifuna to sell land to the highest bidder. Although land scarcity may not have been the impetus for U.S.-bound migration initially, migration and access to land became intertwined during the 1970s and villagers began to feel more squeezed as they had less and less agricultural land on less productive soil, making them even more dependent on wage labor.

The fact that Garifuna have not generally been heavily involved in cash cropping does not mean, however, that land is not important to them. All ethnographers have noted that no matter how far Garifuna men migrate or for how many years, a substantial number of them return regularly to their natal village and most eventually retire there. Some of these retirees invest their savings in land, becoming large landowners who raise cattle and grow sugarcane, bananas, corn, beans, and other crops (Coehlo 1995, 113). Migration rather than agriculture is seen as the *first* avenue of generating capital, which may then later be used to invest in land and agricultural production or in small businesses. So while agriculture has not been the primary source of income for most households it is still important as a resource to fall back on in times of unemployment and as a source of many of the crops particular to the Garifuna diet. Land is also important for collecting medicinal plants and materials with which to build houses and canoes. Most important, agricultural land, the coastal area, and villages are all ideologically constructed as a safe space of cultural and familial reproduction. Even as Garifuna integrate into Honduran society and migrate to the United States, the village continues to be important as a place to call home, especially given the racialized division of labor and power they find outside it.

Exploring New Options: Migration to the United States

During the same period when both men and women began migrating to the cities of Central America in larger numbers, other Garifuna began migrating to the United States. Merchant marines who had settled in the United States became the pioneers who sponsored the migration of family members and friends, establishing the basis of transnational migration networks. As early as 1955, Coehlo wrote that there were enough Honduran Garifuna in New York to have their own club (1995, 51). By the 1970s, some men had already retired to their home villages with houses and land, receiving retirement checks that made them wealthy by Central American standards (Gonzalez 1988, 176). These men clearly served as the example that set the standard for the level of upward mobility that could be achieved and how best to accomplish it. For several decades, U.S.-bound migration was dominated by men who worked in the merchant marine and in factories. By 1970, this changed as more Garifuna women arrived to reunite with family members and because they were attracted by opportunities for employment in the feminized service sector.

Garifuna men who migrated to the United States in the 1940s and 1950s entered an industrial economy still based largely on manufacturing and a large unionized blue-collar labor sector was made up primarily of white ethnics and African Americans. Though many Garifuna men continued to work as merchant marines, some also found employment in factories and in building maintenance, jobs through which they gained union membership. This changed in the 1960s and 1970s, however, as global economic trends led many of these manufacturers to send their operations overseas and/or shift operations in the United States to more high-tech forms of production and assembly that require fewer skills than traditional blue-collar manufacturing jobs. Cities such as Los Angeles and New York that had been major manufacturing centers have shifted to economies based more on this "downgraded" manufacturing sector (that is, sweatshops, nonunionized contract labor, and industrial homework) and on information technology and services (Drennan 1991; Sassen 1994; Waldinger and Bozorgmehr 1996). For example, between 1969 and 1977 many factories and related services, such as warehouses and trucking companies, moved out of New York City to the suburbs or out of state, creating a sharp decline in blue-collar employment in the city. From 1977 to 1987, New York experienced an economic recovery when it became the headquarters of the majority of the 100 largest multinational corporations and related corporate services (finance, insurance, real estate, banking, and so forth). Though new jobs were created, the labor market of this postindustrial economy is highly polarized between high-wage technical and specialty white-collar service jobs and low-wage, low-skilled manufacturing and service jobs (Drennan 1991). As Sassen-Koob (1984) argues, these low-wage jobs are very unattractive to U.S. laborers and have been increasingly filled by immigrants, especially women immigrants. Consequently, Garifuna women found that they had more opportunities for work in the United States at higher wages than what they could earn in Central America.

This shift in the U.S. economy was accompanied by a shift in the racial/ethnic composition of the immigrant population in the United States in general and New York City and Los Angeles in particular. Before 1965, immigration quotas linked to national origins limited the number of immigrants from many so-called Third World countries in Latin America, the Caribbean, and Asia except through labor certification, and the majority of immigrants to New York City were European. In the 1960s climate of protest against racial and ethnic discrimination, the national origins quotas established by the McCarren-Walter Act in 1952 were abolished in 1965, shifting the criteria for legal entry more towards family reunification, refugee status, and skills needed in the United States (Reimers 1987). Thus, after 1965 the number of immigrants from the Caribbean, Latin America, and Asia increased dramatically, and Los Angeles and New York City received the largest share of them. While Los Angeles received more Asians and Mexicans, New York immigrants were more likely to be from the Caribbean and South America. West Indians and Puerto Ricans had been migrating to New York in substantial numbers even before 1965, but their numbers increased sharply after 1965 and they were joined by Dominicans, Jamaicans, Chinese, Haitians, Guyanese, and Colombians (the top six source countries to New York City in the 1980s) and a host of others, changing the racial/ethnic composition of many New York City boroughs (New York City Department of City Planning 1992a).

This shift is readily apparent in the Bronx, where many Garifuna eventually settled. The Jewish, Italian, and Irish blue-collar workforce that dominated the Bronx moved out just as Puerto Ricans, Dominicans, and West Indians moved in. This white flight was related to the loss of jobs and the falling value of rental income, which led landlords to neglect their buildings, at times even torching them to collect the insurance instead of keeping them up. By the 1970s, the South Bronx had become a national prototype of infrastructural and social breakdown, generating images of anarchy and decay such as those in the 1981 Hollywood movie *Fort Apache the Bronx* (Breslin 1995). New York City census data show that from 1970 to 1980, the total population of the Bronx dropped by 20.6 percent. From 1980 to 1990, it increased by only 3 percent. What is most striking, however, is the ethnic dimensions of this population shift. From 1980 to 1990, the Hispanic population rose by 32 percent while the white non-Hispanic population *dropped* by 32 percent. The black non-Hispanic population stayed relatively steady, rising by only 5 percent (New York City Department of City Planning 1994/1995, 7–8).[6] These trends are most pronounced in the community districts of the South and Central Bronx (see Table 2.2).

In the 1970s, as the Bronx became increasingly Hispanic, more Garifuna who had been living in Central Harlem joined the Dominicans and other Hispanics moving to the South Bronx. My informants said that early male transmigrants preferred Harlem, where they could find inexpensive "kitchens" (one-room apartments) and were able to camouflage themselves to avoid the Immigration and Naturalization Service (INS). But many also liked the Hispanic flavor of the Bronx and the larger apartments made cheaper by the real estate devaluation white flight caused, the deindustrialization of the Bronx manufacturing sector, and the growing number of public housing projects that were being constructed there. This search for housing was important because during the

Table 2.2. Population Changes for South Bronx and Central Harlem Neighborhoods Where Garifuna Reside, 1970–1990[a]

	NYC	BRONX	CD#1 Mott Haven/ St. Mary's	CD#2 Hunts Point	CD#3 Morrisania Crotona	CD#4 High Bridge/Grand Concourse	CD#5 Morris Heights	CD#6 East Tremont	CD#7 Fordham	CD#8 Soundview
Hondurans										
Percentage of the total population 1990[b]	0.3[c]	0.6[d]	1.2	1.7	1.7	0.8	0.7	1.6	0.5	0.4
Percentage of the total new immigrant population 1983–1989[e]	1.3	3.5	—	—	5.8	3.4	4.1	3.9	2.8	3.1
Total population change										
Each district from 1970 to 1980[f]	-10.0	-20.6	-43.4	-63.0	-64.0	-20.7	-12.0	-43.0	-46.0	-55.0
Each district from 1980 to 1990	+3.5	+3.0	-1.6	+14.0	+8.0	+3.9	+9.7	+4.7	+10.0	-1.1
Population change										
Non-Hispanic whites 1980–1990	-14.0	-32.0	-56.0	-14.0	-16.0	-60.0	-65.0	-24.0	-46.0	-55.0
Non-Hispanic blacks 1980–1990	+9.0	+5.0	-10.0	-1.0	-6.0	-13.0	-3.0	-13.0	+38.0	+5.0
Hispanics 1980–1990	+26.0	+32.0	+6.0	+19.0	+38.0	+31.0	+31.0	+27.0	+66.0	+19.0

a. All values are percentages.
b. New York City Department of City Planning, *Socioeconomic Profiles: A Portrait of New York City's Community Districts from the 1980 and 1990 Censuses of Population and Housing* (New York, Department of City Planning, 1993).
c. From in 0.2 in 1980.
d. From 0.3 in 1980.
e. New York City Department of City Planning, *Newest New Yorkers: An Analysis of Immigration into New York During the 1980s* (New York: Department of City Planning, 1992). This is not the total percentage of Hondurans living in each area but rather the number that entered and settled in each areas from 1982 to 1989.
f. New York City Department of City Planning, *Community District Needs, Fiscal Year 1996* (New York: Department of City Planning).

1970s the number of Garifuna families living in New York was increasing as men sponsored the migration of their wives and children and as women migrated on their own, forming families in New York and sponsoring their own children. A common mode of entry in the 1970s was through the sponsorship of a relative who obtained either a tourist visa or residency for the transmigrant. Informants say that during this period those with tourist visas (and even those without documentation) had no problem getting a Social Security number and finding employment within a week of arrival (Miller 1993, 140–142, says the same of Belizeans in Los Angeles). As one return migrant told me:

> Garifuna began migrating to the U.S. after World War II, but really massive migration began in the 1960s and 1970s when it was still quite easy. In 1972, when I arrived, I asked what the required documents were to get a job. They told me that basically it is the Social Security card. So the next week my brother took me to the office there in Harlem. We just put the application in one window, waited a half an hour and the card came out from another window. Within a few days I had found two jobs, as a porter and in a factory, and for two years I worked both of those jobs, hoping to save money.

Another transmigrant, Don Felix, left Honduras in 1971 with the help of a sister who got him a tourist visa. He says that he worked for ten years before he got his residency.

> My first job was in construction, then I worked in a rubber factory, then I worked as a dishwasher in different restaurants in Manhattan. One of them was across the street from the INS and employees ate there all the time and didn't bother anyone. They didn't seem to care in those days.

In many ways, Garifuna incorporation into the New York City labor market follows the same pattern their Hispanic Caribbean neighbors followed. In 1970 one-third of immigrant Hispanics[7] were employed in manufacturing (compared to one-fifth of New York City residents in general). Even when deindustrialization accelerated in the 1970s, Honduran Garifuna, like other immigrant Hispanics, still found employment in the manufacturing sector, not because the sector was expanding but because white blue-collar workers were leaving, creating a space for Hispanic workers to fill. In 1980, one-third of Hispanics were still in manufacturing and the rest were in the retail and personal services sectors (as home attendants, domestics, and so forth). Only 9 percent were in professional services (compared to 15 percent citywide; Bailey and Waldinger 1991, 62–64).

IMMIGRATION IN THE 1980S AND 1990S

While Hispanic immigrants remained largely employed throughout the 1970s and 1980s, their incomes declined as the deindustrialization of the New York economy led to an increase in nonunionized manufacturing and service sector employment. While Limoneño informants who arrived in the 1970s told me that they got a Social Security card and employment within a week of arrival, more recent arrivals I met in 1996 had often spent up to three months looking for their first job, accumulating debt to relatives in the meantime. I heard many stories of men standing in line at the headquarters of Local 32E of the Service Employees International Union, hoping to get union membership and a job in maintenance that paid an average of $13.50 an hour plus benefits. But instead many ended up working on contract for companies that bypassed the unions or in one of the factories or laundries where legal status is not questioned. (Interestingly, Limoneños I interviewed who had worked in factories in the 1970s usually cited Italians and Jew as the owners, whereas today they usually mention Koreans and Chinese. See Bailey and Waldinger 1991 for a discussion of how Asians have moved into the manufacturing niche both as owners and workers.) Women who had worked for many years as home attendants also spoke of increasing restrictions on who is hired (employers now demand more workers who speak English and have legal papers and certain types of training) and of having their hours decreased (due to cuts in state spending) to what is essentially part-time work. These women knew that if they switched to agencies where there might be more work, they would have to start at minimum wage all over again. Thus, the picture that is drawn of immigrant Hispanics in general and Honduran Garifuna specifically in the 1980s and 1990s is a population of the working poor who tried to stay employed but whose incomes were declining. (For example, in 1980, 62 percent of Hispanic men and 63 percent of Hispanic women in New York City were in the bottom two quintiles of income distribution, while only 17 percent of men and 18 percent of women were in the top two quintiles; Bailey and Waldinger 1991, 66).

Even though older generations of Hispanic immigrants (that is, Puerto Ricans and Dominicans) were experiencing the decreasing quality of labor conditions in New York City in the 1980s, there was a massive increase in the numbers of Central Americans migrating to the city in that period. From 1950 to 1990, the percentage of Central Americans in the U.S. immigrant population increased from 6 to 14. Most of this growth was due to the influx of Salvadorans, Guatemalans, and Nicaraguans (the top three Central American source countries to the United States in the 1980s, in descending order) who were flee-ing the violence, dislocation, and economic crisis that accompanied long-term civil war.

While Honduras did not experience the levels of political oppression and violence that these countries did, it was affected by the political and economic destabilization of the region and had a military dictatorship that repressed dis-sent and supported U.S. military operations in the region. Thus, the number of Hondurans migrating to the United States also rose in the 1980s as a result of high unemployment and economic reforms that increased the cost of living to the point that even those who were employed were often not able to meet basic family expenses. For example, in the late 1970s, the unemployment rate in Honduras was only 10 percent. By 1989, combined unemployment and un-deremployment had risen to 40 percent, and by 1993, that figure had risen to 50–60 percent of the Honduran labor force, according to one estimate (Mer-rill 1993). In addition, economic restructuring, inflation, and the removal of government subsidies led to an increase in the cost of basic goods, especially food, and reduced the buying power of domestic wages. (From 1970 to 1980, the consumer price index rose by 7.9 percent, and from 1980 to 1990 it rose by 6.2 percent; Calix Suazo and Vindel de Calix 1991, 192).

From 1982 to 1999, El Salvador and Honduras were the largest source coun-tries for Central American immigrants who initially settled in New York City, and Hondurans demonstrating the strongest preference for settling in the city[8] (one-fourth of all Hondurans in the United States settled in New York City in 1990 and one-fifth in 2000). The number of Hondurans arriving in New York City went from an average of 400 per year in the 1970s to an average of 850 per year in the 1980s and 1,050 per year in the 1990s. In 1990, Honduras was the fourteenth top source country to the city; in 2000 it was the nineteenth (New York City Department of City Planning 1992a, 36–37; 2000). This drop in rank is not due to a dwindling number of Hondurans who are migrating but rather to the increased number of immigrants from Mexico, Italy, and Ban-gladesh (none of which were in the top twenty source countries in the 1980s). Though there are no available statistics on what percentage of these Hondurans are Garifuna, the Honduran consulate and members of FEDOHNY who are most familiar with the Honduran population as a whole estimate that Gari-funa make up 70 percent of Hondurans in New York City. Thus, the statistical profile of Hondurans in New York is a fair indicator of the Garifuna popula-tion. (Though New York is the first destination of the majority of Honduran Garifuna due to family connections, New Orleans, Houston, Miami, Boston, and San Francisco are also significant areas of both settlement and secondary migration. According to the consulates of Los Angeles and New Orleans, ladinos are the majority of the Honduran immigrant population in those cities.)

While Central American immigrants in general represent a broad socio-economic spectrum, ranging from urban professionals to rural peasants (since many were fleeing civil war that affected all sectors of society), the statistical profile of Honduran immigrants in New York City generally fits that of a group of poor urban working-class labor migrants. The median age of Hondurans who initially migrate to New York City is 27 (and this statistic does not vary by sex). Seventy-five percent of males reported an occupation prior to migration, the majority in the categories of industrial labor. The rest were in service and professional, managerial, or clerical jobs. Less than 1 percent reported farming or fishing as their previous occupations. In contrast, only 52 percent of females reported an occupation, the majority in the category of service. The second-largest group was in varieties of industrial labor; the third-largest group in professional and clerical work; and less than 1 percent in farming (New York City Department of City Planning 1992b, 70, 74).

While the labor niche Central American immigrants such as the Garifuna occupied in the United States was still available and even growing in the 1980s, working conditions were deteriorating as more employers turned to contract labor to avoid paying benefits and as immigration reform made legal entry more difficult. As U.S. public opinion about migration shifted because of what the public perceived as a massive influx of poor, uneducated, and undocumented immigrants (a group in which Central Americans figured prominently), Congress created increasingly strict criteria for obtaining tourist visas and passed the Immigration Control and Reform Act in 1986, which placed sanctions on employers of undocumented workers. Many studies have shown that after these reforms, the immigration of Central Americans (and Mexicans) not only failed to decrease but actually increased as economic and political crisis in these countries became more acute (Hagan 1994; Mahler 1995; Repak 1995). Central Americans continued to arrive through the mechanism of family reunification.[9] Even though the process could take from three to five years if the sponsoring family member in the United States was only a U.S. resident alien, it could take as few as six months if the sponsoring member was a U.S. citizen. Others decided to forego the bureaucratic hassles of legal migration and enter without documentation, hoping to get residency or political asylum at a later date. Such restrictions on immigration, then, did not decrease the immigrant population; instead, it made it that much more vulnerable.

MORE IMMIGRATION REFORM AND HURRICANE MITCH: A DOUBLE BLOW

Throughout the 1980s and 1990s, anti-immigrant sentiment in the United States grew, culminating in the passage of the Illegal Immigration Reform and Immigrant Responsibility Act of 1996. This legislation was intended to stem the tide of illegal immigration by increasing border enforcement and decreasing the rights of immigrants (both documented and undocumented) to social services, thereby serving as a disincentive to further immigration. The law increased penalties for human trafficking, increased the number of immigration officers and the amount of technology used at the U.S.-Mexican border, streamlined the deportation process, increased the types of offenses for which a person could be deported (including even legal residents and naturalized citizens), and removed access to certain benefits and public services ("U.S. Citizen Fact Sheet," INS Web site). As with the Immigration Control and Reform Act, studies have already shown that the result of this legislation has not been the decrease of illegal immigration but rather the increased vulnerability of those willing to make the passage. Passage across the border has become more expensive and hazardous and is now more often connected with smugglers and drug traffickers who are more organized and powerful than individual coyotes (Andreas 1999, 2001; Nazario 2002). Those in the United States without legal documentation have found themselves even more cut off from family members back home because they are unwilling to risk the trip back home and cannot afford to send for family members (Bibler Coutin 2005; Smith 1998a).

This does not mean that the cross-border flow has stopped. The conditions that created the transnational system in the first place have neither disappeared nor abated. Instead, they have been exacerbated by economic policies that continue to encourage the creation of cheap service jobs in the United States and unemployment in the home countries. The decades-long interdependence of the U.S. demand for cheap labor and the need of immigrant families to send money home is not so easily severed. In the case of Central America, the situation was made even worse by Hurricane Mitch, which hit in late October 1998, leaving approximately 22,000 dead and 3 million homeless. In Honduras, Hurricane Mitch destroyed millions of homes, crops, roads and bridges, and the plantations of Chiquita Brand (formerly United Fruit Company), one of the main sources of employment and revenue on the North Coast, the hardest-hit area. Over 13,000 were killed or are missing there, and the damage done there affected 80 percent of the GDP of the country (NACLA 1999). Although before Hurricane Mitch the number of Hondurans migrating to the United States had been eclipsed by migrants from the war-torn countries of El Salvador, Guatemala, and Nicaragua, after 1998 there was a notable increase in the number of Hondurans entering the United States (Thompson 1999). The number of Hondurans entering legally has remained fairly constant since 1992, hovering between 4,500 and 6,500 per year (*Yearbook 2004,* table 3), but the number of Hondurans deported has steadily increased to the point that in 2003 the number of Hondurans defined as "deportable" by the INS surpassed that of Salvadorans, who had been one of the largest categories of deportees since the 1980s, second only to Mexicans (*Yearbook 2004,* table 36). Peter Andreas (1999) points out that the fact that Mexicans and Central Americans are the largest categories of deportees is not simply a reflection of their sheer numbers but also the result of the fact that the INS disproportionately focuses on apprehending those who use the U.S./Mexico border, mainly Mexicans, Central Americans, and (more recently) Ecuadorians (Kyle 2000), even though visa overstays actually account for half of all undocumented workers. In addition to this, many of the people who are being deported (both documented and undocumented) are immigrants who have committed crimes labeled as deportable under the 1996 law (Arana 2005; Ojito 1998). This has disproportionately affected certain segments of the immigrant population who settled in high-crime neighborhoods and whose children may have become involved in gangs. One of the largest phenomena affecting Central America right now is the deportation of tens of thousands of gang members to El Salvador, Guatemala, and Honduras, many of whom were largely raised in the United States and may speak no Spanish and whose only prospects for survival are to continue their gang activity in Central America (Kraul 2004; Kraul, Lopez, and Connell 2005). Thanks to this policy, the murder rate in Central America has risen dramatically, making it higher than even Colombia's rate (Arana 2005).

It is clear that Honduras as a whole is beginning to rival El Salvador and Guatemala in terms of the degree to which U.S.-bound migration is becoming an integral part of its society and economy. For the Garifuna, for whom immigration was already well established as a social practice and who had already become reliant on remittances, the events of the decade since 1996 have simply reinforced the transnational system and the perceived need to migrate. Because Garifuna migration began at such an early date, they have an advantage over other Hondurans because a higher percentage of them are eligible to immigrate legally through family reunification. I estimate that only about one-fourth of those I interviewed in the 1990s are currently undocumented, and another fourth obtained their documents after entering the United States illegally. The other half entered legally. Even though the number of Honduran deportees has risen, some Garifuna informants suggested to me that Garifuna are apprehended less frequently than ladinos because they can better camouflage themselves as African Americans, whereas the INS targets ladino Hondurans and other "visible" Hispanics. This seems to be true; in my various trips to Limón, I did not encounter anyone who had returned as a deportee.

THE LIMONEÑO EXPERIENCE

Thus far I have discussed the migration patterns of Central Americans in general and Hondurans more specifically, suggesting ways that Garifuna fit or do not fit these patterns. I have also discussed the way that these migration patterns have been affected by the political and economic changes in Central America, the United States, and the global economy. Now I want to describe the way that these macroprocesses have been experienced on the ground by one Limoneño extended family.[10] The following family migration history illustrates the changing patterns of migration and the different conditions Garifuna have encountered in New York in each decade since the 1940s. It shows that Limoneño transmigrants are making choices based on both economic rationales related to macroeconomic changes and ideologies of kinship and family obligations related to Garifuna culture and social structure.

Mario Ramirez is a man in his late fifties. We are sitting on the porch of his house in Limón, talking about his family history and migration experiences. His son Fred sits with us, watching his children play in an inflatable swimming pool he brought from New York for the family's summer vacation. Though Mario's house is only made of wood and is modest by current standards in Limón, where two-story brick houses with garages and modern kitchens are under construction, he assures me that when he built it in the 1970s from money earned in New York it was one of the first "modern" houses to have a concrete rather than a dirt floor and a metal rather than a palm thatch roof. Despite the modesty of his house, Mario is known as one of the wealthiest men in Limón, a model of success who spent most of his youth as a resident of New York, working in the city and as a merchant marine, traveling the world but never forgetting his hometown, where he has now retired with eighty *manzanas* (approximately 136 acres) of land; eighty head of cattle; a sport utility vehicle; a house equipped with a generator, a refrigerator, a television, and a VCR; and a monthly retirement check from the United States.

Mario is one of those men Limoneños often referred me to when I told them I was interested in learning about the migration of Limoneños to New York City. He is the son of one of the original merchant marine pioneers to New

York City, and he was instrumental in sponsoring the migration of many of his brothers and sisters, all of his children, and a number of nieces, nephews, and cousins, who have in turn sponsored others. He, like a few key men I heard about, served as a major conduit of migration for his extended family from Limón to New York City, and his story and that of his family illustrate some of the common threads of U.S.-bound Garifuna migration.

The migration of the Ramirez family began with Mario's father, Franco. Like many Limoneños who had worked for the United Fruit Company on the docks of Puerto Castilla in the 1930s, Franco had to travel farther west to Tela to find employment after the company picked up its tracks and ended operations in Colón in 1937. He worked in Tela from 1943 until he was recruited in 1946 to work as a merchant marine. Though the ship he worked on was registered under the Honduran flag, the crew was a mixed group of Hondurans (Black Creoles, Garifuna, and ladinos) and West Indians, with North American and European officers. For ten years Franco worked as chief chef, and a portion of his check was sent directly to his wife and eight children in Limón. In 1955, he decided to get off the ship in the United States and gain U.S. residency. That way he could join the National Maritime Union and get work on an American ship, where he would earn higher wages. Even though he did not return to Limón for seven years, his wife waited for him (that is, did not take another man) because the company checks continued to arrive. Unlike some other of these early pioneers, Franco (who is now deceased) never brought his wife to New York; she still lives in Limón with one of her daughters and grandchildren.

Finally, in the early 1960s, Franco sponsored the migration of his eldest son, Celio, who then sponsored his brother Mario. Mario arrived in New York City in 1962, leaving behind a wife and three sons. Like many Limoneños, he first lived by himself in a kitchen (efficiency) apartment in Harlem. He worked in a "laundry" (an industrial dry cleaner) until he was able to secure a higher-paying job as a "porter" (doing live-in building maintenance) in an apartment building in the Bronx. During this period the Bronx was still dominated by blue-collar white ethnics (Jews, Irish, and Italians), but this was to soon change as more Puerto Ricans, Dominicans, and West Indians moved into the neighborhood as the whites moved out, giving the South and Central Bronx the primarily Hispanic Caribbean flavor it has today. After only five years of residence in New York, Mario himself became a merchant marine, traveling in and out of New York City ports but also traveling back to Limón to see his wife (with whom he had three more children) and beginning the process of buying land and building a house. At the same time, he formed a union with a Costa Rican woman in New York City, starting a second family there without severing his ties to his family in Limón.

In the 1970s, Mario began to sponsor the migration of more of his family members, eventually bringing his six children, a brother, two sisters, a nephew, and two nieces. One of his sisters, Caterina, had been a teacher in Limón. At first she left her teaching job on leave, reasoning that she would just go to *sondear el ambiente*; that is, check out the conditions in New York City to see what work was available. For several years she worked in New York as a maid and then as a home attendant, returning to Limón to resume her teaching position every six months. Eventually she formed a union with another Limoneño in New York, had a few children, and stopped going back to Limón to teach. She never learned enough English to get accredited as a teacher in the United States, so after twenty years she still works as a home attendant. She and her husband, a former "porter" and now an *embarcado* (employed on a tourist ship out of Hawaii) have already built their respective houses in Limón and are getting ready to retire.

In 1973, Mario arranged for his nephew Hervasio to visit the United States with a tourist visa. At age 23, with no wife or children, Hervasio saw this as merely a visit to see relatives, discover New York, and make a little money. Like many who arrived in the 1970s with a tourist visa, he easily obtained a Social Security number and within a week was working in a factory. After a few months he was ready to return to Honduras, citing the cold weather and long work hours as too much of a hardship, but his uncle convinced him that staying in the United States was the only way to "make something of himself," so he went to a technical school and became an electrician. He eventually married a Garifuna woman from another Honduran Garifuna community and gained his U.S. residency through her. In the 1990s, as the New York economy went into a slump and he went through a divorce, he decided to move to Houston, where he works for a company that ships to the oil refineries of the Gulf of Mexico. He is also in the process of building a house in Limón that his elderly parents will live in until he is ready for retirement.

Mario's sons arrived in New York in the 1980s, leaving behind wives and children, as had their father. Mario's eldest son Fred began by working in a factory and for miscellaneous employers in the service industry until he was able to get a more lucrative position in building maintenance. He did not see his wife and daughter for five years while he was formalizing his residency status and building up enough savings to sponsor their migration. Meanwhile, his wife was living in San Pedro Sula, working as a maid and receiving monthly

Figure 2.1. Apartment building in Harlem neighborhood where author lived with a Garifuna family. On the street level, notice the African restaurant and Jamaican record store. (Photo by author)

checks from Fred. Now in New York, she works as a home attendant and has given birth to another daughter, who is a U.S. citizen. Fred and his family live in a one-bedroom apartment on Grand Concourse in the same building as two of his brothers.

In the 1990s, Mario sponsored the migration of his niece Nora, a woman I had met in Limón prior to her migration. I often visited her in her father's house in Limón (he is the only one of Franco's sons who did not migrate), where she showed me the many photo albums of her classmates at the secretarial school in La Ceiba and her crowning as the queen of the annual village festival. At the time, she was working in the municipality as a secretary and planning her upcoming wedding to her high school sweetheart. Two years later I met her again, this time in a two-bedroom project in the Bronx where she lived with her sister and her brother-in-law and their two children and her own son, who was born in New York. Though she had discovered that she was pregnant only a few months before leaving for New York, she decided to migrate anyway because the papers had already gone through. After a four-month search she finally found employment as a home attendant, where she worked twelve-hour shifts in a home on the Upper West Side of Manhattan. Every morning she left the house at 7:00 in order to drop her son off with another Limoneña, who she paid

$60 a week for childcare. She usually did not make it home until 9:00 at night. She said she wanted to change agencies to get better shifts and benefits, but that would mean starting at minimum wage all over again. Her husband, who was working on a cruise liner, visited her during his vacations. Once he got his U.S. residency (probably a three- to five-year process), they hoped to get their own apartment.

Another niece, Rosa, arrived in 1992, sponsored financially by Mario but without legal documents. Without legal residency, Rosa was not able to secure project housing, so she and her husband lived in a small one-bedroom apartment in Harlem. After many months she finally found a job in a "factory" in East Harlem where she and many other Hispanic women (mainly Dominicans) spend the day packing wallets for shipment. She was hoping to get a better job as a home attendant, but chances are slim given the increasing sanctions placed on employers who hire undocumented workers; this has pushed home attendant agencies to become more strict about requiring green cards and the ability to speak English. Rosa's husband, who is also without documents, worked in a Korean-owned "laundry" in Hunts Point. While both earn slightly over minimum wage, they have little job security; workers are laid off regularly to cut costs and there are no benefits. Fortunately, they had two children in New York who, as U.S. citizens, qualify for food stamps and Medicaid. After four years in New York, Rosa said she was very disillusioned with the conditions there. She had thought she would work for five years and then be able to return to Limón with enough savings to get a business going. But between her insecure work situation, the high rent she had to pay, and the money she sent to her mother, she had been able to save very little. She said she wanted to return to Honduras, but she and her sponsor had sacrificed too much for her to get here. Besides, she was the only one of her mother's eight children who had made it to New York City and she could not go back without something for them. "*Hay que aguantar*" (You have to endure), she told me.

While I have argued that Garifuna U.S.-bound migration was not initiated by economic or political crisis but instead represents a logical continuation of migration patterns set early in Garifuna history, the processes of U.S.-bound migration certainly have been affected by the economic and political changes in both the United States and Central America that took place from the 1980s to 2000. From the 1950s to the 1970s, Garifuna saw the United States as one option among others. In the 1980s and 1990s, they came to see it as the only real option for economic improvement and, for many households receiving the remittances of those migrants, for basic survival. Among the Limoneños I interviewed, a few young men said that they had migrated to the United States to avoid obligatory conscription into the military,[11] but otherwise the primary reason given for migration was economic. Though Garifuna migration has always been primarily economic, what had changed by the 1990s was the sense that much more was riding on migration because more family members in Honduras have come to depend on remittances for a large portion of their monthly income.

Another change is that it is now more difficult for Garifuna to enter the United States with legal documentation. In the 1970s, obtaining a tourist visa merely involved having a sponsor prove his or her ability to support the applicant during the period of visitation. Now it requires applicants to show proof of a substantial stake in returning to the country of citizenship (such as property, a business, a professional post, and so forth). For people coming from poor sectors of poor countries such as Honduras, family reunification has become the surest and most common mode of legal migration. The vast majority of Hondurans entered New York City as the spouses and children of residents and citizens (76 percent in the 1980s and 94 percent in the 1990s; New York City Department of City Planning 1992b, 2000). This follows the trend of immigration to New York in general, where 40 percent of immigrants (mainly from the Caribbean and Latin America) used this class of admission, in contrast to only 19 percent nationwide. This pattern continued in the 1990s as the Immigration Act of 1990 increased the annual quota of visas allocated for family reunification (New York City Department of City Planning 1992a, 59, 17). Though most Garifuna have a close relative in the United States who could apply for them, the process is long and bureaucratically involved, creating long periods of separation between spouses and between parents and the children they have left in the care of grandparents hoping to "send for them" later on. Many decide to take their chances and enter without documentation.

Despite the increasing difficulty of entering the United States legally, Garifuna, like other Central Americans, have not decreased their rates of migration. For those who waited many years to get a visa and for those who entered without documentation, migration is seen as a substantial sacrifice on the part of the migrant and a commitment to family members and the sponsor (who has probably paid substantial legal and immigration fees or a smuggler to get them there). They do not make a commitment to stay permanently in the United States; instead, they commit to the project of being a good *hijo/hija del pueblo* (son or daughter of the village) who stays long enough to support family members and be successful but who also returns. This is often difficult, however, for those who do not have legal documents and whose work does not pay enough to afford travel home. These are the transmigrants who get "stuck" in New York

City, unable to make it in the United States but also unable to return (see Chapter 4).

Ironically, the increasing restrictions on entering the United States legally and the increasing difficulty of saving that nest egg for eventual return seem to have the effect of reinforcing the desire of people such as the Garifuna to eventually return to their home country because of their oftentimes precarious legal and financial status in the United States. At the same time, it forces them to establish more roots in the United States because their ability to travel back and forth frequently is constrained. In the meantime, the geographical gap between the transmigrant community and the home community is constantly bridged and reworked with the arrival of more family members.

CONCLUSION

This brief account of Garifuna history makes it clear that the effect of global political-economic shifts on peoples is not based solely on the logic of the market. Rather, economic shifts and processes are also shaped and justified by racialized and gendered ideologies and hierarchies. For example, the slave trade that brought Africans to the Caribbean was made possible not only by the need for labor but also by racial ideologies that dehumanized and commodified Africans (Smedley 1999). On St. Vincent, ideologies about the significance of race in relation to character and "nativity" shaped different British responses to the "Red" and "Black" Caribs based on assumptions about their potential threat to the British plantation system. In Central America, multinational fruit companies depended on racialized assessments of different labor pools to determine which jobs would be given to whom. They saw Garifuna men as "good labor" because of their association with Black West Indians and willingness to work for wages. Though they were a preferred workforce, Garifuna were hired only in certain capacities, limiting their chances of becoming significant capitalist entrepreneurs or landowners. This same construction of them as good workers based on their blackness had more negative repercussions, however, vis-à-vis the Honduran state and national society, for whom blackness was equated with foreignness, thereby excluding them from full status as "native sons" and from national belonging. In the United States, Honduran Garifuna, as do other Hispanics, face a similar double bind. On the one hand they are seen as "good workers" because they are constructed as "unskilled" and therefore "cheap" labor. But at the same time these assumed qualities also make them undesirable national subjects, encouraging anti-immigration legislation to stem the "brown tide." All of this illustrates how the significance of racial discourses varies in different political and economic contexts to structure and justify systems of inequality.

And yet these ideologies and structures of inequality do not fully determine the decisions Garifuna make within those contexts. In looking at the history of Garifuna labor migration we can see that Garifuna men and women are making choices consistent with cultural orientations and social structures that are more than merely the by-products of political and economic structures. For both men and women, employment opportunities have opened and closed in various locations of the diaspora at various times. The decision to migrate to take advantage of those opportunities is not related solely to economic rationales but also to cultural ideologies of kinship, family obligations, and upward mobility. In the following chapters, I turn to a more detailed discussion of each of these aspects of the transnational community, detailing their operation particularly among Limoneños and drawing conclusions about how those processes are related to consciousness and grassroots political action.

3

Families in Space

The Transnationalization of Matrifocal Kinship

In one of the opening scenes of the film *Spirit of My Mother*,[1] a young Garifuna woman walks down the streets of Los Angeles, past graffiti and broken windows, carrying her baby girl in her arms. Her mind wanders to a dream she has been having about her mother, who died just before the baby was born. The dream always takes place in Honduras, on the beach, with her mother dressed all in white calling to her. As the movie unfolds, we learn that the tragedy of the woman's story is that her mother had migrated to Los Angeles when she was young, leaving her in the care of her grandmother in Honduras. After several years her mother was finally able to send for her to join her in Los Angeles, but by the time the young woman arrived the mother had died and she herself had become pregnant. We find her in Los Angeles, living with an aunt, who takes care of the baby while she works as a maid for a white American family. But the calling of her mother is very strong and her situation in Los Angeles goes from bad to worse as she loses her job and faces the stress of single motherhood. Moving back and forth between the harsh realities of Los Angeles and the dreamlike aura of Honduras, the movie shows the young woman traveling back to Honduras with her daughter in order to carry out a ritual bathing for her mother, hoping to find strength in reconnecting to her homeland and her maternal lineal kin. The movie ends with the young woman, her maternal aunts and uncles, and a *buyei* (shaman) dancing and offering food to the spirit of her mother and the final washing in the sea that ends the ceremony and finally leads to peace between the woman and the mother in her past and her own motherhood in her present.

This film, like no other film I have seen about the Garifuna, captures the core of the cultural and ideological principle of kinship and social structure that characterizes much of Garifuna social life. This principle, which characterizes many of the populations of the African diaspora, is referred to as matrifocality. It is a kinship system in which women, as mothers, serve as the foci of households, extended kin groups, and ritual (Kerns 1983; Smith 1973; Stack 1974). As Virginia Kerns argues in her ethnography *Women and the Ancestors*, the centrality of women in Garifuna society revolves around the important role they play in caring for lineal kin—both the living and the deceased. This importance is manifested in a kinship structure that places more emphasis on maternal consanguineal ties (blood relations on one's mother's side) than on affinal or conjugal ties (with one's in-laws and husband). It puts women at the center of family ritual and household affective relations, is bolstered by the common practice of matrilocal residence, and establishes women as the primary redistributors of resources within the household. Although husbands and wives operate as a conjugal unit, they also invest much of their time and resources in their respective maternal consanguineal kin networks, creating a relative degree of autonomy in the realm of decision-making and resource allocation. Coehlo wrote in his 1955 dissertation that "the position of the woman in the family cannot at all be seen as subordinate, according to the principle that the family is a society in which men and women participate in equal conditions and it does not have to do with one person that orders and the other that obeys" (1995, 81). This is not to imply that matrifocality is the opposite of patriarchy or that women and men face equal sets of opportunities and constraints. Rather, matrifocality is intertwined with elements of patriarchal social structure and ideology, especially because men have an advantage in employment opportunities in the gendered labor market and in political power within the patriarchal state. However, within the family and the village, matrifocality has a distinct logic that is not exactly the same as other principles of kinship and social structures found within Latin America.

Another striking quality of *The Spirit of My Mother* is its movement back and forth between Los Angeles and Honduras, which captures the way matrifocality operates transnationally as one of the threads that knits the community together. As with other transmigrant populations, among the Garifuna kinship serves as a primary avenue through which transnational processes travel and ties are maintained. Children are cared for by maternal kin, housing and jobs are found through kinship networks, money is sent to kin in Honduras, transmigrants return for kinship rituals, and family members remain linked through telephone calls, letters, and other forms of communication. As this film shows, and as I argue in this chapter, the particular character of these ties among the Garifuna is organized around the principle of matrifocality that shapes the character of transnational households, patterns of remittances and investments, and community-level rituals of solidarity. These principles of kinship and domestic structure are practiced not only in Central American Garifuna communities but also among Garifuna in New York City. At the same time, matrifocality is adapted to the different conditions Garifuna encounter in Central America and the United States, especially in terms of the gendered labor market and relations to the state that create different sets of opportunities and constraints for Garifuna men and women in the two places. Thus, manifestations of the principle of matrifocality are present throughout the transnational community but are altered to fit local circumstances.

MATRIFOCALITY AS AN ORGANIZING PRINCIPLE OF DOMESTIC AND COMMUNITY LIFE

The previous chapter showed that for much of Garifuna history, labor migration was mainly the purview of men. Women did not being to migrate to the cities of Central America and the United States in substantial numbers until the 1960s and 1970s. During this early period before 1960, Nancie Gonzalez, one of the first ethnographers to focus on issues of Garifuna kinship and households, conducted her field work in Livingston, Guatemala. She argued that many of the basic characteristics of Garifuna matrifocal social structure such as the relative independence of women, the prevalence of female-centered consanguineal households (households headed by women and consisting of their daughters and their children), and matrilocal residence could be best understood as specific adaptations to the frequent absences of men from the village as labor migrants. Gonzalez's survey of household types, conducted in Livingston during the 1950s and published in 1969 in *Black Carib Household Structure*, found that 45 percent of the households consisted of a focal woman, her children, and her daughters' children. The other 55 percent were nuclear or extended households built around a core affinal couple (a married couple). She noted, however, that even these affinal households frequently converted to the consanguineal type as men moved in and out of the village in search of work and as domestic unions were formed and dissolved. Unmarried sons usually lived in the house of their mothers during their stays in the village, until they either found work or formed a common-law union, in which case they would go to live in the house of the woman. If this union broke up, the man would generally return to live in his mother's house. Other men engaged in "visiting unions" in which they remained in the house of their mothers or of the common-law or legal wife but would visit the other woman on occasion. All ethnographers note the rare occurrence of legal marriage among the Garifuna except among wealthier households and between couples who had already been together for many years; often these couples had adult children. Consequently, most women found themselves in consanguineal households a great deal of the time due to the absence of a male partner (because of the physical absence of a partner from the village or the absence of a relationship). Due to matrilocal residence, the focal woman was actually considered to be the owner of the house, and she, her daughters, and her daughters' children remained the stable focus of the household and the matrilocal compound. Though women ultimately relied on men for cash income, as heads of households women had a considerable amount of leeway to redistribute and invest money as they saw fit. In addition, as the primary agriculturists with networks of reciprocal exchange among female kin, women were not completely reliant on male cash earnings for subsistence.

Gonzalez also noted the centrality of women in the organization of religious rituals and village celebrations and as members of voluntary associations. They serve as *buyeis* that contact the ancestors to communicate cures and coordinate rituals, and they serve as the core members of village dance groups that perform on key holidays and can be mobilized for other types of village events. While both men and women participate in ritual, the main organizers and sponsors are generally women, as are the *buyeis*. Men participate as musicians and workers who help construct the temporary temples, gather firewood, slaughter the animals, and so forth, but women (mainly older women) are the main orchestrators of the event and stay up until dawn, pipes in mouths, distributing and drinking rum, dancing, and singing until dawn.

This picture of women who are at the center of rituals, drink until dawn, and run households is quite different from the patriarchal *casa/calle* (house/street) ideology that is assumed to exist throughout Latin America that limits women's range of motion in public space. Going back all the way to the Moorish presence in Spain even before the conquest of the Americas, Spanish culture was infused with the ideology of the sexual impurity of women and the need to protect and enclose them within the private domain of the home. This led to the cult of domesticity that adulates women as mothers but confines their movements in public and their sexual activity to preserve the honor of the family (Socolow 2000; Stolcke 1991). Even in Spain, however, this ideology was crosscut by class; poorer women were often forced by circumstances to work outside the home, which exposed them to sexual predation and gained them a reputation as dishonorable women, a reputation that ideologically justified the predation. This catch-22 was made even more complex in the American colonies, where indigenous and black women, due to their "racial impurity," were automatically relegated to the category of women without honor. While all women of the poorer classes were to be found in public spaces as market women and in other occupations, which gave them a degree of financial and sexual independence not always enjoyed by middle- and upper-class women, this independence was a source of stigma that justified their subordination in the race, class, and gender system of colonial society (Martinez-Alier 1974; Socolow 2000). Thus, the commonality of female-headed households and women in public spaces has generally been seen as an adaptation to poverty, an aberration of the ideal rather than a distinct cultural and structural principle (see, for example, Lewis 1965; Nash and Safa 1986).

Following this line of thinking, Gonzalez recognized the central role of Garifuna women in both household and village, but she theorized that it existed only as an adaptive strategy in the absence of men. She argued that, as in the dominant Latin American gender ideology, the nuclear family was the ideal and that female-headed households are common only by default because Garifuna villages, like other poor areas, exist on the periphery of national economies and infrastructure, which requires men to migrate and leave women to run the household. This absence of men, in her view, also required women to form economic ties with other women to ensure the reproduction of the household. This leads to matrilocal residence and child fosterage among female kin. Gonzalez also attributed the importance of women in organizing village rituals and in voluntary associations to the absence of a permanent population of men able to consistently form the basis of authority within the village. She predicted that as Garifuna villages became incorporated into the national economy and culture, bringing increased economic stability, the matrifocal consanguineal household would disappear because more couples would be able to achieve and maintain the affinal household structure the Central American middle class preferred.

Ethnographers argue that although the dominant race, class, and gender system described above would have affected Garifuna women who left the village to work in the cities of Central America, gender relations within the village operated on a different logic that has its origins in West African and Carib societies where the *casa/calle* distinction does not make sense because women are expected to work in the fields and participate in rituals and community life as well as tend to the house and the family. Thus, as in many parts of Latin America and the Caribbean, in Honduras, not one but several gender systems operates in different geographical and cultural realms (see, for example, Murphy and Murphy 1985; Silverblatt 1987; Smith 1995; Stephen 1991; Weismantel 2001).

For example, against the image of Garifuna women who have autonomy only in the absence of men, Virginia Kerns (1983) argued that Garifuna matrifocality is more than a temporary adaptation to economic marginalization but rather has deep cultural and ideological roots in the kinship system of the Island Carib on St. Vincent. Her research in a Garifuna village in Belize showed that even in affinal households, women as mothers redistribute economic resources and are the foci of affective relations and ritual. Following the insights of Raymond T. Smith (1973), Kerns argues that like the Black West Indian societies that

Smith describes, matrifocality is a general orientation of the Garifuna society. It should not be assumed to exist only in consanguineal households where women are household heads because it also exists in affinal households. In both consanguineal and affinal households, women provide the stable framework of social life, not because men are absent but because it is the duty of women to care for lineal kin, both the living and the deceased. As mothers, they redistribute money contributed by husbands and children to other members of the household and other consanguineal kin. As organizers of wakes and ancestor rituals (which are sponsored by the deceased's maternal consanguineal kin), they protect their lineal kin from illness and misfortune. Women exhort members of the extended kin group to participate in and contribute to rituals requested by the ancestors. Their influence is based on the ability to invoke the notion of the duty of children to their mothers and the duty of the living to the dead.

Kerns further argued that Garifuna women serve as household foci because of a pattern of male polygyny and female serial monogamy that is also traceable to Island Carib society (Helms 1981; Kerns 1983). Ethnographers have referred to the Garifuna kinship system as polygynous in order to distinguish it from the dominant Latin American gender systems inherited from the Spanish in which legal monogamous marriage is the ideal. In those systems, men may have several domestic partners but only one is considered to be the legitimate wife, while the others are "mistresses" or "outside women" with less social status, fewer rights to the man's earnings, and children who are considered illegitimate. Among the Garifuna, in contrast, a man may have two or more women he simultaneously considers to be his "wives."[2] However, they are considered equally legitimate, the relationships are not generally hidden, and the men are expected to support each wife equally and his children by her. The women in these relationships may be hostile or friendly to one another, but in any case the children consider themselves to be siblings (*hermanos por parte de papa*) and maintain close relations (though not as close as they are with the siblings they grow up with in their mother's house—*hermanos por parte de mama*). There is no concept among the Garifuna of "illegitimate" children (Beaucage 1970). Coehlo (1995), Gonzalez (1969), Beaucage (1970), and Kerns (1983) noted that during the period they were conducting their field work (up through the 1970s), this form of polygyny was basically accepted. However, only about a quarter of men were able to afford this type of relationship—mainly migrants and landowners (20–25 percent of men in Trujillo in 1955, according to Coehlo, 14 percent in Limón in 1965, according to Beaucage's survey data).

The fallacy in seeing matrifocality as simply a by-product of male absence can also be seen when we compare the case of the Garifuna with that of Dominicans and Salvadorans. Eugenia Georges (1992) and Sarah Mahler (2001) argue that although women who remain in the Dominican Republic and El Salvador while their husbands migrate may become the de facto heads of their local households, in order to maintain respectability (that is, to ensure the reputation of sexual fidelity), they often live with their fathers or the family of their husband in order to remain under the watchful eye of a male authority figure. While their husbands may send money that the woman is responsible to administer, the amounts are generally only enough to cover household expenses and are not enough for investment or any other venture in which women would really be making autonomous decisions. In addition, these women tend to spend less time working outside the home both because remittances allow them to support their families without working and in order to maintain their respectability as *amas de casa* (housewives) who do not venture into the realm of the *calle* (street). Women who are the heads of their households (and who have no husband to migrate) are more autonomous in terms of making decisions to engage in wage labor (often for migrant-supported households) or engage in petty trade, but they also have fewer resources. They often face the double social stigma of poverty and of being considered *mujeres de la calle* (women of the street) who have engaged in serial monogamy (not the ideal). The point that Georges and Mahler make is that when a society is already infused with patriarchal gender ideologies where patrilocal lifelong monogamous households are the ideal, the absence of men in the village and in the household does not mean the end of these ideologies and structures. Instead, they are rearticulated to fit the transnational migration system.

What is unique to the Garifuna is not the commonality of female-headed households (as this is common throughout the Americas) but rather the conjuncture of ideologies and structures that create it. Due to the practice of polygyny among some men, the mobility of men as migrant wage laborers, and the relative ease with which unions may form and dissolve, the stable core of Garifuna households tends to include a focal woman and her children by one or several fathers. As a result, the bonds between children and mothers tend to be stronger than the bonds between husbands and wives and between children and fathers. Female-headed households face little social stigma because lifelong monogamy is not expected as the norm. The social value of women is centered on their role as mothers rather than on their role as wives (or their "failure" to become wives).

What Gonzalez identified as the two household types (consanguineal and affinal) can really be more adequately distinguished as three household types (Table 3.1): 1) affinal households in which the husband is present most of the

Table 3.1. Garifuna Household Types in Limón

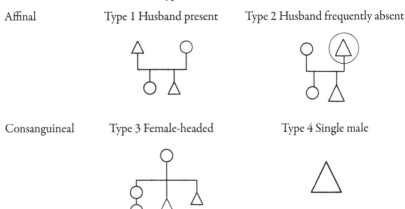

Affinal   Type 1 Husband present   Type 2 Husband frequently absent

Consanguineal   Type 3 Female-headed   Type 4 Single male

time; 2) affinal households in which the husband is absent much of the time due to wage labor but is still an active member of the household; and 3) consanguineal households headed by a core female all of the time (Beaucage 1970). In categories 2 and 3, women serve as household heads much of the time due to male absence, but in categories 1 and 2, men also participate in decision-making, not as *the* head of household but as *one* of the heads of household.

Table 3.2 shows the results of my survey of sixty-three households in Limón. I found that 60 percent of households were affinal and 40 percent were consanguineal; these figures are not much different from those given by Gonzalez. However, if we consider that six of the affinal households are type 2 (husband absent much of the time), then about half of the households are headed by women most of the time (types 2 and 3 make up thirty-one of sixty-three households) and the other half are headed by a woman and a man most of the time (thirty-two of sixty-three households).

I also found that the socioeconomic standing of households varies according to both household type and generational stage. While households run by single women (type 3) are not socially stigmatized, they do tend to be the poorest households because women have less manpower to call on for clearing and cultivating plots, less cash income from men's earnings, and less possibility of finding an adequate job locally. This corresponds with the findings of Kerns (1982) and Miller (1993), who argue that in the Belizean labor market women are paid lower wages than men for comparable work, jobs labeled as "women's work" are less remunerative than those labeled "men's work," and women face more unstable working conditions because of flexible hiring and firing practices. So while there is no Garifuna gender ideology that prevents women from

Table 3.2. Garifuna Household Types in Limón and New York City, 1993–1996

	Limón	New York City	Total
Affinal	38 (60%)	47 (70%)	85 (65%)
Type 1: Husband Present	32	42	74
Type 2: Husband Frequently Absent	6	5	11
Consanguineal	25 (40%)	20 (30%)	45 (35%)
Type 3: Female-Headed	24	7	32
Type 4: Single Male	1	13	14
Total	63	67	130

working, the sexual division of labor in the patriarchal Central American labor market means that women do not have the same earning potential as men. Many women prefer to stay in Garifuna villages where they can get by with the help of female kin, sporadic contributions from the father(s) of their children, and cultivation.

This is not to say that all female-headed consanguineal households (type 3) are poorer than affinal households (types 1 and 2). The generational stage of the household may also play a role in determining socioeconomic status. A consangiuneal household headed by an older woman with working adult children who contribute to the household may have the same amount of resources as an affinal household based around a young couple who rely only on their own work (Beaucage 1970, 406–409). Adult sons and daughters take the place of husbands as financial supporters of the core woman and her household. The poorest households are generally those headed by young women who have no adult children and no husband to contribute resources. Even then, however, there are a few households headed by young women that receive support from a sibling or parent who has migrated. In sum, because serial monogamy is not considered illegitimate and because economic status depends on a combination of several factors, household type is not a sure indicator of economic status or social standing.

All ethnographers agree that regardless of household structure or economic standing, the notion of duty to mother is a central aspect of Garifuna ideology. The mother-daughter bond is especially strong because daughters often depend on their mothers for child care and support. Sons are expected to contribute to their mother's household in addition to the households of women with whom they live or have children. Consequently, they are often less reliable than daughters in contributing to their mother's households because their loyalties and resources are split between their consanguineal and affinal kin groups. Coehlo claims that because of this, Garifuna women are associated with the stable land, while men are associated with the inconstant sea, also obviously a reflection of the traditional division of labor (1995, 82).

MATROFICALITY IN NEW YORK CITY

Thus far I have considered the impact migration has on kinship structures and domestic organization in home communities based on the assumption that the majority of transmigrants are male. But what happens when women become transmigrants? Does their movement away from the village rupture traditional principles of kinship and domestic structures? Is matrifocality reconstituted in the transnational community?

In the migration history of the Ramirez family (introduced in Chapter 1), men dominated the U.S.-bound migration process up to the 1960s, but by the 1970s women were migrating both as dependents (wives and daughters) and on their own as labor migrants attracted by the growing demand for domestics and home attendants in the United States, employment opportunities that are more remunerative than those in Central America. These women have begun to form their own migration networks such that migration among Garifuna is no longer male initiated or male centered (Miller 1993). For example, among the Limoneño transmigrants I interviewed, 84 percent of men arrived as independent adults sponsored by a relative other than a spouse or parent. This implies that the main goal of their migration was for work rather than family. Of the men who came independently, a little over half arrived as bachelors; the rest left wives and children behind. Of the second group, slightly over half never brought their families to New York but rather formed second relationships there. (This pattern was more prevalent up to the 1970s. Now young couples expect eventually to be united, a new pattern that has contributed to the increasing number of wives arriving through family reunification.) Of the women who arrived as independent adults (49 percent), about one-third were single with no children, almost half were single mothers who had left children behind, and a few were married women with children who had left both children and husbands behind. The total sample still shows a tendency for more men to arrive independently (84 percent) and more women arrive as daughters and wives (51 percent). But the fact that just under half of the women arrive independently and that among working-age women in general there are high rates of employment shows that regardless of how they arrived, most women are also labor migrants.

As more women began to arrive, the New York community shifted from the predominance of single-male households (type 4) characteristic of the early years (1960s) to more affinal households (see Table 3.2). There is now a slightly greater tendency for households in New York City to be affinal (70 percent of households in New York City versus 60 percent in Limón) than consanguineal (30 percent of households in New York City versus 40 percent in Limón). Most striking, however, is the difference in the types of consanguineal households found in New York and Limón. There is a significantly lower incidence of single-female–headed households in New York (only 7 out of 67) compared to the incidence of such households in Limón (25 out of 63) and a higher incidence of single-male households in New York (13 out of 67 in New York City compared with only 1 out of 63 in Limón). Thus, in contrast to the commonality of female-headed consanguineal households and matrilocal compounds in Garifuna villages, Garifuna households in New York, which are spread throughout the South and Central Bronx and Harlem, have a greater tendency to be comprised of isolated family units and single males. I believe that this trend toward more affinal households in New York City is related to the fact that immigration is so commonly achieved through the avenue of family reunification that it encourages legal marriage so that one can apply for a spouse; this incentive does not exist in Limón. While immigrant men who are single or are leaving wives behind often live alone in efficiency apartments in New York (thus the larger number of single-male households), women who migrate singly most often live with family until they are reunited with their husbands or form a new union. Thus, female-headed households are fewer because many women form part of extended affinal households.

The increased likelihood that women will be in affinal households in New York City does not mean, however, that the principle of matrifocality ceases to function in the New York context. Kerns's observation that the principle of matrifocality operates even in affinal households in Garifuna villages is also true in the New York context. Matrifocality is not erased in the new setting but is rather rearticulated and continues to serve as an organizing principle of the entire transnational community. Garifuna matrifocal kinship cannot be adequately analyzed in isolation in one locale. As others have shown for Belizean Garifuna in Los Angeles, men and women continue to be as oriented toward their maternal consanguineal kin as they are toward their conjugal unit (Miller 1993), rituals and other community events continue to be organized by and centered on women in both the United States (Macklin 1985) and in the village (Kerns 1983), and female-centered networks continue to operate across national borders (Miller 1993). These trends are consistent with what has been seen among West Indian immigrants, who also have strong matrifocal tendencies (Foner 1986; Ho 1993; Watkins-Owens 2001).

In the following case studies I illustrate the multiple forms households and kin networks may take in the transnational context and the principles of matrifocality that continue to operate within them. Following the insights of Miller (1993) and Parreñas (2002), I argue that Garifuna households and families are not neatly bounded economic or residential units. Because of female serial monogamy and some male polygyny, relations among household members that co-reside can be very complex and can connect multiple extended families. Each member of the household may have a unique set of in-laws and extended kin that are spread across national borders. In addition, men and women continue to be oriented more toward their consanguineal kin than they are toward the conjugal unit. This means that both men and women have many networks outside the residential household and may participate in multiple households simultaneously (in Limón, New York, and other locales in the transnational community) in terms of economic contributions and decision-making. Thus, Garifuna kinship networks often blur the distinction between households and extended kin networks and lead to complex domestic structures that cannot be understood by looking only at the conjugal unit or by analyzing only one location of the transnational migration circuit. Rather, transnationalized households may have members in Honduras and New York City simultaneously who make decisions and share resources in ways that reinforce the principles of matrifocality.

Transnational Limoneño Households and Kin Networks

The four basic household types I have identified can be expanded into seven types if we consider households in their transnational forms (see Table 3.3). Rather than using co-residence as a main criteria for inclusion in a household, I use a combination of consanguineal and affinal ties and economic cooperation and decision-making as variables that identify transnational household types. In these households, some members are in Limón and others are in New York but they are inextricably tied by economic and kinship bonds.

In these case studies I also show how these households change over time. Some households will fall into several different categories reflecting various stages in the household's life cycle. In addition, certain people will belong to several different households and household types simultaneously. For example, in Variation B, the children of the core affinal couple are in the household of the parents in the sense that the parents financially support them, but they reside in a household in Limón, most likely one headed by a core female (Variation F).

Table 3.3. Transnational Household Types

Affinal	Type 1		Type 2	
	Variation A	Variation B	Variation C	Variation D
	Local Affinal:	Transnational	Affinal:	Transnational
	All in	Affinal:	Husband	Affinal:
	one location	Parents are	frequently	Husband is
		transmigrants	absent	transmigrant

Consanguineal	Type 3	Type 4	
	Variation E	Variation F	Variation G
	Local Consanguineal:	Transnational	Single Male
	Female headed	Consanguineal:	
		Female-headed,	
		children are migrants	

Key

Solid circle indicates that the person does not reside in the household.

Dashed circle indicates that the person resides in the household part of the time but works outside the village.

Case #1: Local and Transnational Affinal Households

Tomás is a man in his fifties. In the 1960s, he formed a visiting union with a woman in Limón and had three children. Later, he left to work in the banana plantations of Yoro, and when he returned to Limón the relationship broke up. Soon after forming a union with another woman in Limón, Ninfa, he earned his teaching certificate and began teaching in the local grammar school. Eventually he gained a job teaching in a high school in another Garifuna village, where he formed a union with another woman without breaking off ties with Ninfa. For ten years he traveled back and forth between the two communities and households and had nine children between the two women. This polygynous arrangement lasted for many years and befitted his status as a professional in the village. It eventually ended upon his retirement, when he moved back to

Limón and settled in with Ninfa. At the time I interviewed him, he was culti-vating land bought through his earnings as a teacher and had bought a house in a nearby town. Ninfa and the children spent most of their time in town, where the children attended school, while Tomás traveled back and forth between the land and the town (example of Variation A).

Four of Tomás's children have migrated to the United States, all sponsored by his brother. One son, Daniel, maintains his wife and children in Limón while he works six months out of the year in New Orleans and spends the other six months in Limón tending his cattle. Daniel told me that he sees his periods in New Orleans as part of his family responsibility to earn money to invest at home. He does not want his wife and children to migrate because he does not like the living conditions of U.S. cities. For Daniel, his time in New Orleans is more like commuting to work than migrating to set down roots. He lives by himself in a small efficiency apartment and spends most of his time working to be able to send money to his wife. His is an example of a transnational affinal household (Variation D), in the sense that he and his wife are separated by a national border six months of the year but continue to function as a unit, with him as breadwinner and her as housewife. His wife said that she is also happy with the arrangement because she has her own house and yard in Limón, horses, and other benefits of country living that she knows she could not have in the United States. She would, however, like to visit to know what it is like in New Orleans.

Case #2: Transnational Affinal

When I met Tomás in 1993, one of his daughters, Bocha, was still living in her parents' house in Limón with her two children. Her husband, Tamo, had mi-grated to New York City three years earlier when their youngest child was just three months old. He entered the United States without legal documents, so he had not been able to return to Honduras in all that time. Bocha told me the separation was difficult, but they both knew that this way he would be able to fulfill his duty as husband and father, sending money to build a house and for their children's education. Besides, her uncle had applied for her and her hus-band to migrate to the United States, and she was sure the papers would come through soon. When I returned to Limón a year later, Bocha was living alone with her children in the house built with money sent by her husband (Variation D). She was also working as a nurse in the local clinic, a respectable post within the village, with a salary that could maintain her family. She was still waiting for the immigration papers to come through, although she also confided that she was not that eager to go to New York City because she had a good job and considerable independence in Limón. Although she could be earning dollars in New York, she had heard that many women end up working long hours in factories and as home attendants, unable to spend time with their own children. In the end, however, she repeated the common refrain that given a chance to go to the United States, she would be considered crazy not to take it.

In 1995, I met Bocha's husband Tamo in New York City. He was living in a one-room kitchenette in Harlem and working at a Korean-owned dry-cleaning establishment in the Hunts Point district of South Bronx (Variation G). He told me that he had decided to return to Honduras, although he still did not have his legal residency in the United States and knew he might get stuck there. He missed his family and felt he had spent enough time sacrificing in the United States. He was ready to go back and reap the rewards of his many years of labor. But in 1996, reunited in their remittance-built house in Limón, the couple's situation was not so rosy. Bocha was spending weekdays working in the clinic and weekends washing the family's clothes. Tamo had been unable to find local employment, his savings had run out, and he was spending most of his time with friends drinking. He was ready to go back to the United States. The long-awaited immigration papers finally came through in 1997 and the couple moved to New York City, leaving their children with Bocha's mother (Variation B). After only a few months of working as a home attendant, Bocha had to quit because of an unexpected pregnancy. She then had to rely solely on her husband's earnings and Medicaid to pay for the birth and for support for her and the baby. For Bocha, the change from running a household in Limón to being united with her husband in New York was a bittersweet experience of better work opportunities and loss of a degree of autonomy. Like many Limoneños that I knew in New York, Bocha and Tamo eventually moved to New Orleans, where they bought a house and now live with all of their children. Tamo works for a shipping company in the Gulf of Mexico, a job that takes him away from the house for months at a time, and Bocha works as a maid in one of the large hotels in the French Quarter.

Case #3: Affinal Households in New York and Child Fosterage

Michelle and Franky are a couple in their twenties living in New York City. Both migrated in their teens to live with their fathers, while their mothers and younger siblings remained in Limón. Their fathers had been in New York City for over a decade, working in building maintenance and living with Garifuna women from other Honduran communities. Though Michelle and Franky knew each other in Limón, they became a couple in Harlem and lived together off and on. When their first child was born, they sent her to Honduras to live with Michelle's mother. They sent their second child, a boy, to live with Franky's mother, also in Limón. With no childcare responsibilities, both were able to work full time as home attendants and save enough money to send to their respective mothers for the support of their children (Variation B). When their third child was born, Michelle stopped working and they decided to bring the oldest child, now ready to enter kindergarten, back to the United States to live with them so she could attend school in the United States and be immersed in English. With Michelle out of the workforce, their resources were stretched, but by reporting herself as a single mother she was able to receive food stamps, WIC, and Medicaid for the children (who are all U.S. citizens). With the monthly savings this afforded her, she was able to send $100 a month to her mother, Corina, in Honduras to support her household of five dependent children and to begin the slow process of buying cinder blocks to construct a new house. Michelle also sent money for holidays and for the purchase of food and rum for the *novenario* (one year anniversary wake) for her maternal grandmother. I was told that at one point Michelle was possessed by the spirit of her deceased grandmother to exhort her maternal male cousin, also living in New York City, to send his share of *novenario* expenses to his mother in Limón, who was one of three sisters who would be jointly sponsoring the event. The case of Michelle and Franky shows that what looks on the surface like a simple nuclear family comprised of a couple and their children in New York City really spans national borders and two sets of extended kin. Though both Franky and Michelle contribute to their own household expenses in New York, they also each save money to send to their mothers and other consanguineal kin (mainly siblings) to fulfill their obligations as a good son and daughter.

Case #4: Transnational Female Serial Monogamy

The case of Michelle's mother Corina illustrates the ways in which households in Honduras and the United States are complicated by the transnationalization of polygyny and female serial monogamy. Legal marriage seems to be more common among transmigrants than among nonmigrants, probably a response to the need to be defined as a legal family for immigration purposes. Yet it is still common for transmigrant men to have relationships with other women, although the women tend to be in different locations, most often one in Limón and another in the United States. Women may have children with several men over their lifetime, but they are pressured to have only one relationship at a time, as long as the male is contributing to her household. Failure to send remittances is considered justification for a woman to seek a new partner.

Corina is the head of her household in Limón, which consists of herself and five of her children, who were born from a series of four relationships. Two of the fathers have nuclear households in New York City. The other two have households in other Garifuna communities and work several months at a time on passenger ships. All of these men send money to Corina. It is sent, however, in the name of their children only—they do not claim that they are maintaining another woman. Because the children are minors, the money goes to Corina to be administered as she sees fit. As a result, Corina has several sources of cash entering the household—from the fathers of her children and from her adult children in New York (which makes her household an example of Variation F). With this income she is able to feed her family and send her children to school. Like many women in Limón, she expands these remittances by using them to purchase supplies to make bread, coconut candy, ice, and snow cones to sell in the village. While much of her monthly income comes from the fathers of her children, she has several other sources and she is not fully dependent on any one source. Indeed, her most reliable source of remittances is Michelle, who is working with her brother to finance the construction of her house while simultaneously sponsoring Corina's migration to New York so that she herself may work.

Case #5: Matrifocal Extended Kin Network

Corina's sister, Nina, is another example of an older woman head of household with multiple sources of income (Variation F). Unlike Corina, however, Nina receives remittances and goods only from her nine grown children; their fathers stopped supporting them as they grew older. Nina, Corina, and another sister live as neighbors in a matrilocal compound with a common yard where they wash clothes and meet in the evenings under the mango tree to chat (see Figure 3.1). When I met Nina in 1993, two of her children still lived at home, her youngest son and daughter. Though the son contributed to the maintenance of the household, he spent several months at a time in the Bay Islands working on a fishing boat. When he was not working, he spent his time in the village fishing, collecting firewood, and visiting his girlfriend and new baby. The daughter also had a new baby and the father of the child had moved into the household but periodically left for Tequcigalpa to search for job opportunities. Nina, her youngest daughter, and her son formed the stable core of the household.

Two of Nina's other daughters also lived in Limón, where they had formed their own households. One daughter, Mari, lived next door to her mother within the matrilocal compound. Like her mother, she had been involved in a series of common-law unions and visiting relationships, from which she had borne seven children. She was currently receiving remittances from the father

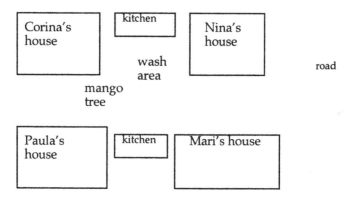

Figure 3.1. Matrilocal compound.

of the last three children, who was soon to retire from New York and join her in Limón (Variation D). The other daughter was legally married with eight children; since her husband worked as a merchant marine, she ran the household most of the time while he was away at work (Variation C). Three more of Nina's children (one daughter and two sons) were in New York. The three siblings in New York had pooled money to build their mother a wooden house with a metal roof, and they sent her remittances monthly, which she redistributed among the household members. Since Nina no longer engaged in any cultivation, the household survived mainly on remittances from all of the working children and from agricultural produce given to her by her daughters and her sisters, who still cultivated some cassava and plantains.

Dani, Nina's only daughter in New York, had migrated just a few years earlier to join her husband Oscar. They lived in a two-bedroom public housing project in the Bronx with their son, who had been in Limón with his grandmother until Dani had worked to save enough money in New York to send for him. At this time Nora, who is Dani's sister from the *casa de papa* (that is, the daughter of Dani's father and his legal wife, not Nina) migrated to New York just after marrying her high school sweetheart in Limón (her story is in Chapter 2). Though Nora and Dani have different mothers and are about the same age, the two grew up as sisters. Nora moved into the two-bedroom project apartment with Dani, giving birth months later to a son. Her husband works on a cruise ship and is able to visit her every few months, but he does not have U.S. residency. Though Dani's husband Oscar has U.S. residency and works in New York, he also earns a great deal of his income as a courier, driving cars and buses loaded with goods from New York to Honduras. Consequently, though the

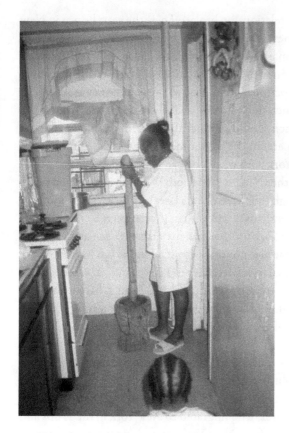

Figure 3.2. Mashing plantains in the *hana* to make coconut-fish soup (*hudutu*) in a Bronx housing project. (Photo by author)

household is based around Dani and Oscar as the core affinal couple, neither of the sisters' husbands are steadily in New York. Dani, Nora, and their children are the more consistent residents of the household, and the two women share finances and baby-sitting (which makes their household a double version of Variation C). In addition to contributing to rent and food expenses, each adult member also sends remittances and goods to the households of their mothers in Limón. Thus, in this group of extended kin, households were focused around women and their children. They exhibited strong networks among female kin and siblings that shared food, money, and child care. Men participated in the household, but their presence was sporadic.

Case #6: Transnational Polygyny

The case of Nina's eldest son Javier illustrates how male polygyny practiced by transmigrants may place men in multiple geographically separated households simultaneously. When Javier left for New York in 1985, he left behind a *compa-*

ñera and a son. Though their relationship broke off over the years he was in New York, he still sends her money and clothes for their son. On his annual trips back to Limón, he met and married another woman, Lilian, who continued to live with her mother in Limón while Javier petitioned for her residency. There are rumors that during this period, Lilian tried to prevent money from reaching the other woman, for which she was criticized; there is a strong belief in the Garifuna community that men should support all children no matter what the circumstances of their birth are. In the meantime, Javier formed a union with another Limoneña in New York with whom he had two children, one of which was sent to live with his mother Nina for a period. When the legal documents for Lilian finally came through (about five years later), Javier left New York for New Orleans, where he currently lives with Lilian (Variation A). He still sends money to the woman in New York for the upkeep of the children and visits her periodically (Variation C). He also continues to send money to his son by the first *compañera* (who earns a salary as a teacher in Limón and has since formed a new union with a man who works on a tourist ship). Though his earnings are spread thin among three households, he also sends money to his mother. She complains, however, that he does not send enough and that his sister Dani is much more reliable.

Javier's case illustrates how polygyny has been transnationalized such that his time and loyalties are split between affinal and consanguineal households that are widely separated geographically. In contrast to the pattern of men in the generation of Mario Ramirez, who migrated to New York in the 1960s and never brought his Limoneña wife to New York, there is now a greater expectation that families will eventually be united by sponsoring the migration of *compañeras* and children. Because the INS requires legal marriage before it will grant sponsorship privileges, legal marriage has become more common among younger couples than it was in the days when Gonzalez, Coehlo, and Beaucage were conducting their field work. Though the increasing prevalence of legal marriage legitimizes one *compañera* over another, during my field work I saw little criticism of men who continue to engage in the practice of polygyny. Criticism was directed more toward men who failed to support their children of multiple relationships rather than because of the relationships themselves. There are, however, signs of female resistance to this practice of polygyny. For example a woman whose *compañero* worked on a tourist ship burned his sea card (making it difficult to get back on the ship) to protest his maintenance of several other women in different ports. Other women are said to use *brujeria* (witchcraft) to sway a man to direct all their energies toward them. Women who seek several male partners simultaneously, on the other hand, are often accused of trying to trick men with affection in order to get their money. This illustrates the contradictions of a matrifocal system that promotes female autonomy and yet continues to constrain female sexuality more than it constrains the sexuality of men (see Kerns 1983 on ritual restrictions on female sexuality during reproductive years).

THE TRANSNATIONALIZATION OF MATRIFOCAL NETWORKS

These case studies clearly illustrate that it is impossible to analyze households in Honduras and New York as separate entities because they exist across national borders within a single transnational formation. Men and women operate as members of both their households of orientation and their households of procreation (which may or may not be in the same locality) in terms of economic contributions, decision-making, and investment. As the cases of Michelle and Franky, Dani and Oscar, and Nora show, both men and women in New York work and contribute to the income of their household of residence but also remain oriented toward supporting their consanguineal extended kin with their own earnings. In some instances their remittances are the primary support of a consanguineal female-headed household in Limón and they are important nonresident participants in the household. This participation in the household from a distance is especially true in cases in which children of the transmigrants are being fostered by family in Limón, be it in a female-headed household, as in the cases of Nina and Corina, or in an affinal household, as in the case of Tomás and Ninfa. In such situations of child fosterage, ties between local households are transnationalized through both economic contributions and the dual locality of the nuclear family. This is also true in cases such as those of Daniel and his wife and Bocha and Tamo, in which the affinal unit itself is split between New York and Limón and yet the unit continues to operate as a household in terms of economic contributions, decision-making, and childrearing.

Just as Miller (1993) documented for Belizean Garifuna in Los Angeles, then, decisions about whether to migrate, how to invest money, which relatives to sponsor, which relatives to educate in Honduras, and so forth are made through transnational networks that are neither male centered nor local but are rather translocal. That is, decisions are made by networks that include both transmigrants and nonmigrants and males and females, who may or may not reside in the same locale. Men are no longer the main instigators and avenues of migration; instead, both men and women have their own networks that operate with a logic based on gendered expectations of kin obligations.

This is not unique to the Garifuna. Many immigrant groups whose members migrate individually (as opposed to in family units) experience long periods of separation between parents and children and husbands and wives and exhibit many of the same household structures I have mentioned (see Ho 1993; Hondagneu-Sotelo and Avila 1997; Levitt 2001; Mahler 1995; Miles 2004; Ong 1999; Parreñas 2002). What is specific to the Garifuna is that these transnational households and networks continue to operate on the logic of matrifocality. For example, one of the primary ways households are transnationalized is through child fosterage. The pattern of child fosterage among Garifuna exhibits the principle of matrifocality because the most common person to foster a child is the child's maternal grandmother. Out of twenty-six cases of child fosterage I documented (from the household surveys in New York and Limón), twenty-two involved the maternal grandmother. A woman who had left her three children with her mother until she was settled in New York City (a seven-year process) told me, "Leaving your children with their maternal grandmother is as though they were with you because she is the same woman that raised you." If the maternal grandmother is not available, then the next best choice is the paternal grandmother (which happened in three cases in my survey) or a maternal aunt (one case). Child fosterage is a common strategy for women to use not only during their initial period of adjustment but even when children are born in New York when child care is prohibitively expensive. Many children are left in Limón or sent to Limón until they are school age so the mothers can continue to work in the United States yet avoid paying for child care at U.S. prices. They send money to Limón for the care of the child, but it costs considerably less there than it does in New York City. As one woman whose son was born in New York told me, "If I kept him in New York I would just be working to pay rent and the baby-sitter." Rather than do that, she sent her son to live with her maternal grandmother in Limón (her own mother was in New York) so she could attend night school and get a better-paying position than the home attendant job she had been in for nearly five years. (Because she was still assigned mainly to Hispanic patients she had not had much time to learn English, much less higher-paying vocational skills.) An alternative strategy to child fosterage for women who choose to keep their children in New York is to sponsor the migration of their own mothers, who will care for their children. If this is not a possibility, they may be able to enlist the childcare services of a few Garifuna women who baby-sit the children of fellow villagers for a fee much lower than most registered childcare providers charge.

Another example of the ways transnational networks are centered on women as mothers is in the patterns of investment and remittances. My survey data showed that one of the first investments both men and women transmigrants make is in the building and furnishing of a house for their mother in Honduras (and the father if he is living with the mother in Limón). Thirty-two of the ninety-seven transmigrants I interviewed said that they had built a house for a family member. Twenty-five specified that the house was for their mother and four said it was for their parents (two had built houses for their wives, and one had built one for a mother-in-law). This is especially interesting given that, as in the case of Corina, children often apply for their mother to migrate to the United States with the purpose of getting better health care for her and free childcare for themselves while they are investing in her house in Limón. Indeed, many older women spend half the year in New York City visiting their children and caring for grandchildren and half the year in Limón caring for elderly parents and other grandchildren. Retired men may also spend half of the year in the United States visiting family and attending to matters related to retirement pay and medical care, but they see Limón as their main place of residence; that is where most have invested in property and businesses.

Finally, the focus on mothers can also be seen in the patterns and politics of sending remittances. In a survey of ninety-seven transmigrants in New York City, I found that remittances were overwhelmingly sent to women rather than to men, regardless of the gender of the sender. Indeed, eight of every ten receivers of remittances in Limón are women. This includes the 57 percent who receive remittances as mothers from children or grandchildren,[3] 10 percent who receive them as "wives" from husbands, 6 percent who receive them as the mothers of children of transmigrant males,[4] and 8 percent who receive them as adult sisters and daughters. Of the men receiving remittances (only 2 percent of those interviewed), more than half are elderly married men. Thus, the predominance of women receiving remittances is not an indication of female dependence on males. Indeed, a significant proportion of remittances are sent by women to women (see also Kerns 1983 for data on Belize). Like Corina and Nina, many women receive remittances from multiple sources that are not restricted to their "husbands" or the fathers of their children but also include their sons and daughters. The fact that the majority of remittances are sent from children to mothers also indicates that the remittance relationship is characterized more by filial duty than by patriarchal authority. (This analysis contrasts with the analysis of such patterns in Dominican transnational communities; see, for example, Georges 1992 and Grasmuck and Pessar 1991).

That very few men receive remittances indicates not only the overriding regard among Garifuna for one's mother as "the one who raised me," a common feature of Latin American transmigrants in general, it also indicates how the ideology of migration as a means of socioeconomic mobility is gendered, placing more social pressure on men to migrate to fulfill their roles as sons, fathers, and husbands. The success of pioneer men such as Mario Ramirez, who went to work at sea and in the United States and retired with a nice house and property in Limón, has contributed to the ideology among Limoneños that the only way to achieve socioeconomic mobility is to migrate, preferably to the United States. All but one Garifuna businessowner and all Garifuna large landowners and ranchers in Limón made their fortunes in the United States. Because of the gendered character of migration ideology, men of working age who stay in Limón are sometimes referred to as *vagos* (bums) with no ambitions. They are seen as losers content to live off the Garifuna "welfare" system—that is, benefiting directly or indirectly from transmigrants' remittances. Those who go to the United States to "make something of themselves" are admired and considered successful members of the community, even if this means leaving wife and children behind and entering the United States illegally to work in unskilled, low-paying jobs.

Transnational migration has fed into notions of masculinity that are tied to success in supporting kin in Limón and building monuments of success such as a cinderblock home, a ranch, and a business. As long as they are sending checks every month and gradually building up the family property, men are considered to be fulfilling their roles as fathers, husbands, and sons. Being a good father does not require fixity in one locale or being present to raise children. Ironically, then, men who stay in the village and reproduce the "traditional" culture transmigrants praise and are so often nostalgic about (fishing, constructing canoes and the implements for making cassava bread, and serving as musicians at wakes and other rituals) do not have as much prestige as those who migrate abroad and return only periodically but with powerful dollars. Nonmigrant males are often positioned in the lower class and are hired as day laborers by transmigrant males who own property and cattle in Limón. Limoneños who make it to the United States but do not return to Limón or send money to their relatives are criticized in much the same way as those who do not leave the village. In this case, however, they are seen as egotists who migrate to New York City only to make money, drink, and party, neglecting their familial and community obligations.

Migration may bring increased community status for men, yet it can also mean estrangement from wives and children and fear of disconnection from a realm of social relations in which men are validated as important members of society. Men's migration stories are filled with ambiguous and contradictory accounts. These stories simultaneously glorify migration as a cosmopolitan adventure for achieving socioeconomic mobility and learning about the world and see it as a dreadful chore that involves becoming wage slaves and living in substandard housing in an environment of racial discrimination. Familial attachments and village recognition of their achievements provide strong motivations for men to remain connected to their place of origin (Goldring 1998). Many men focus on investing in their future in the community and continue to participate in local village politics, even from afar.

Garifuna women, on the other hand, face a less circumscribed set of gendered expectations that gives them more flexibility in relation to migration. Unlike nonmigrant men, women who remain in the village are not criticized for doing so. The fact that many continue to engage in the "traditional" activities of making cassava bread and organizing ancestor rituals is presented by villagers as proof of the resilience of Garifuna culture and the strength of women. Economically, the position of nonmigrant women may actually improve since those who stay in the village reap the immediate material rewards of their relatives' wage work abroad. They typically live in more comfortable houses equipped with consumer goods, receive money each month to cover basic expenses, do not need to engage in agriculture, and can finance their children's secondary education. Women in these households often hire women from nonremittance households to wash clothes and take in young girls to help with cooking and child care. Their ability to do this enhances their status in the community.

The drawback for women in the village is that they face a less certain economic environment in the context of high unemployment and a general lack of state social services. Women such as Corina may be able to make do on remittances, but they cannot control how much they get or when they get it. Women who do not receive remittances face fewer possibilities for employment in Honduras, and those wages are often barely sufficient to meet subsistence needs. Nonmigrant women express wonder at the ability of women like Michelle in New York to receive food stamps, save enough money to buy consumer goods accessible only to the upper middle class in Honduras, and have enough surplus to build a house in Limón. Consequently, many women decide that even if they have to leave children behind temporarily, it is better to migrate to the United States, where they have more chance of finding lucrative employment. Matrifocal support networks that provide such resources as child fosterage facilitate female migration and it is not socially stigmatized. Women can contribute to their transnational households either through domestic labor in the village (such as by fostering a transmigrant female kin's children) or by migrating themselves to send remittances. Both are seen as socially valuable and gender appropriate. The migration of women is not necessarily seen as an abandonment of traditional roles but is often necessary precisely in order to fulfill their roles as good daughters (who support their mothers) and as good mothers (who support their children; see also Hondagneu-Sotelo and Avila 1997).

While the migration of women is facilitated by female support networks that are both local and transnational, paradoxes also come with the transnationalization of matrifocality. While women have better work opportunities in New York and access to state services—resources that many authors have seen as giving women greater independence from men (Hondagneu-Sotelo 1994a), other aspects of the New York context may serve to undermine the other sources of autonomy women have in the village, such as matrilocal residence. In New York City, Garifuna live in apartments and housing projects for which they may have waited many years; many pay large deposits and sign long-term leases for such housing. These apartments and projects are typically small and already crowded with children and temporary residents (mainly recent arrivals just getting oriented to the city) and so are not as extendible as residences in the village. In addition, many men and women have gained legal resident status through marriage and receive state benefits through U.S.-born children who live in their households. For such women, the nuclear family household is not only an affective relationship but also a legal construct that must be maintained in order to receive state benefits and immigration status. (I am not arguing for a clear case of female disempowerment or empowerment but rather am pointing to the complex ways gender relations shift in the transnational context. See, for example, Pessar 1994, 1996. Though this topic was not the focus of my research, it would be a fruitful avenue for further investigation.)

In sum, although Limoneño households in New York City exhibit a lower incidence of single-female–headed households than households in Limón, female networks remain essential for the survival of even affinal households. Women are still primarily responsible for childcare and domestic duties and they must leave the workforce periodically for pregnancies, during which time men's incomes alone may not prove sufficient to meet all transnational household needs. Being in an affinal household does not necessarily mean that the man is always physically present—as in the cases of Dani and Nora, many male partners continue to work in the cargo and passenger ship industry while other men make a living transporting goods from the United States to Honduras. Both kinds of jobs take men away from their New York City homes for months at a time, leaving women with sole responsibility for household affairs. As Gonzalez (1969) has argued, female networks continue to be essential strategies for dealing with the inconsistency of male support and reinforce the relative independence of women in terms of decision-making and resource allocation. The difference in the 1990s was that female networks operated not only in the village but also within the New York community and transnationally.

MATRIFOCALITY AND RITUALS OF COMMUNITY SOLIDARITY

One of the main arguments Virginia Kerns put forward in her book *Women and the Ancestors* is that despite a long history of migration and dispersion, matrifocality has been a major force in keeping Garifuna together, not only by setting standards of what it means to be good daughters, sons, fathers, and mothers who take care of their mothers and children but also through ritual obligations to the ancestors[5] that require the contribution, participation, and return of all family members. Like many other aspects of Garifuna life, ancestor rituals (or rituals of mourning for the deceased) follow the principle of matrifocality in the sense that they are centered on maternal consanguineal kin.

The core organizer of wakes, *novenarios*, and other rituals such as *chügü* and *dügü* is the eldest female descendent of the ancestor involved, and the core group of financial sponsors includes this woman and her sisters and their grown children. *Chügü* and *dügü* are rituals performed by the lineal descendants of a deceased person. The rituals are often performed after a *buyei* has determined that a specific illness or other problem of a lineal descendant is being caused by the deceased person. Part of the cure involves appeasing the ancestor with a *chügü* or the more involved *dügü* (which requires the participation of all the material kin of the deceased in a month-long series of rituals involving singing, dancing, communicating with the ancestor through trance, and offering him or her food).

Other consanguineal and affinal kin and friends (both male and female) with whom the woman has close ties contribute as workers, and anyone who is interested can attend as participants (Kerns 1983, 169–171). In the case of wakes, the organizer would be the closest female kin of the deceased in either the descending (daughter) or ascending (mother) generation. Kerns argues that older women are the main agents who place social pressure on their kin to contribute to and participate in these rituals. Even if these kin have migrated to other parts of Central America or to the United States, they are expected to at least send money for the event. In the case of rituals such as the *dügü*, important events that are planned months in advance, most kin are expected to contribute and attend if possible.

*   *   *

The *dabuyaba*, which was constructed of *caña brava* (a material like bamboo) and palm thatch, contrasted sharply with the pink-and-green Angela Reggae Club built from cinderblocks. The men had built it next to the club for the *dügü* to be held this summer. As I passed by during the day, I could see men and women lounging in hammocks inside the temporary temple, smoking pipes and

Figure 3.3. The *dabuyaba* built for a *dügü* in Limón. This is where the main drumming, singing, and dancing takes place during the month-long ceremony. (Photo by author)

chatting. At night the usual *punta* rock, reggae, and hip-hop of the club was replaced with the drumming and call-and-response singing emanating from the *gayunari*, the main hall of the *dabuyaba*. Men and women dressed in matching red-and-white outfits sewn in New York especially for this *dügü* moved in and out of the temple, dancing and singing, drinking rum, and visiting with family. The entire village was full of transmigrants who had returned to attend the *dügü*. After several members of an extended family living in both Limón and New York City had fallen ill, it was determined by a *buyei* that a *dügü* must be celebrated to honor the ancestors of this family, whose neglect was causing the illnesses. Rumor had it that the New York family members[6] had spent up to $10,000 on expenses related to this ancestor ritual—hiring musicians, buying firewood and cases of rum and beer, and slaughtering a cow and many chickens, not to mention all of the ingredients the women needed to prepare this particular ancestor's favorite foods (coconut bread, coconut and rice pudding, cassava bread, fish stew, and so forth). It was said that even the *buyeis* officiating at the ceremony had charged thousands of dollars for their services. In some ways, this made sense; a few of these women (the *buyeis*) had to travel from their homes in New York to attend the ceremony. In order to recover some of the costs, the sponsors of the *dügü* were charging an admission fee of 50 lempiras at the door of the temple. This caused a great deal of grumbling among residents of Limón, for whom this amount was prohibitively expensive, worth over a day's minimum wage in Honduras. (It was only about $5 for the New Yorkers.)

One of the family members who owns a photography studio in New York was filming the event so that those who had contributed money in New York but were unable to attend could also participate by viewing the video. There was also some grumbling about this among residents of Limón because the *dügü* is considered the most sacred of rituals and they did not want just anyone to see the video. (In fact, I had been told that because I do not have Garifuna blood I would not be allowed to enter the *gayunari*, where family members and *buyeis* were communicating with the ancestors by dancing, singing, and occasionally entering a trance state.) The New York *buyeis*, however, approved of the video, saying that it could be shown to the Garifuna youth in New York in order to teach them about their culture.

*   *   *

The newspaper article detailing the young man's tragic death in an automobile accident in Honduras was being passed around the crowded room. He had died on Tuesday but this wake was postponed until Saturday night, when most family members did not have to work. In the kitchen, women were filling plates with fried chicken, rice and beans, and coconut bread to be handed out among the guests. In the back room, some men were drinking rum and playing cards and dominos. Everyone else was packed into the living room of this small housing-project apartment in Harlem. A few had escaped the heat of the crowded room to the outside hallway, but the cold air entering through the broken windows and the stench of urine emanating from the elevator did not make this a popular gathering place for long.

Normally one of the main activities at a wake is the *punta* drumming and dancing; however, in this crowded project that was not possible. So instead, those seated in the living room focused their attention on the video that was being played on the large-screen television. The video had been filmed some time before in Limón and copies had circulated among family members in New York. It showed the beginnings of a *novenario* celebrated on the year anniversary of the death of the hostess's uncle. We could see women inside the *manaca* (palm-thatch) and *yagua* (palm wood) kitchen preparing coconut-milk *atole* for guests while men drank rum and played cards under a temporary palm thatch awning. Most people were milling about, socializing until the men who would do the drumming arrived. Once it became dark, the drums started. The crowd formed a circle around a candle placed in the sand and began to sing the call-and-response chorus while one couple after another entered the circle to dance *punta*. I knew from attending many a wake in Limón that this drinking and dancing will go on all night. Even when most others had reached their

Figure 3.4. Men drumming *punta* at a wake in Limón. (Photo by author)

limit, the core female organizers and the drummers keep at it until dawn. With the rising of the sun the drums stop and the deceased's female kin go to ritually bathe in the sea.

*   *   *

As can be seen, Garifuna rituals of familial and community solidarity are carried out not only in the village but also throughout the transnational community. While the *dügü* is a ritual that as far as I know is still only observed in the village (it lasts up to a month and requires the construction of the *dabuyaba* out of bamboo and palm leaves), other rituals of mourning can be carried out wherever the deceased has close female relatives and there is a *buyei* to officiate. Because most Honduran Garifuna have a large number of extended family members in the United States, these criteria can usually be met. Most often, rituals of mourning are celebrated in the United States and Honduras simultaneously. Of necessity, they are usually smaller affairs in New York, conducted in the home of the core organizer, who replicates the ritual elements as much she can in small apartments. These events serve as a focus for uniting kin and other village members who are so dispersed in New York City that they may not otherwise see each other on a regular basis. They also allow kin in New York to fulfill their ritual obligations and maintain their status as good *hijos y hijas* who have not forgotten their ancestors and culture. Thus, even transmigrant women in the diaspora are organizers of "traditional" culture, maintaining kin networks across national boundaries and protecting family members from supernatural harm caused by neglected ancestors who travel across national borders, following the diasporic movement of their descendants.

The prominent role of women in ritual is not confined to family affairs. They are also important in the organization of village-level events such as the Christmas *fedu* (a style of dancing and singing performed by the women's dance groups, usually in a large, open-space building), the Easter *ayounani* (a celebration including a procession in which a coffin representing Christ is carried around the village), and the village's festival for its patron saint. In both Limón and New York, dance clubs make up a large part of these community celebrations. They are usually headed by a composer, who can be male or female; a few male musicians; and a core of women who do the dancing and singing. In Limón, the three main clubs are the Mamaristas, Las Pipas, and the Grupo sin Perdón (Group without Pardon). The Grupo sin Perdón has a sister club in New York called the Grupo sin Permiso (Group without Permission). These women also form the core of a voluntary association called the Comité de Damas (Women's Committee) that was created as the female version of the Frente Social Limoneño (Limoneño Social Front; a hometown association). Though the Comité de Damas originally formed in order to organize annual celebrations for the New York Limoneño community, the turnout was so large that participants saw the potential for using such celebrations as a way to raise money for projects in Limón such as providing electricity and potable water. Attendance at these events is another way for Limoneños to show that they are *buen hijos y hijas del pueblo*; they are both networking with other Limoneños and contributing to communal projects.

*   *   *

Vamos a la Peña del Bronx is one of those places you can find only if you know what you are looking for. It is on a back street hidden behind Lincoln Hospital, on the third floor of a building that if you did not know better you would probably think was abandoned, as so many buildings in this part of the South Bronx are. On this evening in December, we arrive from the back way, crossing the railroad tracks from 149th Street behind Hostos College, trudging through the cold air and snow to reach the doorway to the narrow staircase that leads to the club. Even from the street we can hear the pulsating of the drums and the call-and-response singing emanating from the windows left open to compensate for the heat generated by the tightly packed crowd of dancers. Once inside, men and women shed their wool caps, Tommy Hilfiger coats, and Nike sweatshirts to reveal the brightly colored matching dresses and headscarves chosen for this year's Christmas *fedu*.

The scene inside the club provides a sharp contrast to the cold New York winter outside. The walls are painted with depictions of Pancho Villa, the Chilean

Figure 3.5. Women selling food at a hometown association event at Vamos a la Peña del Bronx. (Photo by author)

flag, and scenes from the tropical beaches of the Dominican Republic. In one corner, an altar has been set up with offerings of rum, cassava bread, and mangos. On the walls above the altar hang paintings depicting scenes from Garifuna village life on the North Coast of Honduras: men and women gathered on the beach in the shade of coconut trees waiting to buy the catch of fishermen in small dugout canoes, a woman with a headscarf wrapped around her black braids smoking a pipe while peeling cassava, another woman bent over a *budari* (baking stone) baking cassava bread, and a man playing a mahogany-and-calfskin drum while a group of women dance *punta* around him. As in almost every painting by this Garifuna artist, the ocean, coconut trees, and sandy pathways winding between palm thatch and wooden houses form the backdrops of these nostalgic scenes.

On this December evening, Garifuna from the village of Limón unfortunate enough to be stuck in New York for the holidays have gathered to re-create a Garifuna Christmas as best they can in this South Bronx club. On the dance floor, women line up in rows to sing and dance in unison to male musicians drumming on mahogany-and-calfskin drums brought from Honduras. Men stand near the bar drinking rum, beer, and *horchata* (a rice-milk drink). On a table near the back, women are selling coconut bread, *tapado* (fish stew made with heavy root crops such as cassava), *hudutu* (plantain and fish stew), *bimini*

Figure 3.6. A women's dance group returning from a night of dancing *parranda* at the beginning of the village patron saint's festival. The dance groups go from house to house singing and dancing until dawn. (Photo by author)

katule (rice pudding with coconut milk), tamales, and other Garifuna foods made with ingredients brought from Honduras by returning transmigrants or bought in Dominican *bodegas*. Some of the money generated by the entrance fee and the selling of this food will be used to pay for the rental of the club, and the rest will be sent to Honduras for the electricity project.

*   *   *

Like the ancestor rituals, these village-level events are transnational in the sense that they are held simultaneously in New York and Limón and involve flows of people, goods, cultural symbols, and practices. The dance groups obtain cloth from New York at Christmas for their matching *parranda* dresses, special foods are sent from Honduras for the celebrations in New York, and money raised in New York is sent back to Limón to sponsor more events or village projects. These events do more than simply replicate village-level celebrations in New York (to the degree possible given the different conditions there); these celebrations provide simultaneous participation throughout the transnational Limoneño community that further consolidates the consciousness of belonging among members. They are a way for transmigrants, both men and women, to continue to participate as important members of the village-level community and regenerate their status within it despite geographical distance from the village (Smith 2005).

CONCLUSION

As Kerns aptly argued in her 1983 book and as I have shown in this chapter, the principle of matrifocality, whether enacted in economic kinship obligations, support networks, or ritual, is an important social glue that holds Garifuna society together. It obligates kin to return to the village, it serves as a central ideology of the community in New York, and it provides a mechanism for the simultaneity of social relations and community solidarity in both places. The transnational community is not severely fragmented by geographical distance but can be united by common principles of kinship and community. By expanding the definition of household to include members who are not co-resident but who do participate economically and through decision-making, we can see how households and networks operate transnationally. While this is not unique to the Garifuna (most transmigrant groups have transnational forms of kinship and community), this transnationalization takes place along the principle of matrifocality, and that makes it distinct. This is not to say that matrifocal networks are only maintained by women or that all households are consanguineal but rather that women as mothers continue to serve as an ideological reference point for the Garifuna social system, even if the mothers are mobile. Thus, contrary to assumptions built into unilinear models of immigration and assimilation, migration (especially the migration of women) does not necessarily make traditional kinship systems such as matrifocality disappear. They can be reconstituted in transnational space.

This does not mean, however, that location is unimportant to the form households and social structures take within Garifuna transnational social formations. Garifuna kinship ideologies and domestic structures are also affected by the conditions men and women encounter in New York City and Honduras that offer different sets of opportunities and constraints, shaping the choices about whether to migrate, who to sponsor, how long to stay, what household arrangement to maintain, and so forth. While both men and women often prefer the U.S. labor market because it enables them to better fulfill their economic obligations to kin, migrating to work in the United States also often means that families must be split for periods of time. Many men and women sponsor the migration of their immediate family members to avoid long separations. The emphasis on family reunification in New York is as much a result of the desires of Garifuna to have family members co-reside as it is of the way the

U.S. state constructs the definition of the family, and the rights and benefits associated with it, around affinal ties. For example, the INS stresses affinal ties in its definition of which kin have the first priority in being sponsored through family reunification. This privileges the migration of spouses and children over other categories of relatives, thereby encouraging the reunification of the affinal household. Rights to state social services in the United States, which give benefits for food, housing, and health care primarily to parents through their dependent children, are also defined around affinal ties. This also encourages the reunification of children with parents who may have been separated due to migration or child fosterage.

On the other hand, raising children is much less expensive in Honduras, so some families decide to maintain the split between parents and children until they are school age and no longer need child care. Because employment opportunities in the Central American labor market are not as lucrative as those in the United States, more women are willing to stay in the village and raise their children and those of their kin while receiving remittances instead of doing work in the city *solo para pagar la renta* (just to pay the rent). In the village, women have strong support networks and land to cultivate, so they have a degree of autonomy. Men encounter more social pressure to leave the village to work, so they are often absent from the village for periods of time. This accounts for the greater number of households in the village that are female headed most of the time (types 2 and 3) compared to such households in New York.

But even in New York, where both men and women have more stable employment and there are fewer female-headed households, matrifocal support networks are still important, both for household subsistence and for community solidarity. Thus, Garifuna on both sides of the border call on matrifocal networks for support, be it migrants needing child fosterage or nonmigrants needing remittances. In the Garifuna transnational community, then, there is both continuity (of the principle of matrifocality) and change (in some of the forms that matrifocality takes).

4

"Los Pobres Allá Somos Los Ricos Acá en Honduras"

Navigating the Contradictions of the International Division of Labor

The municipality of Limón, Honduras, is one of those places that is literally at the end of the road. It is the last stop on a typically slow and dusty Central American bus ride that for me usually began in the Department of Atlántida in the port city of La Ceiba. From there, the bus travels down the paved coastal highway (a two-lane road) through groves of bananas and African palm plantations into the Department of Colón, stops at the market in Tocoa, bypasses the Trujillo turnoff at Corocito and proceeds the rest of the way on a dirt road past acres of deforested pastureland dotted with grazing cattle until the final turnoff takes the bus into the village of Limón. There the road transforms from dirt into the sandy pathways of the village that wind their way between palm thatch and cinderblock houses, invariably terminating at the banks of the Río Limón, the Río Salado, or the coconut tree–lined beach. During the dry season the bus can actually make it to one more stop down the coast, to Iriona, on a much more rutted road, but during the rainy season the only access to Garifuna villages between Limón and the Mosquitia is by outboard motor, four-wheel drive, horseback, or simply by walking along the beach. Even the large trucks carrying African palm from the plantations of Honduran billionaire Miguel Facussé and the trucks carrying illegally logged lumber from the stands of tropical forest get stuck in the mud on this last stretch of road. The drivers must enlist the help of the ladino peasants that live in the *aldeas* scattered throughout the municipality to pull them out.

But Limón wasn't always at the end of the road, at least in the metaphorical sense, when roads were not yet the main indicators of national integration. In the 1800s, American schooners stopped there to buy bananas and coconuts that were valuable on the world market, while Garifuna men traveled up and down the coast in their sail-fitted dugout canoes trading in goods between Belize and Nicaragua. In the early 1900s, the Truxillo Railroad Company (a subsidiary of United Fruit) built a railroad through Colón that connected villages such as Limón to the ports of Trujillo and Puerto Castilla, where many men worked loading bananas. But in 1936 the tracks were lifted as United Fruit left for more productive areas, and Limoneños were back to canoes and horses. In the 1960s, Limoneños still had to travel by sea or canoe upriver to get to Trujillo, the nearest town with markets and banks. It was not until the 1970s that the coastal highway was built as a part of the International Development Bank–financed Bajo Aguan agricultural colonization project that brought more people and infrastructure to this area of the North Coast. It was even later in the 1980s that this highway actually reached Limón, bringing with it the peasant colonists, cattle ranchers, lumber companies, agribusiness, and tourism that generally follow such infrastructural development projects of the state. Limón finally got electricity in 1998, but it still did not have telephones or a hospital with a permanent doctor. The main amenities the town had to offer during my fieldwork period from 1993 to 1997 were a potable water system financed in large part by Limoneño hometown associations in New York City, a few privately owned electric generators, a fair number of transmigrant-built homes with indoor toilets and septic tanks, a grammar school, a high school built by the Peace Corps, and one of the most beautiful beaches in Central America. Many women still travel upriver to plant and harvest plots of cassava, plantains, bananas, and coconuts, and every day at midmorning a crowd still gathers on the beach to buy fish from the fishermen who have left in their dugout canoes before dawn. Thus, despite the daily entrance and departure of two buses; the traffic of cattle ranchers, store owners, and former merchant marines in their sport utility vehicles; and the weekly entrance of the ice and frozen chicken trucks, there is still a real sense of being in a rural village at the end of the road.

That is the image, anyway, until you hang out at Black Sugar, a bar on the main street, across from the Catholic church and just behind the municipal office building. It is one of the few businesses in Limón that runs a generator every night despite the high price of gas in order to light the pool table and run the "movie theater"—a set of chairs lined in front of a TV/VCR that plays videos such as *New Jack City, Boyz 'N the Hood, Malcolm X*, and Jackie Chan movies. The movies were brought from the United States by the owner of the bar, a member of the generation of merchant marines who settled in New York City in the 1950s and eventually retired from the sea to work as superintendent of an apartment building in the South Bronx. His nephew sits in the bar every night selling Nacionals and Port Royals (Honduran beers), Coca-Cola, and Teem to the mainly young male clientele that sport the hip-hop fashions of Tommy Hilfiger shirts, B.U.M. jeans, and Nike shoes as best they can from the clothes sent, brought, or wheeled out of relatives living in the United States. The T-shirt logos trace the lines of migration: New York City, New Orleans, Los Angeles,

Miami, San Francisco, even Hawaii and the Cayman Islands. Many of the men are on vacation, visiting family after months spent working on a Bay Island fishing boat or a Carnival Cruise liner registered under the Panamanian flag (what Garifuna call a *barco pirata* because they do not pay U.S. minimum wage; see Frantz 1999) or from a semester at an urban technical school in La Ceiba, San Pedro Sula, or Tegucigalpa. A few might even be visiting from the United States, talking about life in New York City, treating the others to beers, comparing how much this beer would cost in relation to their monthly incomes in U.S. dollars, one of the many indicators of the buying power one gains through migration. The locals, the men who live in Limón and work as day laborers for cattle ranchers or who build the cinderblock houses that are rapidly replacing the *yagua* and palm thatch variety or who are teachers at the local high school and whose daily wage could not even purchase a pair of new jeans, listen to these stories, planning how they might get to New York City. They have a parent, an uncle, an aunt, a brother, a cousin who lives in New York who could help them get a visa or sponsor their trip across Mexico, or they could just get off the cruise liner the next time it docks in Miami and make their way north. Whatever the avenue, the dream is to make enough money to come back and build their own cinderblock house, buy their own land with cattle, run their own business with a stereo sound system playing the hip-hop, reggae, salsa, and *punta* they are listening to that night at Black Sugar.

But this is not just true of men. Women too have their evening gathering place in the homes of those who are hooked up to Cablevision Limón, a business that consists of a satellite dish brought by a New York resident that is run by his mother and sister from 6 to 10 p.m.—just the right hours to catch all of the *novelas* on the Miami-based Spanish-language network Univision. During these hours, some of the homes themselves become movie theaters where neighbors and their children gather around the TV, watching the exploits of the Mexican and Venezuelan rich and famous, commenting in Garifuna on the merits of this or that relationship, this or that shady deal, swatting the few mosquitoes that managed to get in before the doors were closed despite the sweltering heat. At the same moment, Limoneños in New York City are watching these same *novelas* on television sets that will eventually end up in Limón, either sent to a relative or brought for a house being built in anticipation of return migration. Even men in New York City have become hooked on these *novelas* as large home entertainment systems have become a safer alternative to going out at night on the streets of Harlem and the South Bronx and fighting the brutal cold of New York winters. Transmigrants say it is also best to try to save money instead of spending it *vagando en la calle* (hanging out in the street) so they can send that $100 every month to family in Honduras or build that house in Limón sooner or sponsor the migration of children they left behind in the care of a grandmother more quickly. One hundred dollars may not be much in New York City, but in Limón it can provide basic goods for a household of five for a month, supplemented of course by selling bread or coconut oil, growing some cassava and plantains, gathering firewood, and fishing. If Limoneños in New York City do get together for a beer and dancing, it is more likely to be at one of the social clubs in the South Bronx where Limoneño hometown associations enlist Garifuna bands to play to raise money for mayoral elections, for the village patron saint festival, or for the village electrification project that would, as they say, really urbanize Limón, transforming it from a village to a town.

Limón may appear to be an out-of-the-way village on a frontier coast of a country that is seldom heard of in the U.S. media, except when there are tragedies such as Hurricane Mitch.[1] However, the processes that shape the socioeconomic realities of Limoneños can be traced through circuits of kinship, consumption, and politics that pass through multiple locations in both Honduras and the United States. During the slice of time I conducted research, approximately 52.5 percent of Limoneños were living outside Limón. Of that, a little less than one-third were working in other areas of Honduras (mainly the three major cities—Tegucigalpa, San Pedro Sula, and La Ceiba). The other two-thirds were living in the United States. Seven out of every ten Garifuna residing in the United States is a transmigrant; the rest were born there (see Table 4.2 below). It is apparent that the boundaries of the community extend far beyond that of the village, connecting multiple locations through migration and the common experience of being Limoneño.

This is not to say, however, that location is irrelevant for understanding the social relations and socioeconomic conditions of the transnational community. While I argue that the transnational community connects multiple sites, I do not see those sites as static; they are places (or translocalities) created by the intersection of global political and economic structures and ideologies with local cultures, labor market conditions, and ethnic and immigrant compositions— all social relations and power structures that shift over time (Appadurai 1996; Guarnizo and Smith 1998; Massey 1994). While the Garifuna transnational community may transcend borders and manifest continuities, it is also shaped by the socioeconomic conditions of the specific locations where its members reside. Thus, the contours of the transnational community are traceable not only through the cultural forms and socioeconomic activities of Limoneños and their migratory paths; they are also traceable through the paths of transnational capital and the projects of state legislation that have transformed the municipality of Limón into ladino-dominated cattle ranches, African palm plantations, and, most recently, drug trafficking. And they are traceable through global economic processes that have transformed New York City into a pole of Latin American and Caribbean labor migration, and the South Bronx into a "periphery of the core."

The purpose of this chapter is threefold. First, I describe the socioeconomic conditions of the research site—the transnational community of Limón–New York City. I argue that while Limón–New York City can be see as one social space from the point of view of Limoneños, each geographic location has been shaped by the economic and social policies of states, national societies, and international institutions based on particular ideologies about where those societies fit into the hierarchy of nations and hierarchies within each individual nation. In other words, economic and social policies are not based simply on a neutral logic of the market but are also based on culturally embedded ideas about the First World and Third World, economic centers and peripheries, and geographical and cultural frontiers. For example, Honduras has generally been seen as an economic periphery of the global economy and the North Coast as an even more marginal frontier within that economy. This image has contributed to the creation of various development projects aimed at integrating the North Coast into the national economy and bringing Honduras into "modernity" that have had particular effects on places such as Limón. Similarly, the South Bronx has been seen as the Third World of New York City, a "periphery of the core" inhabited by black and Hispanic immigrant labor, leading to structural conditions and development projects not very different from those found in the urban areas of Honduras.

The second purpose of this chapter is to show that the socioeconomic conditions of Limón–New York City must also be understood as the outcome of Limoneños negotiating the circumstances they find in these places through migration, economic activities, and their own understandings of what constitutes progress, modernity, and upward mobility. As others have argued, transmigration can be a means of taking advantage of the different economic opportunities created by political borders. This can be seen as a form of resisting the double marginalization many transmigrants face as members of underdeveloped nations working in the periphery of developed nations (Basch, Glick Schiller, and Szanton Blanc 1994; Portes 1996). The desire of Garifuna to earn more valuable dollars but invest in the home country where they have social prestige and possibilities for upward mobility provides an incentive to maintain ties, move back and forth, return to Honduras to live, and otherwise keep the circuit going (Goldring 1998). While this is one way the transnational community is maintained, it also creates complex class formations in which individual transmigrants may simultaneously occupy different class positions in two countries.

Finally, I conclude the chapter by analyzing the consequences of these multiple class positions for Garifuna consciousness and social practice. I argue that the way transmigrants and nonmigrants experience the gap between labor conditions and the possibilities for upward mobility and entrepreneurship in the United States and those in Honduras leads to competing opinions about whether migration ultimately results in the "progress" of individuals through upward mobility or in the double marginalization of the Garifuna in two national economies. These discourses and opinions are not discrete, however, because members of the transnational community may express both opinions at different moments. Such contradictions have consequences for the ways Garifuna understand and practice migration.

THE DISCOURSE OF DEVELOPMENT AND THE "DISCOVERY OF POVERTY"

Honduras entered the 1990s in a state of economic crisis. With 50–60 percent of the population unemployed or underemployed and 70 percent of the population living below the absolute poverty level, Honduras became the fourth poorest country in the Americas (Merrill 1993; Stonich 1993, 2). According to Susan Stonich (1993), the state of the Honduran economy is a case study of the failures and contradictions of the dominant development model multilateral and international lending institutions have promoted that is based on export-led growth, foreign investment, and international loans instead of the production of basic grains and sustainable growth. This dominant development model, development economics, arose in the wake of World War II and became the guiding ideology for most large-scale development projects of the World Bank, the International Monetary Fund (IMF), and other major lenders. Development economics is based on the assumption that "development" is measured by material signs of "modernization" such as the ability to consume, the construction of infrastructure, and the expansion of industrialization. The implicit standard against which levels of development were measured was the level of development in prosperous western countries that by the 1950s were already achieving high levels of consumption per capita.

Escobar (1995) argues that this particular way of defining poverty—as a lack of consumer goods, industrialization, capital, and a high GNP—was selective and biased towards First World standards. In other words, high degrees of self-sufficiency in food production, small producer access to land, community integration, and other possible criteria were not measured and taken into consideration when determining the level of development of different countries. For example in the framework of development economics small-scale peasant producers are poor because they do not have access to consumer goods though they may be self-sufficient in food. Rather than encourage this small-scale production, proponents of development economics tended to create projects to scientifically and rationally engineer development through the injection of more foreign capital into Third World economies in the form of massive aid, loans, and private investment combined with state-directed development projects. In many cases these projects did not benefit small-producers and in fact led to their displacement from small-holdings and migration to the growing slums of the cities. Thus Escobar argues that development projects that encourage foreign investment and mechanization (based on First World models) have actually contributed to the poverty (in terms of income, access to medical care, and so forth) that we see today in Latin America and other countries. "Thus poverty became an organizing concept and the object of a new problematization. As in the case of any problematization . . . that of poverty brought into existence new discourses and practices that shaped the reality to which they referred. That the essential trait of the Third World was its poverty and that the solution was economic growth and development became self-evident, necessary, and universal truths" (24).

Though development experts discussed assessments of levels of modernization and development in the putatively neutral language of numbers and measures of growth, they were also tied to notions of race, and in Latin America, they often reproduced the language of the rational superiority of Anglos over Latinos. "Development assumes a teleology to the extent that it proposes that the 'natives' will sooner or later be reformed; at the same time, however, it reproduces endlessly the separation between reformers and those to be reformed by keeping alive the premise of the Third World as different and inferior, as having a limited humanity in relation to the accomplished European. Development relies on this perpetual recognition and disavowal of difference, a feature identified by Bhabha . . . as inherent to discrimination" (53–54).

For Latin American countries such as Honduras with a long relationship to U.S. imperialism, this development discourse based on the idea of inadequacy and backwardness was nothing new and can be seen as a continuation of a discourse with origins in the colonial period that was reinforced during the colonial Anglo-Spanish conflict on the Mosquito Coast and continued during the era of the banana companies (Arancibia 1984; Barahona 1991; Euraque 1996b; Floyd 1967). The writings of Anglo (British and North American) colonial administrators, travelers, entrepreneurs, and the like on the subject of Honduras consistently portrayed the country as a place of great economic potential that had a population incapable of ruling itself and thus of realizing that potential (see, for example, Charles 1890; Squier 1970; Young 1847). This attack was often based on an explicit conflation of race and culture in which Anglo writers pointed to the mixture of Spanish blood with that of the indigenous peoples and blacks as the cause of the political chaos and economic inefficiency that was responsible for the lack of "development" in the country and the continued domination of foreign capital. For example, E. G. Squier, an American entrepreneur and trained anthropologist sent as an American envoy in the 1860s, explicitly conflated race and blood in his evaluations of the potential of the Honduran population for economic development and progress. He argued that there are superior and inferior races of man, each with "physical, intellectual, and moral differences" that condition their capacities for progress. In Honduras, where the "Indian or aboriginal predominates . . . in some districts of the state it is difficult to say if the whites have assimilated most to the Indians in habits of life, or the Indians most to the whites," creating what he called "semi-Europeans" (1870/1970, 161). In his opinion, the scarce resource of "superior" "white" blood had been diluted by inferior "indigenous" blood, affecting the inherent ability for development and progress of the Honduran people. For Squier, miscegenation was a degeneration of the national character and therefore of the political and economic potential of Honduras.

Many Anglo writers concluded that implementation of liberal reforms that would encourage further foreign investment and the immigration of Europeans and white North Americans, who would bring "superior" technology and culture of capitalism, was the only hope for the development of the Honduran economy. Thomas Young, the British entrepreneur we saw in Chapter 2 praising the industriousness of the Garifuna, had this to say about Honduras as a whole: "Without the skill and perseverance of the white man, the natural resources of this fine country will never be brought to light, whilst with labour properly directed, many valuable articles, such as mahogany, cedar, caoutchouc, cacao, pimento, hides, sarsaparilla, tortoiseshell, medicinal balsams, gums and other commodities would be produced. At present, I am sorry to say, that everything left to the inhabitants is wasted, and the advantages offered by nature, however easily attainable, however abundant the supply, are refused" (Young 1847, 16). E. G. Squier concurred: "It is only by a judicious system of colonization, which shall ultimately secure the predominance of white blood, at the same time that it shall introduce the intelligence, industry, and skill, that the country can hope to achieve peace, prosperity, and greatness" (1870/1970, 174).

This racialized gaze of Anglo imperialists was reproduced by the owners and managers of the multinational fruit companies and projected onto both the ladino elite and black, indigenous, and ladino workers in a variety of ways that generated a racialized hierarchy of managers and workers based on ideas that conflated constructs about "race" with notions of "productivity" (Bourgois 1989; Euraque 1996b).

Within this racialized ideological context, a central element of state expansion in Honduras has been the promotion of the integration of the northeastern departments into the economy and national identity of the rest of the country. The state considered this to be an important project as the northeast had long been a sparsely populated frontier zone where Anglo dominance had long been a thorn in the side of Honduran national sovereignty. In addition, Honduran state officials often referred to it as underdeveloped and underutilized by its indigenous and black inhabitants (based on a measure of productivity primarily in terms of capitalist market-oriented production, profit-maximizing behavior, and "effective" use of local resources). Thus, while the dominant development model has impacted the entire economy of Honduras, creating poverty, unemployment, peasant evictions, and the highly unequal distribution of wealth and resources in all regions of the country, the Garifuna have been impacted in particular ways based on the notion that the North Coast is an empty space waiting to be filled with "productive" members of the nation.

Policies generated by development economics regarding the agrarian sector have had a strong impact on Garifuna communities. Until the 1960s, concentration of land ownership, proletarianization of rural populations, and impoverishment, which had long been problems in other Central American nations because of the structure of the coffee economy, were not acute in Honduras. This is because of the lower population density and greater availability of national lands and the fact that the main agricultural export, bananas, did not displace peasants. This situation changed in the 1960s and 1970s as international lenders and the state, following the dominant development model's construction of traditional peasant production as inefficient, backward, and unproductive, promoted the "modernization" of the agricultural sector by making credit and technical assistance available to landowners willing to invest in large-scale mechanized production of export crops. While this assistance was theoretically available to all, in reality the large landowners and urban elite with family and political connections to the state and military were strategically placed to obtain the credit and technical assistance (Durham 1979; Stonich 1993; Williams 1986). These members of the elite invested credit in the mechanized production of cotton and other export crops in southern Honduras, where population density is high.

Though this phase of capitalization did not directly impact the Garifuna, its later repercussions did. As many of the peasant sharecroppers in Southern Honduras were evicted and small landowners were bought out (often forcibly) to make room for more cotton production, they searched for alternative sources of livelihood, often on the North Coast, an area still sparsely populated and visualized as a place of *tierra ociosa* (unoccupied or empty land) despite the fact that indigenous peoples and Garifuna did indeed inhabit the area. The situation worsened in the 1970s with the expansion of the cattle industry in response to the growing demand for cheap beef on the U.S. market. Because cattle can be raised in a wide variety of ecological zones, even the more marginal lands of the south that peasants had been pushed onto and the tropical forests of the North Coast became desirable to cattle ranchers (Williams 1986). Cattle ranching spread throughout southern Honduras and into the national forests of the North Coast and the Mosquitia. Garifuna and other residents of the North Coast were faced with the entrance of peasant *colonos* (internal colonists mainly from southern Honduras) and cattle ranchers looking for land to squat on, buy, or simply take over.

As the processes of peasant eviction, land concentration, and unemployment intensified throughout the 1960s and 1970s, campesino organizations formed in southern Honduras (among evicted peasants) and on the North Coast (among former banana workers who were fired after a 1954 strike) that pushed for the passage of new agrarian reform legislation; such legislation was finally passed in 1974 (Posas 1981a). Its purpose was to modernize the agricultural sector through the conversion of *latifundios* (large landholdings) and *minifundios* (small landholdings) to large- and medium-scale commercial enterprises. This was to be done by redistributing unused national and private lands and forming peasant cooperatives and *empresas asociativas* (associative enterprises)[2] that had access to credit and technical assistance. Though the intention of these reforms was the redistribution of the fruits of development, the results were less than equal. Because of the power of the agrarian bourgeoisie (represented by the Federación de Agricultores y Ganaderos de Honduras—FENAGH—which had gained power by producing cotton in the south and cattle in the north), the new agrarian reform did not directly challenge the hegemony of the large landowners. Rather than break up large landholdings, the Instituto Nacional Agrario (INA) encouraged displaced peasants to migrate to the more sparsely populated North Coast and Mosquitia, where land tenure was unclear. In addition, though the new legislation focused on peasants as social actors, the agrarian reform's model of production was still based on export-led economic growth, reliance on international aid, and the capitalization of the factors of agricultural production, which ultimately led to the same contradictions that characterized the 1960s.

Within this context, INA categorized the subsistence agricultural practices of the Garifuna (and indigenous peoples) as summarily unproductive, failing to give the land a "social function"—that is, agricultural production for the market, cattle ranching, or resource extraction. In the end, both large landowners and *colonos* on the North Coast used the agrarian reform of 1974 as a way to expropriate Garifuna agricultural land.

THE DISCOURSE OF DEVELOPMENT REACHES LIMÓN

In 1965, the Facultad de Ciencias Económicas of the Universidad Auónoma de Honduras (Faculty of Economic Sciences of the Autonomous University of Honduras) conducted a socioeconomic study of the development potential of the municipality of Limón. This study provides useful information on demographic change and the history of the village and land distribution. But more important for the present discussion, it also reveals some of the discriminatory assumptions built into the dominant development model concerning ideological connections between culture, gender, ethnicity, and underdevelopment.[3]

The stated purpose of the *Estudio Socio-Económico del Municipio de Limón* was to explain the factors that "enter into an understanding of the present socioeconomic conditions of the municipality" and to suggest ways this type of municipality could be integrated into the national economy.

> Presently, at the level of Central America, there is insistent talk about economic integration, which our country is participating in—but with the warning of those who feel that it is the weakest, economically speaking, of the five countries of the isthmus and fear that it will be converted into a colony of the commerce of those who have reached a comparatively higher level of industrial development. We are going for Central American integration without even having the geographical regions of this country integrated into the economic national life. Therefore, it becomes essential to incorporate the northeastern region of the country into the national economic life, and for this a study is necessary of the ecological, human, and economic factors that make it possible to establish the directions of national economic planning. (Instituto de Investigaciones Económicas y Sociales 1965, 94–95; my translation)

The authors concluded that given the abundance of land and other resources, Limón was characterized by "chronic sub-production" which could be defined as "the permanent deficit of local production in relation to the felt needs of the community. These conditions are the product of a series of geographical, histori-

Table 4.1. Land Distribution in the Municipality of Limón, 1952 and 1963

	1952		1963	
	Percentage of farms	Percentage of surface area	Percentage of farms	Percentage of surface area
Less than 1 hectare	3.6	.2	12.4	.8
1–9 hectares	74.6	25.5	63.2	18.1
10–49 hectares	19.6	32.8	19	34.5
50 hectares or more	2.1	41.4	5.2	46.6

Source: Data from Instituto de Investigaciones Económicas y Sociales, Facultad de Ciencias Económicas, *Estudio Socio-Economico del Municipio de Limón* (Tegucigalpa, Honduras: Universidad Nacional Autónoma de Honduras, 1965).

cal, and cultural factors, the nature and importance of which will be elucidated in the present study" (10).

The main evidence of "chronic sub-production" the researchers presented was the fact that only 2.6 percent of the available land in the municipality was under cultivation and most of this was in small holdings (1–49 hectares). In addition, more of these farms were "occupied" (that is, national land was being cultivated without title) than were *ejidal* (land that was ceded to the municipal government and leased to residents of the municipality for a small fee), which suggests that land was being used not as a commodity or as capital but rather for subsistence cultivation. As can be seen in Table 4.1, there was already considerable inequality in the size of landholdings; 2.1 percent of farms held 41.4 percent of land in 1952 and 5.2 percent of farms held 46.6 percent of land in 1963. The researchers' reading of these numbers was not that *colonos* were steadily encroaching into Garifuna territory but rather that the Garifuna lacked initiative. Their seeming disinterest in large-scale capitalist production did not seem to conform to the economists' standards of profit-maximizing market rationality.

The economists interpreted the fact that Garifuna cultivation is mainly carried out by women as further evidence of the weak potential of agriculture as an economic development activity among that group. In their discussion of the demographics of Limón, they claim that only 2 percent of women were "economically active," while 72 percent of men were. Since they recognized that women are the main cultivators of groundfoods and manufacturers of cassava bread, we must assume that they did not consider these to be "economic" activities, probably because their organization of labor and rules for distribution are governed by reciprocal exchange and kinship obligations as opposed to the logic of market exchange. The economists saw the facts that only 46 percent of the population was between 15 and 59 years old, the years of greatest economic activity, and that of those only 38 percent were male (due to seasonal migration) as a "markedly unfavorable tendency." They felt that the male Garifuna population was "a considerably low percentage of those who could constitute the economically active population" (30). Though they recognized that these men left the village to work, bringing "exterior money" into the village, they interpreted the fact that much of it was spent on subsistence rather than used as seed capital for agricultural enterprises as a lack of economic initiative.

In sum, the authors believed that the factors that "impede or retard [Garifuna] integration into a market economy and a modern society" stemmed from both geography and culture. They recognized that this area of the coast was isolated from exterior markets by lack of adequate modes of transportation and other forms of state infrastructure. Thus, the Garifuna inhabited an area that "was not integrated into the national life and they have therefore remained ethnically pure, conserving their habits, dialect, and the superstitions of their ancestors" (93). This had contributed to the continuation of such "traditional" practices as customary pricing and an "almost subsistence economy and form of life based on women as the main agricultural producer of a reduced number of tubers that constitute the principal element of the diet of the inhabitants" (95), both of which impeded the creation of a market-oriented economy.

According to the study, male migration away from the village was one ray of hope that could bring the Garifuna into the economic life of the nation and modernity. Through migration to port cities, to the capital, and even to the exterior, men had

> come into contact with various cultures and in particular with urban societies. In this manner they have known the benefits of technology, relative comfort, the numerous material facilities that the urban life offers, all of which has elevated the level of their necessities and transformed their aspirations. Limoneños aspire to have comfort in Limón and are disposed to certain sacrifices to obtain them. In particular they easily accept social change, the transformation of customs and traditions; they consider themselves modern and want industrialization, the transformation of primitive technologies and their society; all this despite certain superficial aspects that constitute a primitive and traditional society. (88–89)

This socioeconomic study reveals the discourse of development that emanated from the state that constructed the Garifuna as underproducers who did not bow to the logic of the market in terms of production. The researchers partially attributed this to their ethnic difference. At the same time, the authors recognized that Garifuna had already developed a taste for consumerism beyond subsistence (the sign of a good proletariat that submits to the expansion of "needs") that was satisfied through male migration and led to investment in infrastructure. The drawback in terms of local development was that this exterior money was not invested in large-scale capitalist projects. Men brought modernity and cash but also proletarian dependence; women were both the proud conservators of culture and the obstacle that kept the Garifuna from integrating into national life.

What were the conclusions of the researchers about how to develop this region and integrate it into the national economy? More ladino colonization: "At the moment, and for several years, they have been talking about a colonization project of Bajo Aguan, that once put into effect would be, no doubt, another focal attraction of immigration to the northeastern communities, and would have effects in terms of the intensity of felt needs and projects formulated, because they would see that others do what they would like: increase their standard of living, produce for sale, communicate with other communities, enjoy better housing and schools, etc." (104)

BAJO AGUAN AND THE CONTRADICTIONS OF AGRARIAN REFORM

The Bajo Aguan colonization project is referred to as the "capital of the Agrarian Reform" because it constituted 53 percent of the land expropriated for peasants and affected 38 percent of the beneficiaries of the 1974 agrarian reform (Posas y del Cid 1983, 316–318). Bajo Aguan is an area of the Department of Colón that was part of the concessions given to the United Fruit Company. It encompassed the municipalities of Sabà, Sonaguera, Tocoa, Trujillo, Limón, and Aguan (the last three have a large Garifuna population). After the company abandoned the area in the 1930s, much of this land was haphazardly settled by cattle ranchers and campesinos who often did not have legal title to it. In the late 1960s, the INA appropriated 70,000 hectares of this area for colonization by 6,000 peasant families so they could form cooperatives and *empresas asociativas* dedicated to the cultivation of African palm and oranges (Castro Rubio 1994; Dunkerly 1988). Campesino organizations encouraged peasants to migrate to the area, and the government of Colonel Oswaldo Lopez Arellano (1963–1970, 1972–1975) promised that they would receive titles to this "unoccupied" land, credit, and technical assistance, financed with $21.5 million from the Agency for International Development (AID) and the Interamerican Development Bank (IDB). Most of the peasant colonists came from southwestern areas of Honduras, where land conflict was already acute, such as Choluteca, Comayagua, and Copan. In 1977, the INA, with the support of another $40 million from the IDB, began a more concerted effort to encourage migration and organize the campesinos into cooperatives (Castro Rubio 1994).

In the twenty years the project existed (1961–1982), the population of Colón increased threefold, from 41,904 to 123,448 (106). Paved roads were built connecting La Ceiba to Tocoa and Tocoa to Trujillo and Bonito Oriental. As the center of the Bajo Aguan project, Tocoa grew into a boom town and is now one of the main commercial centers of Colón, where people from the rural areas can bank, buy provisions, and have access to the communications services of Hondutel. But the expansion of infrastructure and population has also brought increasing land conflict. Many of the *colonos* who migrated as part of the project decided to make their way farther east up the Río Sico, settling on national land along the river and closer to the Garifuna and Miskitu villages along the coast, where they engaged in subsistence farming and some lumber extraction. Once they had cleared and cultivated land (to crops or pasture), they were able to petition the INA for title to it because they could claim that they had given it a social function. The problem was that what often appeared to them to be *tierra ociosa* was actually land Garifuna considered to be theirs by use rights (that is, family members had traditionally cultivated it) but that was currently lying fallow or otherwise not under cultivation. Because of the "use it or lose it" standards of the 1974 agrarian reform, *colonos* could easily get legal title to lands Garifuna were cultivating but had no title to. Even worse for Garifuna communities (and even the *colonos* themselves), wherever *colonos* cleared new land, the large landowners were never far behind, ready to buy up (or take by force) parcels *colonos* had spent time clearing, preparing for cultivation, and obtaining legal title to. In this manner, large-scale capitalists managed to buy up large tracts of land for agroindustrial production of export crops.

THE DOMINANT DEVELOPMENT MODEL LIVES ON: 1980–1999

Until the 1980s the contradictions of an increasingly uneven distribution of wealth and resources were kept in check through social welfare programs and government subsidies on basic goods, the *canasta familiar* (family food basket). Because of the government's long-standing emphasis on increasing the gross national product (measured in terms of foreign exchange), credit and technical assistance was largely focused on the expansion and mechanization of export crops rather than on basic grains. So while Honduran farmers were producing crops for export (such as coffee, cotton, bananas, pineapples, African palm, and melons), the government was importing basic grains to be sold at subsidized prices. This trade imbalance generated high inflation and increased the cost of living.

By the end of the 1980s, the amount of loans accrued to finance large-scale development projects, infrastructural expansion, and food subsidies had created an enormous external debt. In 1990, the newly elected Callejas administration complied with the IMF's "economic adjustment program" in order to become eligible for loan refinancing. As occurred in many other countries, this led to increased unemployment and a higher cost of living. Rural areas were especially hard hit. In 1980, the agricultural sector was 57 percent of the labor force. By 1995, it had dropped to 37 percent as people moved to urban areas (Orozco 2002). About half the rural population was unemployed and lived on less than two hectares of land, from which they earned only $70 per year. A majority of the urban population eked out a living either in the poorly paid service sector or in the informal sector. Only one in ten Hondurans was securely employed in the formal sector in 1991 (Merrill 1993).

The structural readjustments the IMF demanded included not only reductions in state spending but also the implementation of policies that would open the domestic economy to more foreign and transnational investment. Throughout the 1990s, economic policy in Honduras focused on expanding the export-processing zones (maquiladoras), agroindustrial production, and the tourist industry (Boyer and Pell 1999; Robinson 1998). The tourist industry is primarily located on the beaches of the North Coast, the Bay Islands, and the Cayos Cochinos; which encompass the total area of most Garifuna villages and their agricultural lands.

This three-pronged focus on maquiladoras, agroindustry, and tourism has continued into the twenty-first century, despite the fact that Hurricane Mitch revealed the immense ecological and economic vulnerability this type of development creates. During the hurricane, the areas of the country that had been most heavily deforested for urbanization and agroindustry were the hardest hit by the flooding. Tourism was halted for a period, and much capital pulled out in the wake of the disaster (Jeffrey 1999). The number of unemployed and those suffering from malnutrition has risen since the hurricane due to the effects of the damage and the competition small farmers face from agroindustry (Replogle 2004). Many scholars argue that this is clear evidence that this form of development does not work and has in fact led to the dramatic increase in immigration from Honduras. Now Honduras, like many other Latin American and Caribbean countries before it, has come to rely on remittances as a source of foreign currency and as a way to stave off poverty at the level of individual households (Orozco 2002).

All of these international and state-directed development projects and economic reforms have had a direct impact on the socioeconomic conditions in Garifuna communities today. Like other rural communities, Garifuna villages suffer from high unemployment. Most people are merely biding their time until they can find an opportunity to leave the village for work, be it in Honduras or in the United States. While those who live in the village have the advantage of not having to pay rent or high transportation costs, the cost of basic foodstuffs is still high relative to the amount of money earned either locally or sent by family in the city. Though agriculture is still practiced in some communities (mainly those in the eastern departments) it tends to be merely supplemental in a household budget that mainly relies on wage income and remittances. This is due in part to the long-standing orientation toward wage labor but also to the fact that the agricultural lands Garifuna communities cultivated have been gradually taken over by *colonos*, cattle ranchers, and agribusiness. It is common to reach a Garifuna village only after driving through groves of African palm and hectares of deforested pastureland that extend right up to the edge of the village. Now with the growth of the tourist industry even the urban plots and the beach itself are being bought by nationals and foreigners who hope to build hotels, restaurants, and resorts.

And yet despite high unemployment (within villages), the high cost of living, and landlessness, Garifuna villages actually look quite prosperous. In contrast to the adobe and palm thatch houses common in the ladino *aldeas* and *caseríos* that surround many Garifuna villages, Garifuna villages tend to have a large number of cinderblock houses. In addition, many Garifuna households have store-bought furniture, televisions, VCRs, and even refrigerators—all consumer goods that are prohibitively expensive for anyone in the lower middle and working class in Honduras. They are not prohibitively expensive for the working class in New York City, though, which is where many of the goods or at least most of the money to buy them originates, a fact not lost on the Garifuna youth hoping someday to migrate. The socioeconomic conditions of Garifuna communities cannot be understood merely as a function of local conditions and nationally bounded processes.

This analysis of the role of international lenders and the state in development illustrates how economic conditions are created at the intersection of national, international, and transnational discursive and material practices. But this only provides the view from above. The socioeconomic conditions of places such as Limón are also shaped by the agency of the Garifuna from below as they negotiate these conditions through economic practices within the transnational community. I now turn to a discussion of the transnational economic practices and discourses of Limoneños.

Limón and "La Cultura de la Sobrevivencia"

The story of national development projects, peasant migration, and neoliberal economic reforms is etched on the social and physical geography of the municipality of Limón today. While the village of Limón itself is still primarily Garifuna—only a few ladino families live there—the rest of the population of the municipality is now primarily ladino who live in the *aldeas* of Francia, Icoteas, and Plan de Flores (the last two were established by ladino migrants from the Bajo Aguan project) and scattered *caseríos*. There are also several large cattle ranches in Laude and Limoncito (on former *ejidal* land cultivated by Garifuna households) that were "purchased"[4] in the 1970s by wealthy families from the capital and the Bay Islands (Bay Islanders are white, which has led to the presence of several "gringo" children in Limón who have blonde hair, blue eyes, and dark skin). Vallecito, the area between the Río Salado and the Río Miel, was also owned by wealthy *capitalinos* (people from the capital Tegucigalpa) until it was rented in the 1980s by the INA to AGROINVASA (an investment group) and then purchased by Miguel Facussé in 1993.

Garifuna households now own and cultivate land only in proximity to the village. These lands are mainly in La Barra (del Río Limón), Limoncito, Amapala, Salado, Malajuaz, and Masicales. Whereas many ladino families live on the same land where they cultivate or tend cattle, Garifuna live in the village (*casco urbano*) and travel by foot or canoe to their agricultural plots, where they may camp for several days if necessary (a practice they refer to in Garifuna as *kampout*). In contrast to what was typical in 1963, it is much more common today for Garifuna to own land as private property, both urban and agricultural plots. Whereas Beaucage argued that the Garifuna did not consider land a commodity to be bought and sold, the long history of usurpation of land by cattle ranchers and *colonos* has convinced Garifuna of the need to get clear title to land to avoid more expropriation. Land is now clearly a commodity, and the demand for it among returning migrants has actually increased its price considerably. The process of land titling and purchase is uneven, however, as getting *dominio pleno* (private title) is bureaucratically complex and costly. Much of the land is still *dominio útil* (use rights) and therefore vulnerable to expropriation. Today many households own no land at all except the plot upon which the house is located in the village. Some households may raise a few chickens or pigs in their yards, have fruit trees, or have a small garden of cassava, but in general the soil in the village is sandy and not good for most cultivation.

In my 1993-96 survey of sixty-three households in Limon,[5] I found that 28.3 percent of households own no agricultural land at all. The majority of the households that own agricultural land (71.7 percent) own only enough to grow a few staples for household consumption such as cassava, coconuts, and plantains (33.3 percent of the total household), or have a few (less than 10) head of cattle (3.3 percent of the total), or a little of both (5 percent of the total). Thirty percent of the households had more extensive holdings,[6] which they used to cultivate crops for sale within the village (mainly *guineo* [green bananas], coconuts, plantains, cassava, corn, beans, rice, but also some sugar cane) and/or for larger herds of cattle (15–100 head). Land and its use provides a significant source of income for only one-third of the households surveyed. For the other third, subsistence agriculture only provides a small percentage of household food consumption, and a final third is landless, relying completely on wage labor.

The Garifuna who are considered to be the wealthiest landowners have dedicated most of their land to cattle ranching. Though cattle require much more extensive areas of land than agriculture and an initially heavy outlay of labor and capital (to clear the fields and plant them in pasture and to purchase the land and cattle), it is more popular among those who have the capital to get started because in the long run cattle require less labor, they can produce income all year round through milk production, they can be tended by someone else while the owner is abroad, and they can be sold or slaughtered if there is an immediate need for cash.

The other main source of wealth in Limón is businessownership. The businesses in Limón include two *bodegas* (large shops that sell dry goods, housewares, clothes, and so forth), a large number of *pulperias* (small shops that sell fresh and dry food items), several restaurants, three hotels, four bars/discos, and a *bloquera* (that manufactures cinder blocks). The *bodegas* and the *bloquera* are owned by ladino families who migrated to Limón, and the rest of the businesses are split between ladinos and Garifuna. With the exception of one of the hotels, all of the larger businesses (that is, those larger than *pulperias*) that belong to Garifuna are owned by transmigrants and are run by family members who live in Limón.

People get by in Limón in other ways that include small-scale entrepreneurial activities such as baking breads—*pan de coco* (coconut bread), *pan de maiz* (corn bread), *pan de ayote* (squash bread), *rosquillos* (fried corn dough), *tableta de coco* (coconut sugar cake), and so forth; making *chicha* (corn, rice, and sugarcane beer); selling ice and *topoillos* (frozen Kool-Aid in a plastic bag); selling cassava bread; and making coconut oil. These small endeavors require very little capital—mainly just the money to purchase the supplies for that day (except ice and *topoillos*, which require a freezer), they generate only a small profit, and they are mainly done by women. Other types of women's work within the village include midwifery and sewing. Informal enterprises of men include fixing radios and other electronic goods, carpentry, fishing, repairing fishing nets, crafting mahogany dugout canoes, and making the implements to manufacture cassava bread (*ruguma* and *hibisi*).[7]

The main sources of formal wage labor within the village are state jobs at the health clinic, the kindergarten, the elementary school, and the high school and within the municipal government. The nurses (ten women), teachers (twenty-two men and women), and administrators (ten men and women) who work in these positions are almost all Garifuna and are considered to be the primary professional class in the village. These professionals make anywhere from L700 to L2,000 per month, depending on seniority. Women professionals often hire other women in the village to wash and iron for them at L25 per wash (a morning's work). Some professional families have *muchachas* that live with them and are responsible for laundry, cooking, and taking care of small children. Often these *muchachas* are actually family members (nieces, cousins) who are borrowed by households without young girls.

Construction is another main source of wage labor for men. Due to the constant stream of transmigrants returning to Limón to build houses for themselves and family members, there is always plenty of work for housebuilders. Some of the houses in Limón are still made of the traditional *yagua* (wood from a particular palm tree) or *caña brava* (a material like bamboo) and have *manaca* (palm thatch) roofs and dirt floors. However, these are quickly being replaced by cinderblocks, zinc and tiled roofs, and cement floors. Indeed, a common sight in Limón is a "traditional" house with a pile of cinderblocks next to it, growing slowly as the owner accumulates enough materials to begin the construction of a "modern" house. Often the old house is converted into the kitchen that stands apart from the main house because much of the cooking is still done on woodstoves (the old house tends to be cooler in the heat of the day because it is more open to the breeze). A few houses have gas stoves, indoor plumbing, and even a two-car garage, invariably built by transmigrants. The most expensive houses in Limón are owned by U.S. transmigrants and often remain empty most of the year until the family comes to visit.

An interesting contradiction arises from this description of economic activities in Limón. I have argued that only a small percentage of households extract a significant amount of their income or household subsistence needs from agriculture or a business. There is very little local full-time employment because businesses are mainly run with family labor, cattle ranching generates little employment, and few people are engaging in the large-scale agricultural projects that would require a consistent supply of *jornaleros* (day laborers). And yet the businesses in Limón are thriving; most households are able to meet their basic needs by purchasing food either in Limón or in the larger towns (Tocoa, Trujillo, and La Ceiba); many households have television sets, refrigerators, and even stereo systems; and more houses are being constructed daily. How is this possible?

One answer is occupational multiplicity; that is, men and women engage in a wide variety of economic activities simultaneously, be it in farming, day labor, microbusinesses, professional jobs, or seasonal migration. In addition, most households rely on a dense set of networks within the village through which they share resources, labor, child care, and so forth. And yet the increasing dependence on purchasing food means that much of what used to take place in the realm of reciprocal exchange is now commoditized. For example, the low levels of cultivation of even staple crops (cassava and *guineo*) among Garifuna households means that many Garifuna now buy these products from ladino farmers instead of cultivating them and exchanging them between Garifuna households. Garifuna informants who try to produce for this internal market complain that their profit margin within the village is small because purchasers often invoke kinship relations or cite a customary price instead of recognizing the cost of capital inputs and the need for a small margin of profit.[8] Just as Beaucage (1970) argued it would, this discourages Garifuna entrepreneurship in agriculture and most Garifuna purchase their food.

As a result of low levels of agricultural production and lack of opportunities for local employment, the real key to survival for many households is remittances from family members who work outside the village and the country. In my sample of sixty-three Limoneño and New York City households, 52.5 percent of Limoneños live outside Limón, about one-third of them in other areas of Central America and the other two-thirds in the United States (Table 4.2). All are households with little or no agricultural land.

Twenty-nine percent rely primarily on U.S. remittances for their cash income. Another 22 percent receive U.S. remittances as a supplement to owning a business or land, having a professional salary, or engaging in small enterprises. A final 17 percent receive remittances from family members working in places other than the United States (Honduras, Belize, Cayman Islands, on cruise liners) combined with other activities. Only 32 percent of households receive no remittances at all. The only correlation between remittances and land is that all of the households that rely primarily on remittances are landless or land poor. But some landless and land-poor households receive no remittances and instead rely on salaries or informal activities, while some landed households and households with two members who earn professional salaries also receive remittances. The wealthiest households have land and remittances, professional salaries and

Table 4.2. Places of Residence of Garifuna Limoneños, 1996

Place of residence	Number	Percentage of total sample
Total	1,347	100.0
Limon	717	53.0
Honduran cities	198	15.0
Tegucigalpa	60	4.4
San Pedro Sula	67	4.9
La Ceiba	61	4.5
Other	10	.7
Other areas of Central America	43	3.0
Islas de la Bahia	9	.6
Bananeros	6	.4
Belize	6	.4
Other	5	.3
Merchant Marine/Cruise Ship	17	1.3
United States	389	29.0
New York City	346	25.6
New Orleans	8	.6
Houston	10	.7
Florida	13	.9
Other	12	.9

remittances, a business and remittances, or all four, while the poorest receive no remittances, rely mainly on informal activities, and are landless or land poor.

To illustrate the importance of remittances even for households that have other sources of income, let us now look at the cost of living in Limón in 1996. Wages ranged from L25 to L70 per day for service work and L800 to L2,000 per month for salaried professional work. For an average household of 6.5, monthly costs averaged L1,742 for provisions (things related to cooking: food, firewood, gas, and so forth). In addition, some households pay for rent, electricity, medicine, school supplies, tuition, and other incidentals. So the highest-paid professionals would be able to support their families on their salaries alone, but they would have little left over for luxury goods or investment. For *jornaleros*, the cost of living is extremely high if you consider that they make L30 per day and the cost of just one pound of chicken at the time was L10. Even households that received remittances often received only enough to get by each month (an average of $150 per month, which in 1996 equaled about L1,500). This is why it is a prevalent belief among Limoneños that as long as one stays in Limón (that is, has not been to the United States yet), one is merely surviving, practicing *la cultura de la sobrevivencia* (the culture of survival). The only way to accumulate wealth or achieve individual upward mobility is through migration to the United States.

LIVING IN THE PERIPHERY OF THE CORE

As we sat in the living room of the small Bronx apartment listening to a presentation about a long-distance phone company, I realized that once again we had been invited to a "reunion" that had nothing to do with Garifuna voluntary associations but rather was an attempt to get us involved in a multilayer marketing scheme. "What is your dream?" asks the Garifuna woman doing the presentation. "Why did you come to this country? Wasn't it to buy some land and build a house in Limón? Or start a little business? We all say we will return in five years, and yet so many of us get caught in this country working low-wage jobs, having children, and never really saving that *principio* [nest egg] to invest back in Honduras." From then on the pitch was like one for U.S. audiences: work at getting people in your downline now and then sit back and receive monthly checks; your future will be secure and work free. The only difference was that this audience envisioned receiving those checks in Honduras, where the astronomical monthly sums that were promised in dollars would be even more astronomical in Honduran lempiras—a much more attractive dream than suffering through twenty to thirty years of hard work to receive retirement checks that are barely sufficient by U.S. standards.

*   *   *

Earlier I showed that the possibilities for upward mobility in Honduras are limited by high unemployment and a high cost of living, reinforcing a "culture of migration" that has already been tightly woven into the social fabric of Garifuna society and directing it primarily toward the United States. But even as there is much social pressure to migrate to the United States to "make something of oneself," there is also much social pressure to return to Honduras. This pressure is partly related to affective ties with home and family and notions of natural belonging and authentic culture. But it is also often related to the living and working conditions transmigrants find in the United States that make any possibility of class mobility within the U.S. class structure unlikely.

While Garifuna labor migration has always had this characteristic of circularity—that is, transmigrants have always expected that they will send remittances and visit and retire in Limón—the current characteristics of this pattern are related as much to economic and social changes in Honduras in recent decades as they are to changes in the United States during the same period. Just as conditions have worsened in Honduras, so they have in New York City for Hispanic immigrants such as the Honduran Garifuna. The jobs that are available are a lower quality than they used to be, welfare reforms have reduced benefits for undocumented and documented residents, and the quality of housing and infrastructure in the Bronx and Harlem has declined (Mollenkopf and Castells 1991).

The effect of this increasing impoverishment is manifest in the living conditions Garifuna transmigrants encounter in the South Bronx and Harlem neighborhoods that have been impacted by deindustrialization and infrastructural decay. In the Bronx, Hondurans are mainly concentrated in southern and eastern community districts such as Mott Haven, Hunts Point, Morrisania/Crotona, and East Tremont; in the 1990s, the top source country for these areas was the Dominican Republic, followed by Jamaica and Guyana.[9] Though Honduras is not one of the top ten source countries to Manhattan, a substantial number of Garifuna live in Central Harlem (where the population is primarily comprised of African American, African, and West Indian blacks) and East Harlem (where the population is primarily African American and Puerto Rican). To give an idea of the socioeconomic conditions of these neighborhoods, in 1990, the Morrisania/Crotona community district, where Hondurans represented 1.7 percent of the total population and 3.9 percent of the immigrant population, was one of the poorest districts in the city. The median annual household income was only $10,487 (about one-third that of the New York average and half that of the Bronx average), 41.5 percent of households were on public assistance, and 46.8 percent of families lived below the poverty level. (See Table 4.3 for other community districts). According to the *Community District Needs: 1996* report, Mott Haven, another area where Garifuna are concentrated, was the poorest congressional district in the nation. Mott Haven and the neighboring district of Hunts Point combined had the same number of AIDS cases as the entire state of Wisconsin (New York City Department of City Planning 1994/1995, 46). Both Mott Haven and Hunts Point were formerly centers of the South Bronx manufacturing sector; now they are filled with empty warehouses and the largest concentration of housing projects in the Bronx. Both have been declared economic development zones that offer incentives to business owners much like those found in the free trade zones of "developing" countries such as Honduras (wage and investment tax credits, property tax reductions, and so forth) (55). On the brighter side, in other areas of the Bronx such as Morris Heights and East Tremont, there has been a move toward neighborhood revitalization through the renovation of burned-out buildings and the construction of individual family homes on vacant lots spurred on in large part by community-based

Table 4.3. Socioeconomic Profiles of Selected Bronx and Harlem Community Districts, 1990

	NYC	BRONX	CD #1 Mott Haven/ St. Mary's	CD #2 Hunts Point	CD #3 Morrisania Crotona	CD #4 High Bridge/ Grand Concourse	CD #5 Morris Heights	CD #6 East Tremont	MANHATTAN	CD #10 Central Harlem	CD #11 East Harlem
Hondurans as percentage of the total population 1990	0.3	0.6	1.2	1.7	1.7	0.8	0.7	1.6	0.2	0.7	0.6
Median household income	$29,823	$21,944	$9,725	$10,165	$10,487	$15,565	$14,605	$12,610	$32,262	$13,252	$14,882
Percentage of households with public assistance income	13.1	23.0	47.0	46.1	41.5	33.1	36.5	38.5	10.9	28.8	34.1
Percentage of families below poverty level	16.3	25.7	49.4	50.5	46.8	38.9	42.6	42.6	17.4	34.4	37.0

Source: New York City Department of City Planning, Socioeconomic Profiles: A Portrait of New York City's Community Districts from the 1980 and 1990 Censuses of Population and Housing (New York, Department of City Planning, 1993).

grassroots organizations that have received federal and private funding (126, 149; Breslin 1995).

On my way to interviews, I often passed this bizarre landscape of burned-out buildings and rundown projects covered in graffiti interspersed with freshly painted rows of townhouses circled by manicured yards just large enough to hold a barbecue pit and a table. None of my interviewees lived in these homes, however. They lived in the nondescript 20-story housing projects, large buildings of small private apartments, and, in Harlem, deteriorating brownstones divided into numerous small apartments. The conditions of the buildings varied from well-kept stairwells and elevators to the images that we associate with the inner-city: graffiti, elevators that do not work, stairwells that stink of urine, and crack vials and other litter strewn everywhere. And yet invariably I would enter an apartment that was neat and clean, crowded with the requisite matching furniture set; entertainment center with television, VCR, and stereo system; hand-crocheted doilies; knickknacks; and photos of weddings, graduations, and christenings in New York City and Honduras. The apartments generally had two bedrooms, though a few families had three bedrooms and single males tend to have one-room efficiencies. No matter the size, however, there was rarely much space to spare. Living rooms served as the bedrooms of recent arrivals just getting adjusted, cribs compete for space with adult beds, and goods ultimately destined for Honduras are piled up in closets and corners.

Though Limoneños live in neighborhoods with high unemployment and poverty rates, most that I interviewed are among the working poor. Limoneños come to the United States primarily to work, and their community feels they are wasting their time and opportunity in the United States if they do not work. While both men and women ideally try to stay employed throughout their stay in the United States, job mobility is fairly limited, especially for women, and they rarely move out of the ranks of the working poor. For example, the first job both men and women get after they arrive is most commonly in a factory or in the service industries (personal, food, and other). Most women eventually end up working as a home attendant. According to Limoneña informants, this is a preferred job for Garifuna women because it has flexible hours and is easy to obtain even with a limited knowledge of English and lack of U.S. education credentials. While the flexibility of the job is an advantage for women who need to juggle work and child care and periodic visits to Honduras, this flexibility can also work against them; if the patient dies or changes agencies, the woman may be out of work for weeks until she gets another case. Also while most feel being a home attendant is easy, the working conditions and workload vary tremendously depending on the patient. Some women (and men) had wonderful relations with their patients, while others had hostile patients (due to the racism or dementia of the patient). Some had patients that were in the beginning stages of illness and merely needed to be watched, whereas others were very sick with AIDS or were bedridden. Some home attendants find themselves working in middle- to upper-class neighborhoods while others work in cramped apartments in rundown neighborhoods. The vast majority of Limoneñas work as home attendants for most of their time in New York. There is little room for advancement within the job and, like domestic work, the job is isolating and not conducive to forming information networks outside of that line of work (Hondagneu-Sotelo 1994b). So for most Limoneñas, home attendant work is often the end peak of upward mobility. Very few first-generation migrants obtain professional jobs in the U.S. and very few are involved in pink-collar jobs. (The exception to this is the few women who are college students and find working twelve-hours at night as home attendants convenient because they can sleep for most of their shift, leaving the days free for school).

While men's employment is more varied than that of women, they also show little upward mobility. Like women, men commonly begin in factories or services. Most aspire to move into maintenance. The most coveted jobs are those in which the man is made the superintendent of the building in which he lives, thereby getting reduced or free rent. Others end up as doormen, security guards, and janitors. Other common jobs include those in construction and installation.

Though not reflected in this sample, jobs in the merchant marine are becoming popular again as men become disillusioned with the lack of unionized labor in New York City. In the two years after this sample was taken, in fact, at least six of the men interviewed moved to New Orleans, where they are able to get a sea card that gives them the right to union membership as a merchant marine. While these jobs entail many weeks and even months away from family, Garifuna men say they like them because they earn a substantial sum of money at once, have no expenses, and get long vacations that enable them to travel to Honduras. Thus, not many men move into white-collar employment, but they are more likely than women to get blue-collar work that is more remunerative than home health care or domestic labor.

Men and women who move into the white-collar professional jobs are most likely to have migrated as children or teenagers and have been educated in the United States. Everyone in my sample who arrived in New York City under the age of 17 received a high school education or equivalent (GED), and 44 percent attended college. In contrast, only 15 percent of those who migrated after age 17 received a GED, and only 12 percent went to college. This suggests that those who migrate young take advantage of access to the U.S. educational system and thus are better prepared linguistically for a broader range of work opportunities in the U.S. labor market. Studies with other immigrant groups have shown that this advantage may be tempered by the process of segmented assimilation in which certain immigrant groups are integrated into the lowest rungs of the racialized class system and labor market even though they attend U.S. schools and speak English because the schools they attend may be in the inner city with low social standing and the English they learn may have low social capital (see, for example, Portes and Rumbaut 1990; Waters 1999). My sample of such 1.5 generation immigrants was too small to come to any conclusions about this issue. (The term "1.5 generation" is a common phrase that refers to those who are first-generation immigrants but have come to the United States so young that their experience is more like that of second-generation immigrants.)

The data on job mobility and educational levels clearly indicate that the possibilities for moving from production and service to professional employment are limited for first-generation Honduran Garifuna transmigrants who migrate as adults (see also Hamilton and Chinchilla 2001 for Central Americans in Los Angeles). The average annual household income levels of the neighborhoods in which Garifuna live, according to the 1990 census, (from $9,725 to $24,440, as shown in Table 4.3) demonstrate that most Garifuna are among the working poor. Many families supplement their incomes with some form of government aid such as food stamps, the Women, Infants, and Children (WIC) program of food subsidies, and subsidized housing (which can be obtained if at least some members of a household are documented). In the community districts where Garifuna live, the median gross monthly rent varies from $286 to $476, which is quite low for New York. The low rents can be attributed to the fact that so much of the housing in the South Bronx consists of housing authority projects and Section 8 subsidized housing. While this low rent is what enables many to send remittances back to Honduras, ultimately their economic situation in New York is not improved by the government subsidies because most of their savings go to family or investments in Honduras. Of the eighty-eight Garifuna I interviewed, only three said they definitely would not return to Honduras to live (all three had arrived as children and had a U.S. college education) and only a few said that they envision going back and forth between the two countries. The vast majority said they would return within five to ten years. They envision their sources of support as (in descending order of frequency of response) retirement checks, running food shops (*bodegas, supermercados,* and so forth) or other businesses (butcher shops, cablevision businesses, and so forth), raising cattle, working in a profession learned in the United States (doctor, accountant,

and so forth), running a restaurant, engaging in agriculture, and continued connections to the United States such as returning there periodically to work or
receiving remittances from a family member. The stated desire to return did not
vary by gender. Other studies of return migration among Latinos have suggested
that women prefer to stay in the United States more often than men because
they have been able to negotiate gender relations within the household to their
advantage (Guarnizo 1997; Hondagneu-Sotelo 1994a). This is not the case for
Garifuna women because of the important role they already play in the economies of their families and communities. But whether the respondent was male
or female, return migration rarely meant a full and permanent return; Garifuna
continued to spend time in both Honduras and the United States with family
members.

For both Garifuna men and women, the "American dream" is to work in the
United States just long enough to generate enough capital to make them financially independent in Honduras. As Portes (1995) has argued, transmigrants
try to take advantage of political and economic border differentials in much the
same way transnational corporations do by using more valuable dollars to invest
in countries with low wages and low property costs. Clearly, however, Garifuna
are doing so under very different conditions and restraints and from a very different set of positions in the international division of labor.

How do Garifuna perceive of these disjunctures between class position, potential for upward mobility, and geographical location? How do they interpret
the fact that they can become independent entrepreneurs in Limón but only
after years of serving as the working poor in New York? How do they understand the contradiction that their communities have been largely marginalized
by the Honduran state (in terms of providing employment and infrastructure)
and yet many of the families in those communities have access to the same level
of consumption as the Honduran middle class? How do these contradictions
and disjunctures impact their understanding of the international division of labor and class exploitation? And finally, how is this consciousness related to the
perpetuation of the transnational migration process?

"Los pobres allá somos los ricos acá en Honduras"

The strategy of migrating to the United States to *mejorar sus condiciones de vida*
(improve one's living conditions) has been successful enough to have become
embedded in the Garifuna community as a central practice, and very few people are really outside of the transmigratory networks. However, there are also
dangers and difficulties inherent in the strategy, such as the challenges of being

undocumented, living in inner city areas, facing discrimination as non–English-speaking immigrants, and the possibility of never really being able to save that nest egg to return at a higher socioeconomic level than when one left. One of the consequences of these contradictions is the existence of a critical counterdiscourse among Garifuna who do not believe that transmigration is necessarily the best path toward improving living conditions. In this section I explore these two positions and analyze how they relate to consciousness and social practice.

Transmigration as Upward Mobility

One of the main explanations Garifuna transmigrants and nonmigrants gave me for why they prefer to migrate to the United States (as opposed to other destinations) is a basic calculation of the value of U.S. wages compared to the cost of living and the price of consumer goods in the United States. This they contrast to the *cultura de la sobrevivencia* that prevails in Honduras, where most earn barely enough to get by.

> One of the most important reasons [Garifuna go to the United States] is the source of employment. Maybe you aren't going to find work in an office, but a woman who wants to work as a domestic can get what she wants because the labor is more parallel, in other words one earns according to the effort one puts in. In contrast, here [in Honduras] a woman who works as a domestic is not going to earn enough to support her family. So this is one of the main reasons people want to migrate from here—the source of employment in the United States. (Danira, schoolteacher in Limón, nonmigrant)

> Inflation in Honduras is too high, and salaries, when we manage to get employment, are not sufficient to cover the costs of the household, especially when there are children. In contrast, the United States has the politics, as a developed country, that the state prevents inflation and a high cost of living by keeping salaries comparable to the cost of goods. For example if the price of meat rises, then they raise the minimum wage. So clearly *el sueldo rinde al trabajador* [wages last for the worker], the only expensive thing that we know of is the rent. When our brothers come from New York they bring us clothes, and shoes, and when they tell us the price we say but how cheap. Of course this is the price in the United States and if we translate that into lempiras it is almost the same [as what it costs in Honduras], but the difference is that here the salary we earn is so miserable that we don't even earn enough to buy that pair of shoes. Whereas in the United States, with the salary that one earns every two weeks one can buy

their shoes, their food, everything, and the other two weeks' wages are for the rent. And when there is no employment and one is a legal resident the government helps. And the single women who have no employment and have children, the government also helps them. Here there is no social assistance. Here if there is no work one has to find a way to survive. (Santos, director of the high school in Limón, nonmigrant)

As these comments reveal, unemployment or absolute poverty is not the only reason people migrate. Garifuna in Honduras are generally able to get employment. However, they argue that since such work is most likely found away from the village, *uno solo trabaja para pagar la renta* (one only works to pay the rent). The salaries are so low compared to the cost of living that they barely cover the costs of basic necessities and nothing is left over to send back to family in Limón or to buy consumer goods, much less to invest in land or a business.

As one young man I interviewed in Limón pointed out to me, a worker in Honduras makes about L150 (U.S. $15) per week and a nice pair of pants (that is, new, not from the *ropa usada americana* [American used clothing] shops) costs L300 (U.S. $30), meaning that for a member of the working class, buying a pair of pants would cost two weeks' earnings. He compared this to the situation in the United States, where $30 might represent a day's wage or less, such that even those earning minimum wage can afford to buy the basic necessities as well as some luxury consumer items. This 18-year-old in fact made a good wage working in La Ceiba as a mason and had saved a substantial amount of money to build a house in Limón, but he was still looking for a way to get to the United States, with or without documents, because he believes that there he can make money even faster, money worth more in Honduras than Honduran lempiras. Indeed, the majority of the working-age transmigrants I interviewed were employed in Honduras before they migrated.

Whether formally employed in Honduras or not, most Limoneños refer to U.S.-bound migration as the fastest way of bettering life conditions or *superando economicamente* (getting ahead financially). Many felt that they were doing fine in Honduras in the sense that they had a roof over their heads and basic food items, but they were just staying at the same level; they were not saving and investing, not getting ahead or changing their situation. Migrating to the United States means getting work where one earns enough to pay all bills and have some left over for consumer items. For example, Rosaria, who was employed as a maid in Honduras before she migrated to New York in 1982, first worked as a live-in maid in New Jersey but got work as a home attendant after she married and had children. Though she works long hours, she feels there is more *seguridad de vida* (security) in the United States because there is employment and government aid and food and clothes are cheap. "It is the only way for nonprofessionals to get ahead."

This sentiment was expressed not only by the Garifuna working class in Honduras (service workers, *jornaleros*, domestics) but even by professionals such as teachers and nurses. For example, Yolani, a kindergarten teacher who lives with her mother and father, who are both also teachers, showed that although they had managed to build a house without remittances, it had been a long and difficult process.

> No matter what it is like over there [in the United States], with the work that they have, those who are in the United States figure out a way to send money back here—and even if it is very little, it comes out to be a lot here in Honduras. And in that way they get their materials [for building a house]. In contrast, the people here, if they are going to the bush every day they are just working to eat, they are not going to get any money to build a house. Maybe now the professionals, the teachers, the nurses, and those that work in the municipality are the ones that know how many years it takes buying the materials little by little, and maybe having to get a loan in order to build a house. Or we have to get together as brothers and sisters and parents and between us all we can build a house.

Based on the apparent success of transmigrants, as demonstrated by their ability to build nice houses, buy land, and start businesses, there is a dominant discourse among Limoneños that U.S.-bound migration is the main way of achieving upward mobility within the context of Honduras. Even if licensed professionals end up working in menial jobs in the United States, it is worth it in order to be able to *independizarse* (become independent) in Honduras, whether it be through owning a business or through receiving retirement checks each month. The discourse is similar to the one in the United States about getting and using a college education for upward class mobility. Anyone who is offered the opportunity to migrate is seen as crazy to not take that opportunity, even if it means quitting a professional job or interrupting a post-secondary education. Those who choose not to migrate are referred to as *vagos* who are not interested in improving their life circumstances (though this tends to be directed toward men more than women).

For example, before she migrated, Eda had attended the national university in Tegucigalpa, where she was trained to work as a laboratory technician in a health clinic. After working at this job for several years in La Ceiba, she got the chance to go to the United States through a relative who had applied for her residency. For two years she worked 24-hour shifts six days a week as a home attendant in order to save enough money to sponsor the migration of her son.

Figure 4.1. Home of a return migrant. (Photo by author)

After that she reduced her workload to twelve hours six days a week, still working well over a 40-hour work week in order to save enough money to contribute to the construction of her mother's house in Limón. She had hoped to get a license as a laboratory technician in the United States, but her limited English and work hours prohibited her from taking the necessary classes. When she was in her late forties, after ten years of working as a home attendant, she received a letter from the Social Security office stating that she had already worked enough hours to receive $300 per month in retirement pay. Soon after that, she packed everything she owned into a school bus her cousin was driving to Honduras loaded with *encargos* (packages sent from relatives) and moved back to Honduras with substantial savings, a house in Limón (her mother Kecha had since migrated to New York City herself to care for grandchildren), and the promise of L3,000 (equivalent then to $300) per month from U.S. Social Security. She now works in the lab of a clinic set up in Limón by American missionaries. In retrospect, she said, those ten years of sacrifice were worth the ability to become financially independent in Honduras.

Aside from wages, another advantage Limoneños identified in the United States is the assistance the government gives to the poor.

The children there have the privilege that the government helps in the feeding and education of children, whereas here no. The only thing the state [in Honduras] gives children is an education, and that only halfway. I understand that there children leave the house at nine in the morning for school, there they eat their lunch, and they do not return until the afternoon. So the mother is free to do the things she needs to do, whereas here no. (Danira)

In Honduras [where] it is not easy to get a scholarship, there are parents that have no way to educate so many children that they have. Whereas in the U.S., I understand that it is easy to get a scholarship from the state, the state helps a lot. So all of those persons that want to study can, whereas here in Honduras no. Our parents have to do everything for our children. (Mery, schoolteacher, nonmigrant)

Many of the comments made by both nonmigrants and transmigrants paint the United States as a place of opportunity and equality, where the state looks out not only for its citizens but also for its immigrant residents (the legal ones, of course).[10] This is in contrast to the situation in Honduras, where Garifuna see the state as neglecting its responsibilities to the citizenry in general and particularly to their own communities due to racial discrimination.

I see that not only the people of Limón want to go to the U.S. but from all parts of the world because it is the fastest way to get money. Generally it is few people who go and stay at the same economic level, rather the majority improve their economic conditions. Others improve in terms of education, getting a university degree, because there it is easier, there is more opportunity for everything, while here in our country everything is more limited. Here only the rich have the right to everything. In the U.S. the laws are made for equality, because there a person without work could take even the president of the country to court and if that poor person is right, he wins the case. Here no. Here we could say that the poor have no liberty. (Edgar, schoolteacher, nonmigrant)

In our case racial discrimination is also a factor. Because no matter how intellectual a Garifuna is, when placed next to a ladino, they prefer the ladino. It is logical that they are going to prefer a ladino because discrimination is deeply rooted here in Honduras. That is one of the barriers to upward mobility. Migrants say there is racism in the U.S., but at a lower level. In the U.S. they take your capacity into consideration, not your color. (Xiomara, schoolteacher, nonmigrant)

In general terms we have been marginalized by the central government. For example, if we look at education, this school was constructed after Hur-

ricane Fifi in 1976, but it was constructed with international funds from
AID, not with national funds, but with international funds. Then there's
the institute [high school], for example. That building was constructed
with international funds from the Peace Corps. The potable water that
we have today, was also made possible by a donation from an organization
[Limoneño] in the U.S. The attention of the central government towards
us has been almost nothing. So the people, upon seeing so much neglect,
have to leave the country in order to find better opportunities as much for
themselves as for their children. The country that more or less offers the
best conditions is the U.S., and so that is why the majority of the population go there looking for better economic, social, living, and educational
conditions—to have a bit of savings for their old age. Although there are
also problems there [in the United States], maybe they are not worse than
that which we confront here, and it is the country that offers the best
working conditions and salaries. So we all risk our lives to get there sometimes with documents, sometimes without. That is why when the U.S. puts
obstacles in the way of our brothers reaching there we get worried, because
when they come from there they could bring us something even if it just a
shirt, some underwear, or pair of shoes. (Rufino, principal of the elementary school, nonmigrant)

For many Garifuna, U.S.-bound migration is a form of resistance to the culture of survival and government neglect in Honduras. Many do not see those
abroad as living on the periphery of the core. They focus mainly on the fact
that working in the United States provides greater opportunities for savings and
consumption through the combination of state aid and a lower cost of living
compared to the value of wages. And yet when Limoneños refer to getting ahead
and *superando sus condiciones de vida*, they always refer to what the transmigrant
is able to achieve in Honduras, not in the United States. While U.S. wages are
valuable for the levels of consumption they provide in both the United States
and Honduras, most believe they could never save enough to become independent (that is, a businessowner) in the United States due to the high cost of property and the limited amount transmigrants workers there can save. But those
same dollars can be converted into capital in Honduras.

There is a saying that says "*los pobres allá somos los ricos acá en Honduras*"
[the poor over there (the United States) are the rich here in Honduras].
They [transmigrants] feel happy because, even though they are poor, when
they buy their little piece of land here, they feel like the rich. They change
their dollars here and end up with a ton of lempiras in their pocket, something that those of us who are here cannot do. (Yolani)

I think that they [transmigrants] achieve their goals because there are people that have a job here in Honduras, but they never changed their social situation. They had their palm thatch house and only worked to eat. But after two years of being in the U.S., they have sent money to build their nice house here in Honduras, they have sent furniture, and for that reason we say they have improved. (Mery)

As these comments indicate, for the Garifuna, transnational migration is clearly about taking advantage of border differentials. Working in the United States is seen as a great opportunity to work for wages that allow for consumption beyond mere survival. Yet they also recognize that if they stay in the United States, the possibilities for upward mobility within the U.S. class structure are as limited in New York City as they had been in Honduras due to their low social capital (as poor Spanish-speaking immigrants). Social and monetary capital may be more quickly generated in the United States but it must be displayed in Honduras to have social prestige and class value.

The case of Don Felix illustrates the way the conditions on the periphery in New York are sometimes obscured in transmigrant consciousness. Don Felix migrated to New York in the 1970s. For many years he lived in Harlem and worked as a dishwasher in a downtown Manhattan restaurant. In the 1980s, he moved to a two-room apartment in the South Bronx with his wife and two children. Since then he has been working as a porter in Riverdale, a mostly Jewish neighborhood in the North Bronx. In the twenty-five years he has lived in New York City, he has sponsored the migration of two different wives and many of his children. Even though he has lived many years in the United States, he has never learned much English and has spent most of his time working two jobs in order to support his family and build up his property in Honduras. He is now being forced to retire early, so his pension will not be as much as he had hoped, but he is still planning his return to Honduras. Despite the hardships he has faced in New York, he feels that "if I had not come here, I would be in even more miserable conditions." He compares himself to two men his same age who had opportunities to migrate but who did not take them. Though these men both own land and cattle in Limón, he says that if they had come to New York to work for a while they could have done even better. Instead, they gained a little bit of capital and have not advanced much from there.

Most Garifuna feel that when a transmigrant dies before he or she is able to make it back to Honduras, it is a tragedy; all of those years of hard work are wasted. This also goes for those who do not return because they are "absorbed by the environment" (*el ambiente los absorbe*). This seems to refer as much to the *"mal ambiente"* (bad environment) of New York (that is, the perils of the inner city) as it does to the culture of consumption that could easily suck up savings so the money does not go back to Honduras. As a man who is considered to be the epitome of a successful return migrant (because he returned in the ideal five years and opened a restaurant in Limón with all the modern equipment) told me:

> In New York there is all the good and all the bad in the world and one's success depends on what one chooses. Just as it [the United States] gives to one, so it also takes away. If we are weak, just as fast as we earn money, we will spend it too. So when we migrate to New York we have to have a strong enough willpower not to get sucked into the *mal ambiente*. We need to just work, take advantage of the dollars and then return here. (Arnulfo)

> As you know in all social circles there are all kinds—there are those who go [to the United States] with this aim of improvement, to elevate their standard of living and they achieve it. There are others that go with this goal but upon arriving there and seeing so much luxury they get confused and don't achieve their goal. Instead of improving they get worse. *El ambiente los absorbe.* (Xiomara)

> Those who meet their goals are the ones that do not go to live the life of the U.S. They know that they must return—they go there, do what they want to do and return to do something here. (Danira)

In brief, the United States is seen as only a place one should go to make some capital before returning to Honduras. According to many, if an immigrant gets too involved in consumption in the United States, he or she is wasting their time. They, like those who made the decision not to migrate, are *vagos* who are not taking full advantage of the opportunities offered to them. Though the rationale for their apparent failure is couched in the language of individual character (they allowed themselves to be absorbed, they gave in to temptation), there are hints that this failure is also related to the structural conditions they find in New York City, the *mal ambiente*.

Andres arrived in New York in 1989 without documents. Like many undocumented Limoneños, he works in a Korean-owned dry cleaning establishment in Hunts Point. He met his current wife in New York (she is Garifuna from another village). As a legal resident, she was able to secure the housing-project apartment where they live in the South Bronx with their two children. His story illustrates the ambivalence I often observed about how to explain the reasons for failure in the United States—sometimes the person's character is blamed and sometimes the structural conditions of poverty and racism are blamed.

> I came to the U.S. to get ahead, to progress. All that I dreamed of having I could not get in Honduras—to dress well, have jewels and so on. But now it is for my family, I want to educate my children and start a business. I had L4,000 in Honduras and I could have used it to start a business but instead I used it to get here. I thought I would do better here. Those who live here and go back to Limón think they are gods, they are humble people there. And so one feels this pressure to get ahead, everyone in Limón talks about this, the pressure to improve. So I migrated. I thought things would be easy here, but I found that one has to sacrifice here in order to achieve what one wants. There is pressure on one here too—starting a new life, learning a new language, one feels a shock. So at first I wanted to return to Honduras. I thought it would have been better if I had stayed there. If I had imagined what it would really be like here I would never have come. Here *te menosprecian* [they despise, undervalue you] because you do not speak English, you feel humble. But this country has all the opportunities one could want to have, so if you do not achieve your goal, it is because you are not working hard enough, or just working enough to get by.

While his initial experience in New York seemed to contradict the image of the United States as the land of opportunity and equality he had learned in Honduras, he eventually was able to achieve his goals of returning to Honduras and opening a business, joining the ranks of the successful return migrants who become entrepreneurs. For many Limoneños, the disadvantages of their place in the division of labor in the United States (as members of the poor proletariat working in the service sector) are mediated by the place they can achieve in the division of labor in Honduras (where they can become entrepreneurs, small capitalists). As a consequence, critical counterdiscourses of the U.S. class structure and the place of the Garifuna in it are often muted by the success stories of transmigrants.

Migration as Double Discrimination

While I argue that this discourse of *superación* (progress, betterment) via migration and return is the dominant discourse among Garifuna, there is also contestation of the idea that migration is always the best means of personal advancement. This opinion comes not only from those who refuse to migrate but also from some who do migrate. Tino's uncle was one of the original merchant marines from Limón to settle in New York City who, much like Mario

Ramirez, is responsible for a large chain of migration, including most of Tino's eight brothers and sisters. In Tino's family, in fact, only he, one sister, and his mother remain in Honduras. For a while he worked in La Ceiba as a carpenter, but then he moved to Limón to take care of the family property. Now he and his wife both work for NGOs.

> This is the general concept, that if we do not leave for the U.S. then we are not going to improve our quality of life. This is what my uncle tells me, he says, look you have not improved your quality of life because you have not wanted to go to the U.S. How many times your brothers have wanted to help you and you haven't done it? And this uncle has always considered me to be crazy because I have not taken the opportunity to go to the U.S.

Tino's wife has also been criticized for not migrating. She said that her uncle applied for her but the papers went through in her last year of secretarial school and migrating would have meant dropping out of the program, so she decided to wait. In the end she made the decision not to go: "What would I have done there? Here I have a degree but there I would have had to start all over again learning English, working in an unskilled job. What would the point of all that education have been?"

> I think there is a lot of confusion around this question [of whether migration really brings progress]. The other day I heard two friends talking. One of the friends wants to go to the U.S. and the other one said "Look why do you want to go to the U.S? You have your family here and your cattle, your business. Life here is more tranquil, there life is very agitated and maybe you'll earn a wage that is not adequate because going illegally they will pay you a wage that is about half what they pay other people." (Miguel, teacher, nonmigrant)

> The other day a guy was telling me that all of those that are in the U.S. would like to return here, but they want to return when they have something secure in Honduras, an investment with their savings from working over there. But then they never manage to get that base and then they get old and it's only when they are no longer worth anything that they come back here. Because the majority of people don't come back here until they've been there for so long that they come back sick. They keep having to go back to the U.S. to the doctor. They come back here after so many years of working—who knows what kind of life they had over there. (Yolani)

There's a man from the U.S., he is already old, he came from there sick. He told me, "Now that I am retired I have come back here to live until I die, I'm not going back to the U.S." When he got sick he told me "I'm going back to the U.S., there they will treat me well." He told me that he got sick because he had worked too hard for the gringos. When the gringos see that one no longer has any juice left, then they send them back here. So I wouldn't want to work for another person, giving my youth to that person and then when I no longer have any juice they send me back to Honduras. (Frasia, unemployed single mother, nonmigrant)

Many of the Garifuna I interviewed expressed the feeling that while things may be bad in Honduras, going to the United States was not necessarily the solution to those problems. These Limoneños recognized that their living conditions and place in the division of labor were based just as much on exploitation and marginalization in the United States as they would be in a Honduran city. In Limón they may be poor, but at least they have the freedom of being independent agents, like Frasia, a single mother of six who gets by primarily by baking bread and selling ice and frozen chicken out of a gas-run freezer. While there may be more employment opportunities in the United States, they are menial and have low status, reserved, as Limoneños often say, for Hispanic immigrants. Thus, migrating to the United States does not provide an escape from the structural racism Garifuna feel in Honduras.

The following opinions were expressed to me by two Limoneños who migrated to the United States and returned after only a few years. Both are currently active in the agricultural cooperative Iseri Lidawamari. Ricardo was brought as a teenager by his mother in 1990 and attended high school in the United States After graduating, he spent time working in a nursing home in upstate New York with mainly white patients; later he worked in the city installing air conditioners. Though he still had plans to attend college, he returned to Limón after six years, where he was spending most of his time working with Iseri Lidawamari.

In the U.S. one loses their dignity and their pride as a person. The system of the U.S. is a system in which you can easily sell yourself in order to get some material belongings. In the time that I was in the U.S. I never had the opportunity to look at myself and say that I am equal to the gringo. My maximum aspiration would have been cleaning floors in a building or to clean the butt of an old lady. All of us who are there are people and we all try to live with dignity, but these are our highest aspirations because we are poor immigrants. Why only give this kind of job to the poor? In the U.S. I saw this phenomenon clearly, that people lose their self-esteem and dignity as people. So even though we are just eating a coconut or a plantain here in Limón, I am doing something that is dignifying. I don't think people would be proud to say of me "There is Ricardo, who spent his life washing the butts of old ladies or cleaning floors."

Teofilo Lacayo, one of the founders of Iseri Lidawamari, migrated to New York City in 1972 at the request of his sister. He had recently received his teaching degree, but he left the country after just three years of teaching. "I did not go to the U.S. motivated by the interest to change my economic level. I went with the idea to see for myself what I had already known through reading and conversations with people." He worked in a factory and in building maintenance and sees his time in New York as mainly a negative experience. He returned after just two years. Though he was able to buy a small piece of land with the money he had saved, he also spent much of it on the medicine he needed to recover from the cold and overwork he experienced in New York.

In the U.S. there is discrimination, there are jobs there strictly relegated for *la gente nativa de allá* [Americans]. They continue to see us as people from an undeveloped country, so they establish a low wage for us. There is employment but it is only because there are some spaces that need to be filled by Latinos. The natives don't want to do the work because they would not be earning enough. So this marginalizes us. In general, the Europeans who migrate to the U.S. come with a *formación técnica* [technical background]. We leave here without that. For example, a teacher. A teacher goes from here and can't aspire to much more than being a porter. If they are ok with that they stay there all of their lives. If they do not want to stay at that level they will have to go to night school after work, and those are not as high status as other schools. All of these problems converge in determining the economic and educational levels that we Latinos occupy in the U.S.

Likewise, Lombardo, the man who was mayor of Limón at the time of the interviews and the founder of Iseri Lidawamari (and a nephew of Teofilo), had visited New York to meet with the Limoneño community there. Like Ricardo and Teofilo, he was struck by the "miserable conditions" Limoneños live in and the number of hours they must work in order to save enough money to send back to Limón. He said that even after they manage to build their house and return to Limón, they find they have gotten used to the consumer lifestyle of the United States and so return again and again to make more money. For these men, the consumerism that others had identified as a form of upward mobility, progress, and freedom enslaves them to ideologies of wealth and regimes of working for others.

Others questioned whether progress should be measured only by material wealth. What about education, health, and family life? For Lombardo, *superación de condiciones de vida* means more than earning dollars:

> If we talk about *superación de condiciones de vida*, I see it as housing, health, security, food, education, and other fundamental life necessities. If we consider them in this way the people who migrate only achieve some of them. Many improve their housing—here in Honduras, not in New York, there they live in a terrible poverty. They make a huge sacrifice to send money from there to build their little house here. Very few improve their educational levels there. There is no security in either place. The food they get there is actually bad for their health, they're only eating to survive and send money back here. Health, well in fact there are so many that just when they come back here to live in that house they spent so many years to build they either come with high blood pressure or die the next year of cancer. If we say that we go to the U.S. to improve our conditions of life, we don't achieve it.
>
> Too many of those who go to the U.S. go in search of dollars only and not education so they return with a *cultura baja* [low culture]; they just talk about money and do not take advantage of the other things the U.S. has to offer. (Felicia, teacher, nonmigrant)

Others also talked about the *disentegración familiar* (family disintegration) migration brings about in terms of families that are separated transnationally and even among those that are united in New York.

> Migration also brings the problem of family disintegration because I think that in the last few years the majority of migrants have been women because they believe that even without papers women can get work as home attendants, they have more opportunity than men. So the women leave their children here in Honduras and if there is no relative that will take them in, they remain practically abandoned. The effects of this are felt in the schools. There are students that feel abandoned, without affection, and it is a negative factor in their development as students. There are many students who do not even try in school because they have parents in the U.S. and they just assume that one day they will go there so why should they work here? Students with parents in the U.S. are the worst disciplinary problems here in Limón. (Santos)

And yet many argue that even when women (and men) work hard to sponsor the migration of their children to New York, the conditions they find there also lead to family disintegration. Teofilo's reasons for returning to New York after just two years focused largely on the issue of family unity.

> In the winter of 1993 I told my sister I was going to return to Honduras. She hit the ceiling and asked why did I want to return to Honduras to ruin my life again. I told her my work as a teacher is more important. It's true that here I could earn more money, but then what about the social significance of the work for which I went to school? For each new citizen that I form I am happy. I saw that the more years I stayed there the more I was going to be obligated to bring my family. I was opposed to this because the concept that I have of family is that the children in their formative years should be constantly relating to their parents to establish confidence and communication. And in the environment of New York parents lose authority over their children. I saw that this link between parents and children was getting stretched. When the father leaves for work the children have not gotten up yet and when he returns they're in school. In one week perhaps they hardly even have time to greet one another. And the same with the mother, maybe not until the weekend does the family have time to get together. And this is due to the pace of life, maybe the father even has to work on Sundays. And that's why I did not want to bring my family and instead I decided to return myself.

While Teofilo blames migration for the disintegration of the family, he also challenges the normativity of masculinity and mobility, the idea that being a good father is mainly being a good provider, even if from far away. These same sentiments were expressed by Felicia's husband, who went to New York in 1971, leaving her behind with six children. He wrote asking her to come to New York, but her mother was sick and she refused. He decided that the best thing to do was to return to Honduras to be with his family. It is significant, however, that both of these men are teachers, so unlike some other transmigrants, they had a fairly prestigious and somewhat lucrative position to return to in Honduras.

In contrast to these men are other transmigrants who said that while they recognize that the conditions in New York are not what they had believed they would be, they feel that they are stuck there until they can return with something to show for their years of hard work or people will say that they were absorbed by the environment. This is especially true for those who are undocumented and for whom return is seen as more definite than a mere visit. As Lombardo eloquently put it:

> I met Limoneños in the street who had gone *mojados* [undocumented] and cannot return to Honduras because they don't want to return without

something to show for their time in New York. They cried when they saw me. They were like spirits who died in Limón, left the world of the living and are stuck in the world of the dead in New York and cannot return.

Victor is a man from another Garifuna village I met in New York through Garifuna organizations. The first time I spoke with him he told me that he felt deceived by his experience in New York. In Honduras he had been an artist and made a living painting billboards. He owns a house in a Honduran city and has a wife and two children. He came to New York hoping to make enough money to open a workshop in Honduras, but without documents he had a very difficult time finding and keeping a job. "I have been trying to work in construction but as an undocumented worker they just lay you off after each job is over and then you never know when you'll be hired again." He has survived mainly by doing artwork (T-shirts, posters, logos, and so forth) for the many Garifuna voluntary associations in New York City. Yet the second time I spoke with him he said that he wanted to bring his family to New York so his children could get a U.S. education. He hoped that if they had legal papers they could have more leeway in deciding whether to live in New York or Honduras. Despite the hardship and debt he has incurred in his journey, he still believes that the United States is a place of opportunity.

The contradictory ways in which the ideology of migration is ultimately maintained came home to me again one day when I went to visit Rosaria in Limón, where she and her six New York–born children were visiting her mother. When I arrived, a neighbor, also a single mother of six, was looking through a selection of used clothes Rosaria had brought from New York to sell. The woman was trying to invoke neighborly relations in order to get a discount, but Rosaria would not budge. She complained that things are so expensive in Honduras that in just one week she had spent L5,000 on bus fare, visas, and American food bought in the city for her kids. To the neighbor this seemed an incredible sum of money, a real luxury. But Rosaria defended her position by arguing that while those in New York make what seems by Honduran standards to be a substantial amount of money, they also have to spend a great deal of money on rent, clothes, food, the subway, and so forth. Besides, in the U.S. you have to work long hours and always be on time and then work all weekend doing family chores. The neighbor, a woman with no formal employment or male provider in Honduras, seemed unconvinced, however, as she converted Rosaria's monthly salary of $1,500 into lempiras (L15,000, about twice what a day laborer would make in a year in Honduras).

In these last years those that come to our house say that life is hard in the U.S. But then they are only here for one month and they go back and if they can take a brother or sister or their mother or father with them they try to do that. So that is when we do not believe them. Because if life is so hard over there then why take your brothers and sisters to live there? So I say life can't be so bad over there. (Yolani)

And so the ideology of U.S.-bound migration as the main means of social and economic mobility lives on despite (or perhaps because of) the many contradictions Garifuna face on both sides of the border. Transmigrants go back and forth between Honduras and the United States in order to take advantage of the best of both worlds. Some members of the transnational community (both transmigrants and nonmigrants) accept that this is the best strategy for rising above the marginal conditions they face in both Honduras and the United States. Other members of the transnational community question whether transmigration is the best strategy when the achievements are mainly based on participation in the culture of consumerism. Most members of the transnational community express both opinions at different times. They recognize that Garifuna face discrimination in the United States but they have also seen enough cases of transmigrants who have managed to return at a higher socioeconomic level to be convinced that there is some merit to the transmigration strategy as a form of upward mobility. Thus, despite changes in the U.S. economy and the advent of more restrictive immigration policy, migration has become embedded as a social practice with ideological and economic dimensions essential to the Garifuna community.

CONCLUSION

The economic activities and decision-making processes of Limoneños cannot be understood in relation to just one national context or labor market. Households operate through the generation of resources in several labor markets (both in Honduras and the United States) and make economic decisions about the possibilities for employment and consumption in two national contexts simultaneously. These strategies create different sets of opportunities and constraints for Garifuna according to whether they have migrated to the United States or stayed in Limón, whether they are documented or undocumented in New York, whether they have completed an education in Honduras or New York, and so forth. Some transmigrants may succeed in buying land in Honduras and becoming financially independent, while others may never save that nest egg to return as a "successful" member of the community. Some nonmigrants may never get a chance to go to New York but may achieve upward mobility through an education financed by remittances, while others may have only distant family ties in New York and rely solely on the Central American labor market. This has led to an increase in class differences among Garifuna compared with the 1960s, both within Limón and between migrants and nonmigrants.

These class differences cannot, however, be understood solely in terms of an individual's relation to the means of production; it also must be understood in terms of access to consumer items that signify middle-class status. For example, while the households in Limón with the most disposable wealth are obviously those with the most capital (land and cattle or a large business), some households are equally able to consume because they receive a large amount of money through remittances. So while land- and business-owning households produce value for themselves and remittance households produce value for others (through the labor of the U.S. transmigrant, a difference that would normally divide them into capitalist and proletariat), in terms of the power of consumption they are equal due to political and economic border differences (dollars buy more in Honduras than lempiras do). In addition, while there are differences in relation to capital and the means of production in Limón, local capitalists do not monopolize employment opportunities. Money earned through wages is not generally earned locally—Garifuna are proletarians working for capitalists, but those capitalists are positioned outside the village and outside the country. Similarly, businessowners in Limón make their profits from sales within the village, but the money that is spent at these businesses is generated outside the village (and the capital to start and maintain the business is also often generated outside the village). Class relations are complicated and not locally bounded; they are crosscut by kinship relations and span transnational space (Kearney 1996). Economic differences in Limón are not really reducible to "class" in the classic sense of the relation to the means of production but are also manifested in the power of consumption. Limoneños feel that socioeconomic mobility is most often measured by the ability to consume at middle-class levels, no matter what relations of production generated the money to do so.

These complexities lead to the conflicting interpretations of economic success or failure I have illustrated in this chapter. The gap Garifuna often encounter between the ideology of upward mobility and consumption and the experiences of racialization and marginalization in two national contexts at times leads them to question whether migration and consumption are really bringing progress to individuals and families. At other times, Limoneños support migration as ultimately aiding them in overcoming racialization and marginalization. These seemingly incongruous views reveal how the disjunctures between ideals of "modernity," "progress," and "development" and the practical experiences of racialization and economic inequality generate forms of consciousness and social practice that appear contradictory. In the next chapter I analyze how these differing interpretations of the origins of racial and economic inequality lead to different ideas and strategies among Garifuna grassroots organizations about how to bring "development" to the community.

5

¿Superando o Desintegrando?

Disparate Discourses of Development in Transnational Grassroots Organizations

The Honduran sun is hot, so they've placed a chair in the shade for me to sit while I wait. As I enjoy the sea breeze that reaches me in this strategic location, I watch Carlos on the roof of his house, where he and another man are carefully shifting a huge satellite dish, adjusting the angle ever so slightly to try to capture the channel they are looking for. I have been trying to get an interview with Carlos ever since I met him in New York, but like many Garifuna in the United States he was working two jobs and was hard to find at home. Now he has come to Limón for two weeks to visit his mother, his sisters, his "other" wife Ana, and his son, who all live in this house, and to connect more villagers to his satellite dish. He is my neighbor in Limón, and I thought I might have a better chance of catching him here for the interview than in New York City.

I had been hearing about Carlos ever since I came to Limón in 1993. He is one of the Garifuna who arrived in New York City in the 1970s as a young man and has done pretty well for himself, marrying an African American woman through whom he gained residency; getting a job as a janitor at a nursing home, where he was able to connect other Limoneños with work; and saving enough money to build this nice cinderblock house in Limón for his mother, fully furnished and equipped with a stereo system, TV, and VCR all run on an electric generator brought from New York. The $100 a month he sends to his mother along with Ana's salary as a teacher at the local primary school keeps the household afloat and even allows Ana to hire a young girl to supplement the cooking and cleaning activities of Carlos's mother and sister.

I had been introduced to Carlos at an Easter *ayounani* celebration held in a South Bronx community center. After the procession carrying the coffin of Jesus and the cross had finished circling the gym and the prayers were invoked, the requisite DJ music began and people began milling about, dancing, socializing, and moving into the kitchen area to buy food from the Comité de Damas (Women's Committee). It was there that Carlos was pointed out to me as the man I had been looking for, one of the original organizers of the Comité

Pro-Agua Potable (Pro-Potable Water Committee), which had raised money through community events like this *ayounani* to pay for a potable water system to be built in Limón. He is also a current member of the Comité Pro-Electrificación (Pro-Electrification Committee), which is trying to raise enough money to finally get Limón connected to the national electricity source, and the man who introduced Limón to cable television.

As I sat in the shade of the coconut tree waiting to talk to him about his involvement in these groups, I watched different channels flicker across the screen of the television they had set up to monitor their progress. They were looking for Univision, the channel that attracted neighbors to gather every night to watch *El Premio Mayor*, *Tu y Yo*, and *La Dueña*, all *telenovelas* I was already familiar with after watching them in Limoneño households in New York. Carlos had been working all morning trying to capture Univision again before the evening. Progress was slow, however, as he seemed to get every channel except the one he wanted. For a brief "postmodern moment," I was watching *Gilligan's Island*, reliving the Hollywood images of a deserted tropical island I had watched religiously as a child, feeding my fantasies about a life of survival through self-sufficiency in the tropics, a fantasy that in many ways I had been living out through participation with the agricultural cooperative Iseri Lidawamari. At the cooperative in Vallecito (about ten kilometers east of Limón), we fished for our lunch, pulled up cassava for dinner, slept in hammocks in a rudimentary house of wood and palm thatch, and gathered water from the creek. During the day we weeded the cassava plants, tended the pigs, built *nasas* (fishing traps), and gathered medicinal plants—all in the name of "returning" to a system of communitarian self-sufficient production. Out in Vallecito there was no cablevision, only an occasional *Malcolm X* video on the VCR and hours of *concientización* (consciousness-raising) about the Garifuna situation.

As Carlos continued to search for Univision, the Home Shopping Channel flashed by and I had to chuckle to myself. When Carlos came down to adjust the television, I jokingly told him that as the person who decided which channels the whole town of Limón was going to watch, he had a lot of power. Assuming that after twenty years in New York, he shared my reading of the Home Shopping Channel as an absurd element of American consumer culture, I asked him if he was going to try to capture it too. Not picking up on my sarcasm, he answered seriously that yes, he hoped that one day Limón would be able to watch the Home Shopping Channel and many others.

To many Limoneños, Carlos's life history—his involvement in community organizations, his fulfillment of his obligation to support his mother and sisters, and his efforts to bring cable television to Limón—are shining examples of a *buen hijo del pueblo* (good native son) who has contributed to the development of the community. In this dominant discourse among Garifuna, the history of migration to New York City is understood as one of gradual *superación* (progress, getting ahead), both of individuals and of the community, as members create more linkages to the global economy and the culture of consumption. Limoneños often pointed out the benefits migration has brought the community—transmigrants have built nice cinderblock houses that are nicely painted and furnished with goods bought in La Ceiba; they have brought televisions, VCRs, refrigerators, electric generators and other *comodidades* (conveniences) from New York; they have established businesses that provide services to the community such as discos, restaurants, butcher shops, and the cable service; their remittances have enabled Limoneños to participate in the culture of consumption and to pay for education in a way local Honduran wages never could; and through voluntary associations in New York City they have helped to bring infrastructure to the village that the Honduran state alone has not been willing to invest in. In this scenario, "traditional" Garifuna culture was characterized by poverty and isolation and migration has brought individuals and the village into modernity.

There is, however, a competing version of Garifuna history that argues that instead of *superación*, migration has brought *desintegración* (disintegration). Proponents of this version see migration as having contributed to the progressive disintegration of the economic autonomy of Garifuna villages and the gradual deterioration of Garifuna cultural values. In this scenario, "traditional" Garifuna culture was based on a self-sufficient local economy of cultivation and fishing within the bounded moral community of the village. Garifuna men participated in wage labor outside the village but were not dependent on it for the basic necessities of survival because food, housing, and so forth were all produced locally. "We were materially poor but we were never hungry" is a common refrain. This has been ruptured, continues this argument, by the increasing connection to and dependence on the U.S. labor market and a transnational culture of consumption as opposed to production. Proponents of this view point out that entire households depend on U.S. remittances for their survival; many families have abandoned or sold landholdings within the municipality to "outsiders," thereby increasing their dependence on external sources of income and allowing for the increasing penetration of the municipality by non-Garifuna with suspect motives. Class divisions and the creation of a consumer and profit oriented culture are dissolving the former spirit of community solidarity and cooperation in favor of individualism, and the improvement of village infrastructure has actually contributed to further penetration of outsiders with more economic power who are beginning to dominate the local economy. The idea that Limón is *desarrollando* (developing), then, is presented as an illusion that is based on the power of Limoneños to consume instead of on a self-generating local economy of production. Modernity has come as an outside force that has penetrated the bounded community with foreign capital, inserting Garifuna into the global economy as oppressed proletarians and exploiting the local resources (labor, environment, land, and culture) for the needs of a neoliberal transnational capitalism rather than for true local development.

The contradictory experience of achieving upward mobility in the context of Honduras only through continued reliance on transnational migration and exploitation within a racialized and gendered international division of labor leads to complex interpretations of the loci of exploitation and the possibilities for "progress." This contradictory consciousness is not only manifested in the varying strategies that individuals and families use to get ahead in the transnational community but it is also converted into social action among community organizations. In this chapter I focus on the goals and strategies of grassroots organizations. In particular, I analyze the links these grassroots organizations see between migration and *desarrollo comunal* (community development) and how they mobilize different discourses of development to raise money and support for certain projects.

I will do this analysis through a comparison of two main Limoneño grassroots organizations—the Limón-based agricultural cooperative Iseri Lidawamari and the New York–based hometown association Comité Pro-Electrificación. Though both organizations seek community development as their primary goal, they have different ideas about how that development should be brought about. As in the case of Garifuna views of migration and individual progress, the two views of development laid out above may seem dichotomous and are often espoused in such terms by the members of the two organizations. But the transnational community as a whole cannot be divided neatly into two opposing camps. There are adherents of both positions in both New York and in Limón, among transmigrants and nonmigrants, and of all generations. Indeed, it is more useful to see the two discourses of community development as representing two poles of a continuum, and most people shift between the two views depending on the context. This speaks to the multiple class positions Garifuna occupy and the lack of coherence among ideologies of development emanating from the state, the media, and the international arena and the practical experience of the Garifuna operating in transnational space.

A History of Limoneño Transnational Organizations

Transmigrant Hometown Associations and Development as Infrastructure

The issue of development is not new in the Limoneño community. As early as the 1960s, there were organizations within the village that could be mobilized for development projects such as the women's dance groups, the Consejo de Maestros (Teachers' Council), and La Nueva Juventud Limoneña (The New Limoneño Youth). The last group was founded by Limoneños working in the port city of Tela in 1957, who later established a branch in New York. In 1962, Alfonso Lacayo, the first Garifuna medical doctor in Honduras and son of a Limoneño, went to live in Limón, where he initiated a number of projects such as a free medical clinic and an agricultural cooperative with the cooperation of colleagues from the Universidad Nacional Autónoma de Honduras (where he had obtained his medical degree), La Nueva Juventud Limoneña, anthropologist Pierre Beaucage, and the liberal reformist government of Ramón Villeda Morales (1957–1963). Based on his popularity because of these development initiatives, which included getting fellowships for Garifuna to study nursing and other professions, and his former activism within the university's student body, Dr. Lacayo was proposed as a candidate to Congress for the Department of Colón. Though at this time there was considerable support for community development projects under the Liberal Party administration of Villeda Morales and John F. Kennedy's Alliance for Progress (which was initiated in 1961), the traditional conservative elite and many American officials were suspicious of any activity perceived of as communist—one of the contradictions of the politics of development during the Cold War (embodied in "containment liberalism"; see Bello 1994). In response to the liberal reformist policies of Villeda Morales (such as the first agrarian reform law of 1962), Colonel Oswaldo Lopez Arellano led a coup d'etat in 1963, beginning an era of military rule during which members of the Liberal Party were suspected of communism. Many were arrested, including Alfonso Lacayo and his cousin Teofilo Lacayo (Lacayo Sambulá 1998).

Before his arrest in 1963, Dr. Lacayo wrote a letter to the voluntary associations in New York City requesting that they send money to build a system of water pumps that would replace the open wells Limoneños had been using for drinking water that had been contributing to an epidemic of dysentery and other water-borne diseases. Limoneños in New York already had a system of social clubs and merchant marine mutual aid societies that could be mobilized to raise money for the project through raffles and fiestas. These associations (including La Nueva Juventud Limoneña) organized themselves as the Patronato Pro-Mejoramiento de Limón (Patrons for the Betterment of Limón) and raised a portion of the money needed to complete the project.

In the 1970s, the New York organizations were again mobilized at the request of the Patronato to improve the system of pumps with a potable water system that would bring water from the mountains to a water tank, where it would be purified and distributed throughout the village through a system of tubes and faucets. In conjunction with this effort, a new group was formed in 1977 called Frente Social Limoneño; a committee of this organization called the Comité Pro-Agua Potable was dedicated exclusively to the water project. Though Frente Social Limoneño was largely focused on issues dealing with the development of Limón, it was also concerned with issues within the New York City Garifuna community. In addition to raising money for the water project and the construction of the Centro Comunal (Community Center) in Limón (the group's two most successful projects), it also sponsored events in New York such as Madre Garifuna celebrations, fiestas, and Garifuna dance troupes and it published a bulletin entitled *Voz Garifuna* (Garifuna Voice) that was distributed throughout the Honduran Garifuna community in New York. It is clear from this publication that many of the members had gone to college in New York and were becoming concerned with issues of ethnic identity as well as development. Several articles deal with the history and language of the Garifuna and calls for efforts to maintain Garifuna culture among young people. It is also evident that voluntary associations representing many other Honduran Garifuna villages were already present in New York; their fiestas and excursions are advertised in the bulletin.[1]

During the 1980s, several other groups formed among Limoneños, namely soccer clubs and the Comité de Damas. The soccer clubs play in leagues in New York and have raised money through ticket sales for projects in Limón such as building a soccer field there, soccer uniforms for the village team, and a drum set for the high school marching band. The Comité de Damas participated in the water project and financed the reconstruction of the Catholic church in Limón. The gender differences in these two types of organizations are clearly marked. Not surprisingly, the soccer clubs are mainly the purview of men, while the women's clubs are generally involved in celebrations that have to do specifically with Garifuna culture (such as Christmas *fedu*, Easter *ayounani*, and other community celebrations). Though this is a sexual division of labor, both types of organizations have the goal of uniting the community through cultural and sporting events and raising money for different projects. In the hometown associations such as the Comité Pro-Agua Potable, however, men and women participate equally. Both serve on the *junta directiva* (board of directors), both are vocal in meetings, and both participate enthusiastically in raising money, giving speeches, making flyers, contracting clubs for fiestas, and so forth. Though some women find it difficult to devote as much time to hometown associations as men do because of childcare responsibilities, no gender ideology prevents them from participating.

Through the work of the Comité de Damas, the soccer clubs, and the Comité Pro-Agua Potable, the water project was finally completed in 1990. The state matched the money raised by these hometown associations, and residents of the village contributed the labor of installing the tubes and faucets.[2] Limoneño households now pay a small monthly fee for the service.

Frente Social Limoneño, like other organizations before it, had disappeared as a functioning group by the end of the 1980s due to internal conflict. After the water project was completed in 1990, the remaining members of the Comité Pro-Agua Potable turned their efforts to getting the government to connect Limón to the national system of electricity (which would enable Limoneños to replace generators with power lines), forming the Comité Pro-Electrificación. In 1993, Comité Pro-Electrificación joined with the soccer clubs and the Comité de Damas to form Unificación Limoneña, whose stated goal is to coordinate the events of each of the member organizations so their schedules do not conflict, thereby maximizing the ability of community members to participate in multiple organizations. Unificación Limoneña also declared that the electrification project was the main priority and that all money raised should go toward its completion (which took place in 1998). The main rationale of adherents of the electrification project was that it would improve the standard of living in Limón with a cheaper source of light (formerly provided by kerosene lamps), energy for televisions and refrigerators (formerly provided by gas-run generators in a country where gas prices were quite high—L25 a gallon in Limón in 1996 [U.S. $2.50], nearly a day's wage), and enable carpenters, welders, butchers, mechanics, and so forth to create small businesses. The following opinion expressed by a transmigrant who has lived and worked in New York for over twenty years and now owns a restaurant in Limón exemplifies the view expressed by most members of the Comité Pro-Electrificación:

> Electricity is really the basis of development. It is one of the reasons that people move to the city, to have refrigerators, blenders, fans, and other conveniences that make life more comfortable. It also can create sources of employment, we could open factories and other businesses. So if we have these things in Limón people will not have to leave the village. They can have the luxuries of the city here. From my point of view, electricity is the fundamental factor in development.

Thus far, the development efforts of Limoneño organizations I have described fall in line with the dominant development model the Honduran state and international organizations have promoted since the 1960s. That is, the efforts are mainly focused on improving the standard of living in Limón through infrastructure related to hygiene, education, consumption, and industrial production. On the one hand, these efforts have been spurred on by the fact that the state has generally ignored Garifuna communities, which has forced transmigrant organizations to mobilize their own resources for community development projects. But on the other hand, these development efforts have not been hindered by the state because they coincide with an ideology of development economics that is centered on increasing consumption, constructing infrastructure, and expanding industrialization (Escobar 1995). Representatives of the state (teachers, politicians, bureaucrats, and so forth) and businessowners see these efforts by the *hijos del pueblo* as contributions to the integration of Garifuna communities into national life and modernity. Participation in these voluntary associations enhances the status of the primary organizers, proving their dedication not only to their families but also to their natal village and (indirectly) to their country.

A ceremony I attended in the community center in Limón illustrates how participation in such voluntary associations can enhance the prestige of organizers in their communities and promote notions of national belonging and civic duty. The ceremony was organized to honor members of one of the Limoneño soccer clubs from New York as it officially handed over a drum set for the marching band (rumored to have cost $2,000) to the high school. All of the schoolchildren were made to attend and the school director gave a speech congratulating the soccer club members for their selfless efforts in contributing to the development of the community. The soccer club members replied in speeches emphasizing their loyalty to Limón and their duty as transmigrants to contribute to their *pueblo*.[3] A few months later this marching band set was proudly displayed in the annual 15th of September parade put on by all the schoolchildren in celebration of Honduran Independence Day.

In sum, these voluntary associations are simultaneously transnational and local in their scope of operation because they are mainly focused on the needs of a particular village whose members are of a particular ethnic group. While this dual focus may appear to counter the state ideology of integrating all Hondurans into one national identity and economy, the goals of the organizations ultimately do seek to bring Limón and Limoneños into "modernity" through participation in consumer culture (Sklair 1995), institutions of the state, and national life.

Iseri Lidawamari and Development as Social Justice

During the time when the electrification committee was gaining momentum, a problem was brewing in the municipality of Limón that temporarily united the various organizations around a somewhat different set of development issues: land tenure, agricultural production, and "foreign" invasion. This new struggle was inspired by the information that a military investment group, Agroindustrial Vallecito, SA (AGROINVASA), was threatening to take over the last remaining unoccupied portion of Vallecito—an area of fertile agricultural land between Limón and the neighboring community of Punta Piedra that had been under dispute for a number of years. A large portion of Vallecito had already been bought up by AGROINVASA and cultivated in African palm plantations. Limoneños were worried that if the whole area was taken over by this group and planted in African palm there would be no possibility for the local communities to engage in any kind of agricultural enterprise. In response, a group of young men formed the Movimiento Negro Iseri Lidawamari, vowing to redress decades of land usurpation in Limón (and other Garifuna villages) and to establish an agricultural cooperative that would bring a different kind of development to Limón based on cultural autonomy and economic self-sufficiency. In contrast to the long-standing emphasis on infrastructure and national integration within Garifuna voluntary associations, the goals of Iseri Lidawamari are more critical of the dominant development model and national society. The group argues that the basis of development is not infrastructure alone but rather infrastructure combined with agricultural production; not private ownership but communal ownership and production (that supposedly correspond more closely to a traditional Garifuna peasant and ethnic communitarian past); not acculturation (in the sense of culture loss) but rather cultural autonomy. The group's goals are integrationist in the sense that it wants full participation in society in terms of rights and political participation, but it also wants autonomy as an ethnic group.

This was not the first time the issues of land tenure and expropriation had come up within Limoneño organizations. An article in a 1978 issue of *Voz Garifuna* details the history of land expropriation in the municipality of Limón, making a call to Limoneños in New York and Honduras to unite in an effort to combat the problem.

> Limón is a village fighting to overcome multiple problems. It has been more than 12 years since one of its prominent sons [Alfonso Lacayo] fought to integrate it into national life in terms of active progress, trying to resolve and channel the success of the most urgent public works such as the aqueduct, electricity, school buildings, etc. If anything has been achieved it is nothing in comparison to what is left to do.
>
> Why is this? Could it be because of the tribal vices, local and family disputes, and departmental interests that divide the municipality? More

than anything it is the lack of progressive vision of those who with hard work have achieved a certain status and economic capacity, while their civic blindness has not allowed them to work more objectively for the community they say they love; and in the end the richness of the municipal soil has favored them only for them to deny it a tribute. Frente Social Limoneño asks: what are they doing, in what civic activity are people like Brooks, landowner located on the *ejidal* lands of Limón, participating in? Like him there are the Goffs, the Molinas, the Ordoñezes (owners of Vallecito), Arturo Moya, los Lacayo, Leonardo Marin, Luciano y Manuel Pereira,[4] and others who are taking over the municipal territory—Lauda, Francia, Limoncito, Farallones, Sico, Masicales, etc. There are also those who exploit the lumber riches through outside companies. There are foreigners taking minerals under the pretense of the scientific investigation of the municipal subsoil, taking advantage of the blindness of the municipal government in this respect. And in this industry, where there is so much economic possibility, instead of filling the municipal treasury, they pay taxes to the department head, adding to the poverty and incapacity of the municipality to carry out its community tasks.

If the main branches of civic organizations were in accordance with one another and presented a gradual plan to the different branches of their organizations that have arisen in different cities within the country and outside it, these branches would respond better and stop suffering once and for all the negative feelings of their brothers, tired of giving money without seeing the fruits of what they have invested in. ("Voz del Frente")

As early as the 1970s, then, some Limoneños were critiquing the presence of "foreigners" in Limón—the ladino (and some Isleño) *colonos* who arrived in the 1960s and 1970s. The authors of this article argued that *colonos* worked for their own interests and not that of the community. Like the relationship between the First and Third Worlds depicted by dependency theorists, the authors of *Voz Garífuna* believed that these "foreigners" saw Limón only as a place to extract resources and exploit cheap labor, not as a community to which they belonged and should contribute.

Though it is clear that Limoneños in both Limón and New York City were already identifying this as a serious social problem, there does not appear to have been much mobilization around the issue until the 1990s. This is probably due in part to the fact that in the 1980s a military dictatorship ruled Honduras, part of the economic and political crisis throughout Central America that militarized the whole region. The 1980s was a dangerous time to be involved in social movements. The military governments of General Alvarez Martinez and General Walter Lopez Reyes (both of whom were supported by the Reagan administration and the U.S. military, which was using Honduras as a base from which to fight the Nicaraguan contras) jailed and "disappeared" numerous peasant and labor union activists accused of communist activities (Lapper and Painter 1985).

In 1990, this political climate changed when Rafael Leonardo Callejas (1990–1993) was elected as the first civilian president in a decade, bringing the new Nationalist Party to power. Though the Nationalist Party administration had a strongly neoliberal economic agenda (it implemented austerity measures and encouraged transnational investment), international human rights organizations, the United Nations, and other international bodies pressured the state to be accountable for issues of social justice. It is a striking paradox that at the same time that international economic and development policies were being increasingly constructed around the globalization, privatization, technification of production, and the neoliberal ideologies of the free market (pushed by the World Bank, a UN specialized agency, and the IMF), such development strategies were being heavily criticized (often by other UN entities) as having contributed to environmental degradation, growing gaps between the rich and the poor, and social unrest (Fisher 1993; Stiefel and Wolfe 1994). In the late 1970s, in fact, UN entities such as the United Nations Research Institute for Social Development (UNRISD) and the International Labour Organization (ILO) began to criticize the dominant development model. These organizations argued that instead of alleviating poverty, such policies were leading to environmental degradation and were nonparticipatory—that is, too state-directed, not taking into account the views and needs of local communities that might have cultural differences from agents of the state (Stiefel and Wolfe 1994).

This ideological shift was supported by UN-sponsored and academic research that revealed the links between the dominant development model, structural adjustment, transnational corporations, environmental degradation, and poverty (cf. Durham 1979; Franke and Chasin 1992; Guha 1989; Hecht and Cockburn 1990; Stonich 1993). An alternative paradigm emerged called sustainable development, which seeks to empower local communities through the formation of *organizaciones de base* (grassroots organizations) and other types of NGOs that would ideally be able to design community development projects (with the aid of experts) that speak more to their reality, are based in the community (rather than in a distant think tank or UN entity), and are more environmentally sustainable (that is, can produce for the market but in a way that does not cause ecological harm). The new ideology of community-based sustainable development is still within the development framework in the sense that the goal continues to be market production and increasing the power of consumption, but it is an alternative vision of development as small scale, culturally sensitive, and environmentally sound (Fisher 1993; Stiefel and Wolfe 1994).[5] As Stiefel and Wolfe argue:

> The ethnic movements most relevant to the original conception of the UNRISD program are those of tribal and peasant peoples distinguished by language, culture, forms of livelihood, and sometimes physical traits, living in rural hinterlands, and forested, mountainous and arid or semi-arid regions. They are usually minorities within the national population, but sometimes constitute majorities among the rural poor. In such groups ethnic identification has coincided closely with degree of exclusion from control over resources and institutions. They have experienced continual aggression from the state, in the name of assimilation and modernization, and from participants in the nationally dominant culture appropriating their land and other resources and exploiting their labor under systems equivalent to serfdom or debt peonage. (1994, 171)

Like its development economics predecessor, the alternative visions of sustainable development, community-based development, and so forth that became popular in the 1980s both reflect an alternative reality and discursively construct the subjects of development. Where development economics constructed "traditional" modes of peasant and indigenous production as inefficient and backward, sustainable development constructs these same practices as naturally conservationist and in harmony with nature. Where development economics constructed large-scale, privately owned, technified production as "modern" rational relations of production, sustainable development constructs small-scale, community projects as communitarian and socially just relations of production. Because indigenous peoples, peasants, and women have been marginalized by the processes of development economics (not in the sense of not being affected but rather in the sense of not having benefited), they are seen as reservoirs of an alternative knowledge of the environment and communitarian values that exist apart from the western values of individualism and the profit motive. Much of the literature assumes that while they want the benefits of development (medical clinics, clean water, education, etc.) they do not propose to achieve this through free market models so dominant in many development programs.

To say that these alternative visions of development were often generated in international organizations is not to say that all indigenous, peasant, and women's organizations were manufactured from above. As Fisher (1993) notes, grassroots organizations often emerge from already existing forms of organization that are simply formalized through the process of being funded. Indigenous peoples, peasants, and women do have critiques of the logic of the free market, the effects of the dominant development model, and structural adjustment as a result of their experiences of marginalization (Escobar and Alvarez 1992; Nash 1993; Taussig 1980). Thus, the explosion of the numbers of NGOs, indigenous rights groups, sustainable agriculture programs, women's movements, and so forth in the 1980s and 1990s was a reciprocal process of pressure from below and changing ideas from above that opened an international space in which to speak (Escobar and Alvarez 1992; Mato 1996; Nelson 1999; Rogers 1996). This *coyuntura* (conjuncture) has challenged the integrationist policies of the nation-state and forced a political *apertura* (opening) for grassroots organizations and social movements of *lo indígena, negro, y popular* (indigenous peoples, blacks, and popular sectors (Brysk 2000, Escobar 1997; Hale 1994a; Nelson 1999; Sawyer 2004; Selverston-Scher 2001; Stavenhagen 1992; Varese 1994; Wade 1995; Warren 1998; Whitten and Torres 1998).

In the early 1990s, the Garifuna movement around land issues found a national political opening and international support and began functioning in a much more open way on a national level. The Organización Fraternal Negra Hondureña (OFRANEH), founded in 1977 by Alfonso Lacayo and others, was already working against racism in Honduras, but in the 1990s land became a major issue in the organization. As the 1992 Quincentenary of the Americas approached, organizations of indigenous peoples and blacks throughout Latin America were mobilizing around land issues. In Honduras, the main NGOs involved in the land struggle initially were OFRANEH, the Consejo Asesor Hondureño para el Desarrollo de las Etnias Autóctonas (CAHDEA) and the Confederación de Pueblos Autóctonos de Honduras (CONPAH) (the final two represent indigenous peoples and the Garifuna under the umbrella term "autocthonous"—an issue of identity politics I explore in more detail in Chapter 6). Like indigenous and black organizations throughout Latin America, these Honduran organizations focused their energies initially on pressuring the state to ratify the International Labour Organization's Convention (No. 169) concerning Indigenous and Tribal Peoples in Independent Countries (known popularly as ILO Convention 169, written in 1989), which obligates states to protect the rights of indigenous and "tribal" people to land, territory, and cultural autonomy. The basic philosophy of ILO Convention 169 is that indigenous and tribal people, due to their cultural difference, have a special relationship to the land that conflicts with the western notion of land as merely a commodity

Figure 5.1. Protest march in La Ceiba on October 12, 1993, organized by black, indigenous, and popular groups. Their primary demand was that the government ratify the ILO's Convention 169. (Photo by author)

that is individually and privately owned. The convention argues for the right of ethnic peoples to have land that is legally recognized as their territory, which they use for cultivation but also for their "functional habitat"; that is, for hunting, collecting medicinal plants, sacred sites, and so forth (ILO 1996, article 13). Garifuna and indigenous organizations pushed the Honduran state to ratify this international convention in the hope that they could use it as a tool to legally recuperate and further protect much of their community lands that had been taken over and are under threat of being taken over (see Cruz Sandoval 1984 for statistics on land tenure in Honduran indigenous communities).

For Limoneños the local manifestation of all of these processes—conflicting ideas about development from the state and international aid organizations, ethnic social movements emerging from below and supported from above—is centered on the land struggle in Vallecito, an area about ten kilometers east of Limón between Cabo Farallones and the neighboring village of Punta Piedra. It is within the boundaries of the municipality, but according to informants it was not really a center of Garifuna cultivation because it had been "given" to the prominent *capitalino* Ordoñez family in the 1930s. Though the Ordoñez family owned the property, they did not cultivate it or pay taxes on it, which made it eligible for expropriation by the INA under the 1974 agrarian reform law (all land within the municipality that is not *ejidal* or within the *catastro* [town limits] is under the jurisdiction of the INA). In the 1970s and 1980s many of the *colonos* who had left the Bajo Aguan project moved into the area and occupied the land, carrying out subsistence agriculture, some cattle ranching, and extraction of lumber. In 1985, the INA rented the land to AGROINVASA, which planted the area in African palm. The peasants were removed, threatened, and jailed by the military, as was common practice throughout the 1980s (cf. Williams 1986 on the massacre of ladino peasants in Olancho).

In 1990, a group of about ten young Limoneños led by Lombardo Lacayo (who was a university graduate, teacher, and the son of Alfonso Lacayo) decided that the land situation in Limón had become critical. This group of men learned that AGROINVASA had plans to take over the remainder of the Ordoñez property in Vallecito to expand its plantation. Because it was the last fertile area of the municipality of Limón that had not been taken over as private property (with full legal title), members of Iseri Lidawamari decided that it was important to "recuperate" the land, both in the legal sense that is used in the agrarian reform law—that is, retaking *ejidal* or national lands that had been expropriated by large landowners—and in the sense of *recuperando* (recuperating) or *rescatando* (rescuing) land that belongs to the Garifuna *ancestralmente* (ancestrally), a tactic that implied that the ownership of the land by outsiders disrupts more

Figure 5.2. Members of Iseri Lidawamari on their way to the National Agrarian Institute to demand titling of the land in Vallecito. (Photo by author)

than a legal relationship of Garifuna to the land. Iseri Lidawamari occupied land neighboring the plantation of AGROINVASA by both living on it and beginning to clear it for cultivation, thereby giving it a "social function." Based on this, the organization began the process of petitioning the INA for legal title to the land as a group of six *empresas asociativas* (associative enterprises).

Though Iseri Lidawamari used the same tactics many peasant organizations use to declare rights to land—tactics made possible by the agrarian reform law of 1974 (that is, squat on the land, give it a "social function," form *empresas asociativas*, petition the INA for the title, and so forth)—they also have a strong critique of the agrarian reform law as discriminatory toward indigenous peoples and the Garifuna. One of their main issues is a critique of the term "social function," which, they argue, forces landowners to engage in production for export, monocrop agriculture, lumber extraction, and cattle ranching, forms of production that are detrimental to the environment. They argue that Garifuna and indigenous forms of production are naturally ecological and sustainable because they use swidden agriculture and natural fertilizers and do not deforest. They feel that the dominant development model, which has served as the basis of most state-sponsored development projects thus far (including agrarian reform), harms not only small producers but also indigenous peoples. Armed with this philosophy and the support of international organizations, Iseri Lidawamari and other organizations fighting for land pose a much more direct challenge to the Honduran state.

Initially Iseri Lidawamari received no support from the Honduran state. In fact, the members of the group who lived in Vallecito were threatened and shot at by employees of AGROINVASA. They appealed to the department governer for justice, but nothing was done. But they did get support from national-level organizations such as the Comité para los Derechos Humanos de Honduras (CODEH), OFRANEH, CAHDEA and the Catholic church and from international bodies such as the United Nations. By gathering international support and keeping the issue in the forefront locally with a series of public denouncements and marches to Vallecito, Iseri Lidawamari created enough negative publicity for AGROINVASA that it entered into a dialogue to settle the matter. At a meeting between representatives from Limón, the INA, the Catholic bishop of Trujillo, and AGROINVASA on April 13, 1992, the parties agreed that AGROINVASA could keep the lands already under cultivation in African palm as long as it began to pay municipal taxes and left the uncultivated portion (about 10,000 hectares) to Iseri Lidawamari for its agricultural cooperative (Miralda 1992).

Unfortunately, this only marked the beginnings of the struggles of Iseri Lidawamari. One year later it discovered that AGROINVASA had sold its shares to Miguel Facussé, one of the wealthiest capitalists in Honduras and a notorious enemy of peasant cooperatives (he now owns much of what was once the Bajo Aguan cooperative). What was worse, the mayor of Limón had also clandestinely sold Cabo Farallones to Facussé. Cabo Farallones is an area of about 500 manzanas situated on the beach between Limón and Vallecito that includes a forested ridge, dramatic cliffs overlooking the ocean, a beautiful secluded beach, and an abundance of wildlife—in sum, an area perfect for a tourist resort, and that is exactly what it was rumored Facussé had planned for it (Steiner Bendeck 1993). The sale of Cabo Farallones had Limoneños up in arms because the mayor had done it illegally without following the proper procedure of consulting with the *corporación municipal* (the municipal body, which is made up of the mayor and four *regidores* who are appointed by the two parties and function somewhat like a U.S. city council). He also pocketed the profits himself (CONPAH July 14, 1993). Any purchaser of land in Honduras must acquire a *constancia de vecindad* (proof of residency) and a *constancia de catastro* (proof of tax payment), documents the mayor did not obtain in the sale of Cabo Farallones. Without these documents from the municipality, the sale was not fully legal, and members of Iseri Lidawamari sought to have it annulled.[6]

As a consequence of these events, Lombardo Lacayo decided to run for mayor of Limón as the Liberal Party candidate in the national elections of 1993. His platform was based on his reputation as an educated youth (in contrast to the incumbent mayor, who had no postsecondary education), the recuperation of Vallecito, and projects in the village that would bring sustainable development. In his presentations to the community he argued that the *base para el desarrollo* (basis of development) should be the production of food and other goods locally, which would lead to the development of infrastructure and other linkages with the state. He further contended that the acquisition of infrastructure from the state should come second, as it would lead only to dependency on the state and urban markets if the community was not self-sufficient in food production first. For example, rather than use a paved highway to bring food stuffs to Limón, he believed that the highway should be used to transport food from the village's own local production to the produce markets in the cities.

In sum, while the formation and philosophies of Limoneño grassroots organizations such as the Comité Pro-Electrificación and Iseri Lidawamari emerged from very local histories and experiences, they are also engaged in a long conversation with current global ideologies of development and national ideologies of belonging. For much of the history of Garifuna grassroots organizations, activists have been in dialogue with the dominant models of development economics and mestizo nationalism. Today international bodies and transnational organizations are changing their views on development and social justice; now they pressure nation-states to rethink the dominant development model and support programs for sustainable development that put ethnic peoples and peasants at the center of projects. This does not mean that the dominant development model has disappeared. Ironically, international aid organizations and the state often support both models simultaneously, creating a contradictory situation in which the politics of development among Garifuna social movements coincide with those of the state and international aid organizations at some moments and not at others. The construction of some development philosophies and projects as deviant at certain historical junctures and as in line with nationalist projects at other moments provides some of the context for how possibilities for Garifuna social action are variously enabled and constrained. But it is not enough to look at the contradictory politics of development emanating from above. We must also consider the complex ways discourses of development, modernity, and social justice are filtered through the culture and practical experiences of poverty and racial discrimination among Garifuna to generate their particular understandings of what constitutes development.

THE GARIFUNA "WELFARE" SYSTEM

When members of Garifuna grassroots organizations discuss the problem of "development" in their communities, the issue that is most often at the core of the debate is remittance dependency. There is a consensus that the need for more ethnic rights and the problems of the lack of jobs, infrastructure, and land are all related to the lack of economic power Garifuna communities have in Honduras, a lack that is most clearly manifested in the substantial dependency Garifuna communities have on remittances and the decline in local agricultural production. Activists have a favorite image that illustrates the absurdity of this situation—the image of Garifuna emerging from their houses once a week at the call of a loudspeaker to buy sacks of *guineo* (green bananas) and cassava from trucks that circle the village, driven by ladino farmers coming from the bush. This is pointed out as absurd because the Garifuna have such a long history of producing *guineo* and cassava, at least for their own communities and households, and now they mostly buy them from outside sellers. This is seen as especially absurd in the case of cassava, which (even more than *guineo*) is not only considered to be a staple of the Garifuna diet but is also a powerful symbol of Garifuna culture. Cassava and the unique set of implements for making cassava-derived products (everything from bread to starch to soup stock) were brought to Honduras from St. Vincent as a part of the cultural heritage learned from the Island Carib. Now not only has cassava been superseded in popularity as a staple by store-bought rice, but what cassava is eaten is often bought from ladinos.

To many Garifuna individuals and members of organizations in both Honduras and New York City, this is the ultimate sign that what they call the Garifuna "welfare" system has gone too far. All are in agreement that the system of sending remittances, while based on the good intentions of supporting family members, has had the unintended consequence of leading to dependency on remittances and a lack of local production. Most agree that sending remittances to elderly parents is justifiable since they are getting too old to go to the bush or to work. Sending remittances to a woman who has children and/or grandchildren in the house to whom she redistributes the money (as opposed to using it for drink or other vices) is also justifiable. The problem stems from those in the household who could be working but instead live off the money the mother or elderly couple receives from relatives abroad.

> One of our dreams in coming here [to the United States] was so that our mothers and fathers would no longer have to go to the bush [to cultivate] or go fishing. They could retire and rest. So we always sent money to them. But now they are all resting and even the youths are too. They are bums who live off the Garifuna "welfare" system. They don't want to do any work anymore, they just want to live off the dollars we send and they even complain when they do not get the money. So it's really been a *dólar de doble filo* (a double-edged dollar) that has helped out our family but also led to this dependency. (Edson, transmigrant)

> I believe that there is a social problem that has been brought on by migration. The youth spend more time imitating musicians, doing their hair, playing their music, and they have ignored the issue of how to get the money to continue walking around with these luxuries. Their parents are the ones that are developing themselves in the U.S., sending dollars, so the children are satisfied. They don't see any problems because the clothes are always there. Many of these youth become delinquents, they are unemployed, they have empty minds, they don't have to invest their time, so they dedicate themselves to planning mischief. (Xiomara, nonmigrant, schoolteacher)

What I found interesting is that not only do the Garifuna use the term "welfare" to refer to remittance dependency, but the discussions around it are strikingly similar to national debates around welfare in the United States (Wilson 1996). On the one hand, there are the deserving poor who really need to be helped and for whom welfare (or remittances) is seen as justified—these are elderly parents who are not able to work and mothers who need help in raising children. But then there are also the undeserving poor, in this case grown children, live-in boyfriends of daughters, and other *vagos* who should be out making their own living. These youth are seen as not having the right values, as not wanting to work hard and get ahead. Just as opponents of welfare programs in the United States blame them for having created a "culture of poverty" where nonproductive values are instilled in the youth, transmigrants similarly blame remittances for having created a "remittance culture"[7] in which young people assume they will either survive on remittances or migrate to New York themselves, an assumption that gives them no incentive to engage in productive activity in Honduras. As Arnulfo (the transmigrant we saw in Chapter 4 who had achieved the goal of returning in five years) explained, these young people have become accustomed to a *cultura de mándame* (culture of send me money/goods).

> The fault is with we who are out of the country. We are used to sending anything our family members want—clothes, tennis shoes, and so on. They see the brand on TV and that is what they want. We have created a *cultura de mándame*. Before everyone went to the bush to cultivate cassava, they raised chickens, and so forth. Now there are few who raise cassava; they buy it from the ladinos who come in their trucks.

Another interviewee was one of the original merchant marines to leave Limón in the 1940s (but never settled in the United States), always sending a portion of his check back to his family. At 75, he is now retired in Limón with land and cattle. He had this opinion:

> We, men and women, are used to going to the bush. But the youth do not want to. They assume that their mothers and fathers will send them money and clothes from the United States, and so in the end who can get them to go to the bush? They just spend time hanging out. They start to drink *guaro*, why? Because they have the money to buy it.

I heard this type of complaint voiced many times by Garifuna transmigrants. As one man said, "We all have the experience of receiving that monthly 'bill.'" He was referring to a letter that lists all of the things a family member wants to have sent. Transmigrants tend to invoke individualist/culturalist explanations of the origins of remittance dependency—it is the result from the weakness of those in Honduras who have preferred to live the easy life of dependency in which money is used for consumption instead of being invested in some form of production. (Although most transmigrants send only enough remittances to cover living expenses; few who receive remittances have enough left over to invest.) In the view of many Limoneño transmigrants and nonmigrants, transmigrants have the initiative to better themselves and the community, at least in terms of infrastructure (such as housing, water, electricity) and services (such as cablevision, discos, shops). The dominant narrative is that transmigrants have brought what development there is to Limón, partially because of a sense of civic duty and partially because of the desire to recreate the conveniences of the United States in Limón. This corresponds with the liberalist discourse of upward mobility in which most Garifuna explain individual achievement as primarily the result of hard work in what they see as the meritocracy of the United States. In general, this is the position adherents of the Comité Pro-Electrificación espouse—that transmigrants have worked hard in the United States and so it is natural that they would come to enjoy the fruits of their labor in the form of capitalist enterprises in Limón. Though these businesses are individually owned, the benefits will eventually trickle down to their extended family and the rest of the community. With increased economic power comes movement away from generalized poverty and toward respect of the Garifuna as a people. Consequently, in their view, individual class mobility is the key to overcoming economic, political, and cultural marginality.

GARIFUNA "WELFARE REFORM"

In contrast to this dominant view, other Limoneños believe that the individualized path of migration is the wrong path to community development. Among both transmigrants and nonmigrants, the "culture of send me" is often counterpoised to an imagined former ethic of self-sufficiency in which migration was only a supplement to other forms of production, not a primary means of survival. For example, Teofilo, Lombardo's uncle and one of the founders of Iseri Lidawamari, has this version of Garifuna history.

> In the 1950s it was difficult to find a malnourished child in our communities because food was abundant. The basis of the Garifuna diet was fresh foods, for example fish, plantains, *guineo, ñame, malanga*. There was material poverty, but people were healthier. Clothes, shoes, furniture, good beds, all of these things—who dreamed of having a refrigerator in this area in 1949? It was in the 1950s that things began to change with migration. But we have to recognize that migration out of the country has affected the system of production because the emigrants that have gone have sent money back here to their relatives to cover their living expenses, but

I would say that in a way these relatives have not known how to use this money—because instead of it having served to better their economic situation, they have limited themselves to consuming it instead of investing it. There has been a regression in the productive system. Since there is money to buy whatever one needs, then who cares about production?

Lombardo also draws a picture of the gradual decline of the community in terms of self-sufficiency and production. However he implicates both nonmigrants and transmigrants for contributing to a reliance on transnational migration and remittances. The following quote is from the opening speech Lombardo gave at a seminar on community development sponsored by the Universidad Pedagógica in 1996.

We Garifuna arrived here in 1797. Our ancestors were very skillful. They had a very efficient production system through which they were able to provide their housing, food, clothing, and just about all of the necessities of life. In those days there were no doctors, only mothers with great knowledge of medicinal plants. But then the banana companies came. It was with the arrival of the banana companies that an attitude, a mode of conduct, was created in our communities that is the culture of dependence. Before the banana companies there was a great level of production in our communities, but then the banana companies created a situation of dependence and began a process of the destruction of the economy of the Garifuna people because then the word "*salarismo*" was introduced in the Garifuna community. Before that no one had worked for anyone else, but instead we all worked together, helping each other out. But after this *salarismo*, we also see the beginning of the word "*awaduhani*"—that is, migrate from the village—to supposedly look for better money. This is when our grandfathers and great-grandfathers left in the merchant marines to send money to those left here so they could survive. And since the situation of the world economy was different then, many saw that this was good, and they decided to go too, forming a whole chain of migration. But this form of resolving economic problems has its limits. We can see that this process created a pattern in which we feel that what we have here is not sufficient; our mind begins to wander to other paths, and we forget the great richness that is around us. In addition, there was a time until the 1970s that Garifuna gathered *corozo* and harvested copra to sell and then buy whatever we did not produce like cement, shoes, clothes, some food—and that is how we survived. It was more dignified than the way we survive today. Now many people have migrated to the United States and many people have sold their land. This creates a system of survival that is very precarious in both places.

To speak of the history of the economic development of the Garifuna community, then, is to speak of a situation of decadence—from something superior to something inferior—because mothers have to send their sons to sea or to the city to make maybe L30 per day to send maybe L20 per day and see if they can't figure out a way to get to the United States where they can send $50 per month. This is a process through which we have lost the value of the land, we have lost faith in the land. We no longer visualize it as part of our identity, we just live on it, and to see it in such a mundane way there comes a time when we believe that the land is no longer useful, that it is not productive, that the land is for others and not for us—those people that sell the land, that is the concept that they have.

On the other hand, members of Iseri Lidawamari invoke explanations that use individualist/culturalist explanations for remittance dependency and lack of production. In Lombardo's story, the attitudes of the people had changed over time and they had lost their love of the land and become satisfied with just getting by with what relatives send. However, he also implicates the transmigrants, who brought urban images of themselves mainly as workers and not as cultivators and the land as a commodity instead of a collective territory and spiritual homeland. He often argued that transmigrants were responsible for introducing notions of individualism and consumerism in the community, values that he saw as clashing with "traditional" Garifuna values of cooperation and self-sufficiency. A Honduran anthropologist who interviewed members of Iseri Lidawamari for an article that appeared in the national newspaper El Tiempo in July 1992 described this version of the impact of migration on Garifuna culture:

Those Garifuna who travel to the U.S. change rapidly based on the influence of North American society, but also the migration of Garifuna to the cities of Honduras generates mental schemes that, in large part, clash with communal values. In Trujillo, La Ceiba, San Pedro Sula, and Tegucigalpa there is racial segregation and this provokes a marked social division. This is reflected in the supply and demand of labor because the color of the skin can mean a lower salary to a black for the same work that a ladino does. There are some Garifuna who appreciate their blackness and their culture and are ready to transform themselves based on who they are, but those who come from outside try to impose the modernity they bring with them, thereby destroying the original cultural pattern. The official educational system also contributes to the deterioration of family tradition by prohibiting the use of Garifuna in the schools, based on the assumption that if blacks speak Spanish they will develop more. Nevertheless, instead of bettering themselves, the Garifuna have been confused to the point of rejecting their own language, denying their blackness, seeking instead to flee from *el pueblo*. Many Garifuna families would like to see their children working in the United States so they can bring them Nikes without thinking about the fact that this luxury means having to bow down before others. (Miralda 1992)

Members of Iseri Lidawamari point out that while workers who migrate may acquire personal wealth, they do so at the cost of remaining proletariats subject to the constraints of a racialized division of labor. For members of Iseri Lidawamari, migration is a system in which all people of the community remain dependent: nonmigrants depend on remittances and transmigrants depend on the vagaries of the racialized and gendered labor market. For them, saying that investment in housing and businesses has brought the "development" of the community is based on the illusion that consumption increases power. They would prefer production and autonomy (both economic and cultural). Lombardo clearly outlined this critique of what he calls the culture of consumption.

What is the position of the people with regard to production? What is the concept they have of development? If we do a survey about this, we will discover that there is a confusion in the people. Why? If I propose something to you, there should be a *coherence* in everything I am proposing. But if we ask the people of the community what is development, they are going to tell you that it is that there are good streets, that we eat well, that we have pretty houses. All of these concepts they will give about development are just concepts of consumption. This concept is the response to a formal education that is systematized in grammar school and high school. If we analyze it, we will see that it is not an education that teaches us to better our place in life, it is an education that tricks us, it is an education that teaches us to act like a robot. So we cannot expect great things from this education. And if we look at informal education, for example political campaigns, they promise things to the people and the people see the politicians as gods who, once in government, are going to resolve their problems. This creates a mode of thinking, a magical mentality, without reason. Another form of informal education is the advertisements we hear on the radio—Coca Cola, Salva Vida [Honduran beer], etc. And also the conduct of migrants within the community becomes a pattern that people follow. So to have any impact we have to *orient the people to see their reality*, to not be clouded by that of the politicians and the rich into believing that development is just about consumption and to not be taken in by an *alienating education*. (my emphasis; Lombardo, Iseri Lidawamari round table 1996)

Iseri Lidawamari's analysis of the problems of remittance dependency and lack of production is very Gramscian. Lombardo explicitly names the national educational system and the national media as agents of the state and the rich who have duped the people into following a *patrón cultural* (cultural pattern) that is not a true reflection of their reality as an ethnic people with a different relationship to the land and to each other. They have become robots who buy into the culture of consumption and modernity without critically analyzing the way it further impoverishes them. There is no coherence between their practical experience and their theoretical understanding of the situation. In the end they remain proletariats, alienated from their labor power (and ethnic communitarian values) and sell their land to buy consumer goods, thereby reinforcing the plans of the state and the wealthy, whose interests it represents.

While much of Iseri Lidawamari's critique is leveled at the changing internal values of the Garifuna community, especially toward those who sell their land to *foraneos* (outsiders, implying both non-Hondurans and non-Garifuna), ultimately it blames external structural forces for having pushed the community in this direction, forcing its members off their land and into a situation of dependency. This can be seen in the two slogans of the movement that appear on all official documents they produce: *Mua lubuñebai ibagari, miguira wamai* (Land is the basis of life, don't abandon it) and *Miguira wamai wamua haun chilüdügütiñu o risitiñu* (Don't leave our land to the foreigners or the rich). In the second discourse they point the finger at structural causes for poverty. The cause of land loss is the prejudices toward the poor built into the dominant development model. State and international economic policies favor large-scale export projects that require a great deal of start-up capital. The result is that peasant producers are not able to compete and ultimately are dislocated from their land (Stonich 1993). While this issue affects all rural communities (ethnic and ladino), Iseri Lidawamari also points to the racism of Honduran national society for discriminating against the Garifuna in education, in the labor market, and in land struggles. This linking of class and race is clearly articulated in the following quote from a proposal Iseri Lidawamari wrote in 1993 to request funding from OXFAM Canada. The authors argue that Garifuna cultural difference from national society is the foundation of an alternative vision of development and relationship to the land.

Our communities have been based on our own culture, with its own customs, language, dances, forms of organization, forms of production, in the end all of those qualities that make up a differentiated people with its own identity. This has never been taken into account by the rulers of this country and so they make decisions that violate our rights as an ethnic people such as rights to territory, the sea, the forest, customs, etc.

Every day more foreigners arrive in our communities and from day to night they get rich off the backs of our people. Our communities, because they are on the edge of the ocean, are wanted for tourism, so the government has signed agreements with German, Mexican, and Spanish investors to begin large-scale tourist projects such as TORNASAL that are displacing the communities of Tornabe and San Juan. For the last twenty years, Limón, as all other Garifuna communities, has been stripped of its most fertile lands. Large landowners have let their cattle and horses graze over Garifuna crops, forcing them to abandon their lands. Today there are more cattle on the lands of the village than there is cassava, *ñame, malanga, camote,* sugar cane, corn, beans, plantains, etc. and the people have no alternative but to cultivate in the sand.

We as a people need an answer to all of these problems and that is why the Movimiento Negro Iseri Lidawamari was born in the village of Limón as an alternative for generating an integral development for the area of Limón that will be a base for the defense and production of Garifuna lands throughout the country.

Iseri Lidawamari's analysis of the current situation of the Garifuna is that poverty (class), which can be solved through individual upward mobility, is not the only problem for the community. The deeper problems of racism and cultural discrimination also create obstacles to healthy community development. In the organization's view, migration is not the solution to poverty and marginality because all it does is move people from one realm of class and ethnic marginalization to another. In each location of the transnational community, Garifuna are dependent proletariats and racial minorities. While working for thirty years in New York City may bring individual class mobility, it does not develop the whole community because it does not address the systemic problems of structural racism and poverty.

The critique of reliance on migration and remittances is based not only on the experiences of poverty and marginalization in Honduras but also on a growing sense of insecurity in the United States. This comes from worsening economic conditions in New York City and U.S. legislation such as the welfare and immigration reforms passed in the 1990s aimed at curbing the flow of immigrants from poor countries by increasing security at the border, facilitating deportations, and restricting the access of immigrants (both legal and illegal) to state services such as Medicaid and public assistance. In many meetings I attended in New York, Garifuna mentioned this issue in a way that revealed a profound insecurity that was rooted in a feeling of being outside the national imagined community, a disposable population that could be kicked out at any time (Chavez 1991). Even successful upwardly mobile transmigrants and those waiting for their papers in Honduras have begun to question whether migration is still a viable alternative.

Those who have already invested many years of their working life in the United States generally feel that the answer to remittance dependency is not to stem the tide of migration but to spend the money that is earned abroad more wisely. Garifuna activists concur that one of the main problems the Garifuna community faces is that the money that is earned in the United States and sent to Limón does not circulate within the community—that is, it is most often taken immediately to a bank in the city, where it is exchanged for lempiras and used to buy provisions for a month or more in urban shops owned by ladinos or *turcos* (Arab Palestinians). Some of the money is spent in the Garifuna villages, but even there the majority of the larger businesses are owned by ladinos. A number of studies in Central America have shown that indeed the majority of remittances (up to 80 percent) are used for immediate needs instead of for investment (Andrade-Eekhoff and Silva-Avalos 2003; Orozco 2002). This use of money has few multiplier effects in rural communities because most recipients go to the larger towns to exchange the money and buy goods. A study conducted by a German service agency on the use of remittances in Garifuna communities found that once wire transfer fees, transportation costs, and bulk purchases in the towns are taken into consideration, an average remittance of $110 would leave the recipient with only $24 to spend in the community (Cantor, Schoenharl, and Valerio 2004).

Many activists in New York refer to the African American strategy of "buying black" and propose the same solution: more Garifuna-owned enterprises (be it businesses or agricultural production) need to be established so that remittances benefit not just the banks and business of Honduras but instead benefit and promote the self-sufficiency of the Garifuna community. As one activist in New York said:

Here [in the United States] we have Garifuna who are being trained as doctors, nurses, mechanics, accountants, and so forth, so why should we rely on outsiders to do those jobs for us? We can fill those positions ourselves and have those services in our communities so that people don't have to go to the city.

The director of the high school in Limón concurred:

Suppose I am a barber, I have my relative in the U.S. who sends me $30 a month. I would say, "Buy me a barber's chair, all the tools of a barber, don't send me dollars anymore." They would no longer be obligated to send me dollars anymore because they have given me a source of livelihood, I will depend on my small business.

In sum, while most Garifuna grassroots organizations agree about what the problem is (remittance dependency and lack of local production), they part ways about where to place the blame for this system (the Garifuna themselves, the state, ladino *colonos*, or foreign investors) and how to remedy the situation—that is, what kind of production would be most useful for achieving development and what that development should look like. Contradictions between the promises of development, modernity, and national integration and the reality of continued economic dependency and racial discrimination in both Honduras and the United States have led to critiques of the dominant development model and the culture of consumption. As Iseri Lidawamari members often argue, they are discriminated against *por ser negro y por ser pobre* (for being black and poor). Their solution is to attack discrimination on the two fronts of race and class. One way to do this is through a reemphasis on ethnic solidarity, cultural autonomy, and economic self-sufficiency through agricultural production. Yet in many ways Iseri Lidawamari's discourses of ethnic autonomy and economic self-sufficiency do not correspond to the practical experience of many Garifuna and their family members who have achieved upward mobility through migration and are now able to consume at Honduran middle-class levels. The main foe, as members of Pro-Electrificación see it, is the lack of individual motivation to work *within* the system, not *against* it. For them, the primary strategy for *superando sus condiciones de vida* continues to be hard work and achieving success within the class system and the national educational system, not what they perceive to be the "ethnic separatist" politics of Iseri Lidawamari.

ELECTRICITY VERSUS LAND

In 1993, Lombardo Lacayo was elected mayor of Limón after a heated election campaign against a *colono* candidate. The Limoneño community was excited that a *hijo del pueblo* had won. In addition, Liberal Party member Carlos Roberto Reina, a former member of the human rights organization CODEH, was elected president. Iseri Lidawamari hoped that the politics of the state would be in their favor. Indeed, during his administration, Reina ratified ILO Convention 169 and implemented several programs such as Nuestras Raíces (Our Roots) that help finance community-based development projects of ethnic peoples. In

Figure 5.3. Lombardo Lacayo, founder of Iseri Lidawamari and mayor of Limón from 1994 to 1997, in his mother's house in Limón. Notice the posters of President Reina and Lomabardo's father, Alfonso Lacayo, on the wall. (Photo by author)

addition, he appointed a Fiscal de las Etnias (Minister of Ethnic Groups) whose job is to advocate for the interests of ethnic communities before the state—in this case mainly involving land and cultural rights as laid out in ILO Convention 169. The United Nations also implemented a program called Rescate Cultural-Ecológico that supports sustainable development projects in indigenous communities and projects of cultural recovery such as bilingual education, ecological conservation, and craft production. During Lombardo's administration (1994–1997), Iseri Lidawamari received funding from all of these national programs as well as from some foreign agencies such as the U.S.-based Inter-American Foundation and the Dutch embassy. The money was received either directly by Iseri Lidawamari or indirectly through the municipality to support three main projects: 1) the agricultural cooperative (which includes a *porqueriza* [pigsty]); 2) a Centro de Capacitación (training center), built on the cooperative land, meant to serve as a school of agriculture and Garifuna "traditional" culture (such as learning about Garifuna farming techniques, organic fertilizers, language, history, knowledge of medicinal plants, and so forth); and 3) the Banco Comunal (community bank) in Limón, where Limoneños can exchange dollars and deposit their money in savings accounts. The money was to be invested in projects that would fund the cooperative, such as selling fish within the municipality. All of these projects were meant to provide alternatives to buying food in the cities, using national (non-Garifuna) banks, and relying solely on the national educational system, where Garifuna receive what Iseri Lidawamari sees as an *educación alienante* (alienating education).

This new focus on community-initiated projects is part of a trend throughout Latin America to modernize the state by decentralizing the government (Willis, Garman, and Haggard 1999). The intention is to give local governments such as municipalities more autonomy to decide how they will spend funds on community-based projects and thus increase participatory democracy. As an indication of the changing politics of the state in favor of decentralization, community-initiated development, and ethnic rights, Iseri Lidawamari was often featured in meetings of national programs as an exemplar of a community-based development initiative. The president of the Fondo Hondureño de Inversion Social (FHIS, of which Nuestras Raíces is a part), the Fiscal de las Etnias, UN representatives, and even the governor of Colón visited Limón and Vallecito to see this innovative project.

And yet, in spite of its differences from the previous administration in the recognition of ethnic and human rights, the Reina administration still basically supported neoliberal economic policies that deviated little from the dominant development model. Often these policies worked against the goals of protecting ethnic rights and achieving sustainable development that other branches of the state had set in place. Even as the state was displaying Iseri Lidawamari as an exemplar of community-based development, it was doing little to stem the tide of land usurpation on the part of Facussé. In fact, Facussé is the author of the Reina administration's Plan Nacional de Desarrollo (National Development Plan), ratified in 1996, which features private investment in agribusiness and large-scale tourism on the Caribbean coast as the main engines of economic growth. This dovetails with the strategy to decentralize the state in the sense that the rationale is to replace government-sponsored and -financed projects with private capital, which most often comes from foreign capitalists.

Thus, ironically, while the move toward decentralization provided an opening for grassroots organizations such as Iseri Lidawamari, it also coincided with neoliberal economic policies and the ideology of the free market by placing more control at the local level and focusing on privatization instead of on state-directed projects. This gave municipalities such as Limón more autonomy, but it also pitted them against private capitalists such as Facussé. Thus, the municipal government (headed by Lombardo) and Iseri Lidawamari were in the contradictory position of being in line with state policies in some respects (as exemplar of a community based development initiative) but against state policy in other respects (as an opponent of large scale agribusiness and tourism).

In Garifuna organizations there was ambivalence within the community about whether the goals of Iseri Lidawamari and Lombardo's administration were in line with the desires of the *pueblo*. On the one hand, there was growing support from New York, where the recuperation of Vallecito became both a Limoneño and a pan-Honduran Garifuna issue. A new Limoneño organization, Lemenigui Limun (The Hope of Limón), began to campaign for support of Iseri Lidawamari throughout the entire New York Garifuna community, including Belizean and Guatemalan Garifuna, arguing that land struggles and the like are issues that affect the whole ethnic group, not just individual villages or even countries, and should be addressed as such. Through the efforts of Lemenigui Limun, Iseri Lidawamari received support from many Garifuna organizations in New York and even organized two benefit concerts with the popular *punta* rock group Garifuna Kids, one in New York City, and one in Vallecito.

On the other hand, many Limoneños in Limón and New York were not happy with Lombardo's administration and the trajectory of Iseri Lidawamari. More and more there was grumbling in the transnational community that Lombardo was devoting too much of his time and energy and municipal funds to Iseri Lidawamari (although he was no longer the president) instead of to infrastructural projects directly within the town of Limón, namely paving the roads and electricity. Though he argued that he and Iseri Lidawamari were working for the *pueblo*, a growing majority of Limoneños began to see the group's strategies as misdirected and out of touch with the wishes of the *pueblo*. Though there was support for the idea of saving the land, few Limoneños were willing to go out to the cooperative to work. By 1996 (my second period of field work in Limón), Iseri Lidawamari had constructed the Centro de Capacitación that, while much more accommodating than the building that had preceded it, was still seen by many Limoneños I talked to as uncomfortable; it had no water tap and was not close to stores and other village conveniences. Also, transportation to Vallecito was still a problem, as it was mainly reached by walking or by private car on roads that are treacherously muddy during the rainy season. Many Limoneños I talked to thought Vallecito was too far from Limón, had too few amenities, and was still a dangerous place to be.

In addition, the prevailing view I heard from young people was that they would prefer to migrate since it was already a tried and true method of earning cash rather than wait around for the cooperative to finally make a profit. Getting an education, migrating, and owning a business were the strategies young people most commonly told me they hoped to use. Few mentioned agriculture. I was also often told that the men in Iseri Lidawamari were failing as good fathers and husbands because their work in Vallecito (and in grassroots activism in general, which requires a lot of voluntary work) was not adequately providing for their families. As one retired merchant marine told me, "You've got to think of your family first, make something of yourself, then worry about others." By the time I returned to Limón in 1999, many of the people I had known as staunch supporters of Iseri Lidawamari in 1993 had migrated to New York after papers filed by a relative (often years before) had finally come through.

While it is easy for members of Iseri Lidawamari to explain the contradictory position of the state as the result of embedded racial and class discrimination, it is more difficult to understand the lack of broad community support from Limoneños for the group's agenda. Members of Iseri Lidawamari interpret this lack of community support as a form of false consciousness, the result of an *educación alienante* that has taught Garifuna the values of market society and the illusion that modernization will benefit them. Thus, one of the main goals of the organization is to serve as the vanguard that will *conscientizar la gente* (raise the consciousness of the people), creating a coherence between what Iseri Lidawamari sees as the practical experience of the Garifuna and a critical consciousness of race and class exploitation. One strategy they use is to bring members of other NGOs (such as CODEH, OFRANEH, and UN entities) to hold meetings and seminars open to the whole municipality (*a cabildo abierto*) to educate villagers about the Honduran Constitution, ILO Convention 169, the Universal Declaration of Human Rights, and other decrees they can use to claim rights to land and cultural autonomy. One problem with these meetings is that often the main attendees are the already converted. In response, Lombardo devised a strategy that required the members of the Teachers' Council and municipal workers to attend a three-day seminar in Limón organized by students from the Universidad Pedagógica on the topic of community development. In this seminar, the university students (who were all ladinos from the capital) discussed alternative notions of development, the rights of ethnic peoples under ILO Convention 169, and the new Ley de Municipalidades (Law of Municipalities) and its role in the decentralization of the state and the promotion of community development.

At the seminar, the teachers were asked to list the development needs of the municipality. Most listed electricity, paved roads, health, and education (in that order); only a few mentioned land. These results coincide with the findings of my surveys among Limoneños in both Limón and New York. Members of Iseri Lidawamari who attended the seminar stated a clear opposition to this vision of development:

> We are not ready for electricity and the [paved] road. Many people think that those will bring development to the community—but it is just going

to be used by Limoneños to watch *novelas* and drink cold water. Only those with capital are really going to benefit from the electricity—they will come in and take advantage of the *pueblo* and the dollars they have. What we need is to produce food first. (Manolo, nonmigrant, member of one of the few households that produces a substantial amount of its food and income from the land and receives no remittances)

The *pueblo* needs to be educated about this new Ley de Municipalidades so they do not make a disaster of it. When the "highway" came, everyone was very enthusiastic, but we did not take advantage of it. Other people have used it to come in and take our lands and now they sell us food. We have struggled for the electricity, but once we get it, it will just raise household costs. So in addition to electricity we must also create a source of income (other than remittances). Before we get electricity and a paved road we need to create the economic conditions to be able to take advantage of them. (Fernando, municipal jefe de catastro [head of the land register], nonmigrant, receives no remittances)

In sum, at the seminar, the university students and Iseri Lidawamari argued that if Limón did not create an autonomous base of development before it built infrastructure such as electricity and a paved road, these amenities would only be luxuries that would increase consumption and could not be sustained locally. Family members in New York would have to continue to pay for them while Limoneños would continue to lack the capital to start their own businesses based on the new infrastructure. While electricity is a common good, it would lead only to individual profit. Iseri Lidawamari members argued that getting electricity and the paved road before the agricultural cooperative could generate funds for its members would only make Limón that much more attractive to outsiders such as Facussé, who see it as an ideal place to take advantage of an economically dependent population.

During the seminar, the teachers did not offer clear refutations of the views Iseri Lidawamari and the Universidad Pedagógica students expressed. Limoneños generally agree that they do not want their municipality completely bought up by foreigners in a way that provides no benefit to them. Also, few object to the idea that some kind of business venture (be it agriculture, industrial, or service) should be established by Garifuna in Limón. However, a few months later when I conducted a round table with the Consejo de Maestros and asked for their definition of development and how best to carry it out, they expressed opinions that were much more in line with the liberalist discourse I heard within the Comité Pro-Electrificación.

It should not frighten us that once we get electricity, foreigners that have economic power will come here. Because if a foreigner who has capital comes here, we can learn something from him, we cannot deny him the opportunity. Because if we look at how San Pedro Sula has progressed, for example, if we do a survey of who are the most powerful people in San Pedro Sula, we are going to see that almost all of them are foreigners. (Rufino, school principal)

I think that the struggle of us Limoneños should be to prepare ourselves [educationally], so that if the capitalists come, we will be able to take the employment they offer us so they do not have to bring in workers from outside the village. (Bernabe, Schoolteacher)

I have heard the comments of various people who live in the U.S. They say they are there for the dollars, not because they want to be there. They are there to improve their lives. They say that if there was electricity in Limón, with the capital that they have, they could easily come to Limón to establish something, some kind of business, but this requires electricity. There is Arnulfo with his restaurant. He has a ton of electrical appliances, but he cannot improve his business because there is no electricity. There is Don Ovidio, he came from New York City and said he was going to set up a butcher shop, but he does not have a freezer. So there is his business but he is not doing all that he wants because the meat will ruin. There are so many Limoneños in the U.S. who are just waiting for the electricity. (Guadelupe, Schoolteacher)

The teachers, like members of Pro-Electrificación, believe in the strategy of individual capitalist investment as a means of bringing jobs and other benefits that will trickle down to residents of the village. They recognize that the Limoneño transmigrants are most strategically placed to take advantage of such infrastructure as the electricity and the paved roads because they are the ones with enough capital to start businesses and have the luxury of owning a car. Since many of those transmigrants are their relatives, they would also reap the benefits of the individual upward mobility earned through the hard work of those who have the initiative to leave and *desarrollarse* (make something of themselves). Consequently, much of the rhetoric of Iseri Lidawamari about the ills of private property, about returning to an existence of living off the land, and so forth does not appeal to them. The reality that most Limoneños have seen is that transmigrants leave the village and come back with capital, education, retirement checks, and the ability to become small-scale capitalists. This contradicts the story Iseri Lidawamari tells of a former communitarian past characterized by cultural autonomy and self-sufficiency; the Garifuna have a long history of involvement in the wage economy and migration (Chapter 2). As Wilk argues in the case of Belize, current consumer behavior of Garifuna cannot be attributed to a "disoriented response to the invasion of a new global mode of production." Participation in the world economy is an integral element of Garifuna history and culture, not a recent phenomenon that has disrupted a "kind of stable and traditionally-bound regime of consumption beloved of anthropologists" (Wilk 1990, 82).

And yet Iseri Lidawamari argues that participation in the world economy and consumption regimes has come at the expense of racial discrimination and class exploitation in multiple national contexts. One of its main arguments, then, is that ethnic solidarity should come before class interests and the desire for individual upward mobility. As one university student put it at the seminar:

> In this confusion in the municipality you all have forgotten that you are an ethnic group, as though this were a municipality like any other. But the ILO Convention 169 says that this territory belongs to the Garifuna. The people who are not interested have forgotten that they are Garifuna, they are trying to think as though they are just a normal citizen of the country that has no ties that unite them. You all do have a tie that unites you. You have a culture and you have a territory that is yours.

Both sides of the struggle over the meaning of community development draw on pieces of Garifuna history and the present reality. The discourses they construct around these images appeal to members of the transnational community at certain historical junctures, mobilizing them to action, but not at others. As Hale (1994b) has argued in the case of the Miskitu, who are similarly caught between national ideologies, international politics, and local ethnic experience, this is not a matter of simple false consciousness but rather one in which people are drawing on historical realities, some of which they highlight and others of which they obscure. The case of the Garifuna is made even more complex by the fact that this construction of history, identity, and class consciousness is being produced within a transnational community.

Conclusion

In much of the literature on new social movements, the concept of critical consciousness is used to refer to moments when social movements articulate ideologies and strategies that are critical of and counter to the dominant ideologies of state apparatuses and the cultural elite. Most often theorists complicate the basic Marxian and Gramscian understanding of critical consciousness centered on class to also include a consideration of other loci of oppression, such as race and gender. Whether considering social movements articulated around race, class, gender, or a combination thereof, theorists tend to maintain the position that spaces of contestation, ambiguity, and reinterpretation emerge out of a lack of coherence between practical experience and dominant ideologies. In the case of ethnic peoples, cultural difference plays an important role as well. As Escobar writes:

> At the bottom of the investigation of alternatives [to development economics] lies the sheer fact of cultural difference. Cultural differences embody possibilities for transforming the politics of representation, that is for transforming social life itself. Out of hybrid or minority cultural situations might emerge other ways of building economies, of dealing with basic needs, of coming together in social groups. The greatest political promise of minority cultures is their potential for resisting and subverting the axiomatics of capitalism and modernity in their hegemonic form. This is why cultural difference is one of the key political facts of our time. (1995, 225; see also 168)

In the case of the Garifuna, experiences of continued poverty brought on by land loss and structural adjustment in Honduras, the deindustrialization of New York, and the peripheralization of the South Bronx have led many members of the transnational community to critique the principle tenets of development economics and discourses of modernity and progress. This critique is based in some ways on a cultural and historical difference from the national societies of the United States and Honduras that include different ways of understanding land ownership, land use, and community relations. Cultural difference and the experience of confronting racial and cultural discrimination in two national contexts has led Garifuna to question whether working within the system through upward class mobility is the only way to overcome social, political, and economic marginalization. The experience of double marginalization has led to a critical consciousness of the racialized nature of the division of labor and promises of national belonging.

But this critical perspective on the international division of labor and the dominant discourse of development is not just a minority or border zone position from below. It is also the product of a long conversation with international ethnic rights and development organizations and even with agents of the state. As Fisher (1993) and Stiefel and Wolfe (1994) demonstrate, notions of sustainable development and other alternatives to development economics that emphasize the importance of local participation in designing and implementing development projects, salvaging indigenous knowledge and forms of organization, and the notion of cultural difference as a basic human right have originated as much from the First World as from the Third. As groups such as Iseri Lidawamari become connected to these transnational networks of aid organizations, NGOs, and so forth, they draw on these global discourses and are simultaneously constructed and constructing themselves into "global structures of common difference, which celebrate particular kinds of diversity while submerging, deflating, or suppressing others" (Wilk 1995,118). Thus, in the cultural history Garifuna activists often present, their ancestors were natural conservators of the land and their communities were reservoirs of precapitalist social relations that were rooted to territory, all of which are familiar tropes in indigenous organizations and international documents such as Convention 169 of the ILO.

Though these characteristics are certainly present within the Garifuna community, they are not necessarily hegemonic because of the group's long history of participation in migratory wage labor and the deep embeddedness of urban and U.S.-bound migration as a means of social mobility and masculine identity. Some members of the transnational community do not agree with Iseri Lidawamari's version of Garifuna history or their vision of future development because they do not resonate with what they see as the Garifuna reality. Their experiences as migrant workers and consumers make obvious the gaps in the ideal of economic self-sufficiency and cultural autonomy. They argue that migration has brought upward mobility and that their primary goal should be integration into national society through education, political participation, and capitalist entrepreneurship. As Glick Schiller and Fouron (2001) argue, access to the benefits of living in a "core" country may squelch much critical discourse about neoliberal legislation and economic reforms among transmigrants. Like transnational corporations, transmigrants are strategically placed to invest in places such as Honduras that offer cheap land and labor. Their nonmigrant family members also benefit from investments that enable them to achieve levels of consumption not available to most working-class Hondurans. To many Garifuna, then, transmigrant and state projects of infrastuctural development, even those that are primarily designed to benefit a transnationally financed tourist industry, appear to offer opportunities, not constraints.

The discourses of development economics and sustainable development both rely on certain (re)constructions of Garifuna history and present reality that in some instances correspond to Garifuna practical experience and in other instances do not. The consciousness of members of the Limoneño transnational community on both sides of the debate concerning community development can be characterized as contradictory. Members of Iseri Lidawamari are critical of the hegemonic premises of development economics and assimilationist national integration but do not critique emergent models of sustainable development that have become dominant within NGO circles and are not always coherent with Garifuna history and practical experience. Limoneños who adhere to the philosophy of the Comité Pro-Electrificación also exhibit a contradictory consciousness in the sense that they are critical of the emergent ideologies of NGOs and international ethnic politics but continue to accept the hegemonic premises upon which the dominant ideologies of modernity and development economics are based.

This case illustrates the argument that while it may be true that disjunctures between practical experience, cultural difference, and hegemonic state ideologies create spaces of contestation, the forms this contestation takes cannot be assumed to be uniform, even within an ethnic group whose members share a cultural difference from the national society. Social actors adopt dominant discourses but also rearticulate them through the lenses of culture, history, practical experience, and consciousness as they participate in and are impacted by the economic, social, and political processes of transnationalism.

6

Black, Indigenous, and Latino

The Politics of Racial and Ethnic Identity in the Garifuna Diaspora

In this book I have discussed several aspects of the Garifuna transnational migration process and the relation of those processes to political consciousness by focusing on the transnational community of Limón–New York City. These processes and political struggles have implications that reach much farther than one transnational community. The transnationalization of matrifocal kinship structures, economic exchanges, class relations, and grassroots organizations affects all Garifuna communities in ways that are broadly similar but also specific to their location within the Garifuna diaspora. Even the struggle around Vallecito is not just a Limoneño issue but rather forms part of a larger social movement that encompasses Garifuna communities from throughout Central America and the United States. Organizations such as Iseri Lidawamari do not act only in the interests of Limoneños, and they do not act alone. They are connected to many organizations that represent the state, international bodies, Garifuna in other Central American nations, and other ethnic and popular groups whose interests intersect with Garifuna interests. To understand current Garifuna social movements, it is important to analyze them not just in the context of transnational migration but also in the context of the diaspora and the global arena of ethnic politics.

This chapter analyzes the politics of race and identity as manifested in Garifuna social movements. Though I continue to focus on the role of Honduran Garifuna transnational communities, I do so by analyzing their particular location within the larger Garifuna diaspora. Analytically speaking, the distinction between diaspora and transnational migration is that diaspora implies the dispersal of a people from a homeland, whether voluntarily or through exile, to multiple nation-states rather than the bilocality generally associated with transnational migration. In addition, in contrast to the more intense contact transmigrants have with their country of origin, diasporic populations often have a more tenuous relationship to the "homeland" or society of origin because there is little hope of return; the relationship is more remote, or even mythical.[1] Following Clifford (1997), I understand diaspora to be both a condition (of dispersal to multiple nation-states) and a form of consciousness. As a form of consciousness, it is the collective identity and politics that emerges from the experience of dispersal and disconnectedness from a source of roots, an identity that draws on myths or memories of the homeland, is supported by the desire for eventual return, and is defined by the relationship of the diasporic population to the homeland. Diasporic identities are defined both against and through notions of territoriality, nation, and indigeneity. Such identities are defined against territoriality in the sense that they privilege the solidarity and identity of the geographically dispersed diaspora over the territorial nationalism of the countries of residence of its members. At the same time, members of a diaspora define their own identity as rooted somewhere, as primordially connected to some particular nation and territory, whether that connection be in the recent or distant past. For the Garifuna, the politics of diaspora are complex because they have several different homelands and different relationships to them—from the mainly symbolic relationships to Africa and St. Vincent to the more immediate relationship to Central America. The specific form the identification with each homeland takes has different political implications. Tracing the processes of this identification and the politics attached to them reveals the intersection of local, national, and transnational processes as well as the complexity of Garifuna identity in diaspora and the global arena of ethnic politics.

MULTIPLE IDENTITIES, MULTIPLE HOMELANDS

One of the most complete manifestations of the identity politics of the Garifuna diaspora I witnessed during my fieldwork period was the Garifuna Bicentennial celebration held in La Ceiba, Honduras, in April 1997. The event was a celebration of the 200th anniversary of the arrival of the Garifuna in Central America and their contributions to that region. The event included dances and other displays of multiculturalism as well as appearances by Honduran president Carlos Roberto Reina, minister of the Fondo Hondureño de Inversion Social (FHIS; Honduran Fund for Social Investment) Manuel Zelaya, and Prime Minister James Mitchell of St. Vincent, all of whom lauded the cultural accomplishments of the Garifuna and promised that the state would give more attention to their communities. At the same time, however, the event was a forum of protest against the racial discrimination, economic exploitation, and political marginalization Garifuna face throughout the diaspora. In addition to the dances and speeches, there were seminars on the topics of racism, women's issues, land struggles, economic development, and Garifuna youth. Each panel had representatives from various locations in the Garifuna diaspora (Belize, Guatemala, Honduras, Nicaragua, St. Vincent, New York, Los Angeles, and New Orleans)

Figure 6.1. Garifuna attending the Bicentennial gather around a statue of Satuye, the Black Carib chief who led the Black Carib of St. Vincent in their fight against the British. (Photo by Catherine England)

who elucidated the particular circumstances of the Garifuna in those locations. Many of the panels also had speakers from other social sectors with whom Garifuna organizations have created alliances: indigenous peoples, Afro Latinos, and African Americans.

Despite this range of participants and activities, the pervading aesthetic of the Bicentennial was clearly an identification with the African diaspora, as evidenced by the abundance of dreadlocks, cowry-shell earrings, Senegalese clothing, and Bob Marley T-shirts. The event was given full coverage by the staff of *Diaspora: A Global Black Magazine;* its featured report consistently praised the Garifuna as having "authentic African culture in its untouched and undiluted form" (John-Sandy 1997, 27) and as an example of cultural, spiritual, and linguistic conservation, an inspiration to all members of the African diaspora looking for their roots in an African homeland. At other times, however, Garifuna leaders referred to the group as "autocthonous" to the Americas (meaning native to a particular geographical region and culturally rooted in that place). They pointed to the long-standing legal definition of the Garifuna as indigenous by Central American states and the current alliance of Garifuna grassroots organizations with indigenous organizations struggling for rights to territory, cultural autonomy, and economic development as ethnic nations within nation-states.

At these moments, leaders stressed the importance of Garifuna villages in a Central American homeland—a territory occupied "ancestrally" that must be defended and maintained as the economic and cultural base of the Garifuna people.

Yet the most insistent claim Garifuna organizers of the event made was that the Garifuna constitute a single ethnic "nation"—unified by their common language, culture, and origins in St. Vincent despite their current geographical dispersion and fragmented citizenships. Leaders referred to St. Vincent as the homeland from which the Garifuna have been exiled and as the territorial base of their culture, race, and identity. This diasporic politics emphasizes the historical reality of displacement, exile, mobility, and multiple communities and the possibility that the Garifuna diaspora may be reunited across nation-state borders as the Garifuna Nation, not through literal reinhabitation of St. Vincent but through consciousness of constituting one people and reconnection to an authentic cultural origin.

What I found fascinating in the Bicentennial was the simultaneous evocation of three homelands—Africa, St. Vincent, and Central America—each of which carried different connotations of racial identity, national identification, and political alliances. In some instances participants identified with blackness as a global racial identity, in others with Afro Latinos as a transnational hemispheric identity, in others as citizens of particular nation-states; in others as ethnic/autocthonous nations within these nation-states, and, most interestingly, as one ethnic nation that transcends the borders of individual nation-states.

In this chapter, I trace the political and ideological contexts within which each of these identities is formulated. I argue that the complexity of this formulation of identities is intimately connected to the negotiation of rights vis-à-vis nation-states, international human rights and development organizations, and ethnic social movements where ideologies of race, ethnicity, nation, and citizenship carry different implications for rights and belonging. I begin with a consideration of the way the Garifuna negotiate the tropes of autochthony and blackness generated by the Honduran nationalist discourse of *mestizaje*. I argue that in struggles around issues of land and cultural autonomy, Garifuna organizations privilege the image of themselves as indigenous/autocthonous to Central America while simultaneously identifying with a global racial identity of blackness. I then turn to a discussion of the experiences of Garifuna transmigrants in New York City, where racial identities of blackness and ethnic identities of culture and nationality lead them to negotiate between seeing themselves as black, Hispanic, and Afro Latino. This is followed by a consideration of how transmigrants express their identity vis-à-vis the Honduran state from abroad.

Such expressions reveal ambivalence toward identifying with Honduran nationalism and citizenship and a simultaneous promotion of Garifuna nationalism in which some Garifuna leaders maintain that their nation-states of origin and citizenship should be irrelevant because they belong to the Garifuna "nation in diaspora" first and foremost. I conclude by considering the ways this may lead to a reconceptualization of our thinking about how identities and political consciousness emerge from global processes, transnational networks, and local contingencies.

CHALLENGING THE MESTIZO STATE: CONTRADICTIONS OF BEING AFRO INDIGENOUS

Two days after the grand finale of the Bicentennial, an editorial appeared in the Honduran newspaper *El Tiempo*, written by Rodolfo Pastor Fasquelle, the Honduran minister of culture. In response to the obvious afrocentricity of the Bicentennial, he wrote:

> [I must] remind the Garifuna where they come from. One cannot invent oneself according to one's whim or preference. To try to pass as African is just as questionable for a Garifuna as it would be for [President] Carlos Roberto Reina to dress like a Lenca or for me to presume to be a Briton or a Pech Indian just because I have these ancestors. Like all other Hondurans, the Garifuna are mestizos, from the Arawak Indian and the African black. To pass as the product of just one of these ancestors is to falsify one's identity, to forget the other complementary component, to betray the ancestors they are trying to erase from their collective historical birth certificate. (April 14, 1997)

In the current moment, when Latin American states are espousing a politics of multiculturalism that celebrates cultural difference, why would the minister of culture be concerned with the growing tendency of Garifuna organizations to identify with blackness while minimizing their indigenous heritage? Why does it matter whether the Garifuna locate their identity in Africa, St. Vincent, or Central America, whether they identify as black, indigenous, or mestizo? What are the political stakes involved in this excavation of history and construction of identity for Garifuna social movements?

To answer these questions it must first be understood that at least since the 1930s, the Honduran state has promoted the idea that Honduras is primarily a mestizo nation with little racial and cultural difference and consequently, so the logic goes, no racial discrimination. In a direct challenge to this ideology of racial harmony, however, both black and indigenous organizations in Honduras have become increasingly vocal in arguing that they have been the victims of just such racial discrimination for 500 years. Black and indigenous organizations are now demanding the redress of this situation through bilingual education, economic opportunities, political representation, the protection of basic human rights, and the legal protection and titling of village lands. The most dramatic display of this activism was a series of marches on the capital during which indigenous and black organizations (sometimes jointly and sometimes separately) mobilized busloads of protesters from their villages, camped for days in the central plaza, burned effigies of Columbus, and carried out religious rituals for the ancestors in front of the presidential palace (*La Prensa* October 12, 1996). This activism and these spectacles of cultural difference have brought the issues of racial discrimination and multiculturalism to the forefront of national debates, challenging the formerly hegemonic elite, academic, and state ideology that Honduras is a homogenous mestizo nation in which race is not an issue of social concern. Pressured by indigenous and black activism from below and by an international political arena from above that is increasingly sympathetic to the plight of indigenous and tribal peoples in the world, the Honduran state has responded with a series of gestures toward recognizing Honduras as a multiethnic nation and toward protecting the economic, cultural, and human rights of ethnic peoples.

Yet state policies around issues of economic development, multiculturalism, and ethnic rights are not always coherent, either with each other or with those of the international arena. Even as agents of the state pass laws that nominally protect the land and rights of indigenous peoples and blacks, they support large-scale development efforts such as those of the tourist industry that threaten those same lands and rights. And even as they promote a politics of recognizing cultural diversity, they often do so more in the spirit of protecting the "national heritage" rather than truly challenging the premises of *mestizaje*. As the minister of culture's comments illustrate, the state is willing to listen to the demands of indigenous peoples and blacks only to a certain extent. For the Garifuna, the historically ambivalent relationship of blackness to Honduran nationalism is particularly relevant for revealing where those boundaries lie.

In this section I show that though Garifuna organizations are joined in the struggle against Honduran mestizo nationalism with indigenous peoples, they also face unique contradictions as blacks. I do this through an analysis of how the Honduran nationalist ideology of *mestizaje* has constructed the Garifuna as both black and "autocthonous" and how Garifuna organizations negotiate those identities in their political struggles for land and state recognition of multiculturalism.

Blackness, Indigenismo, and Mestizaje

As it is in other Latin American countries, *mestizaje* is the dominant nationalist ideology in Honduras, promoted at the turn of the twentieth century by elites who were embroiled in the process of nation-building. The mestizo is posited as the result of the "natural" miscegenation of the three races (European, Indian, and African) during the colonial period, which led to the formation of a racially and culturally homogeneous nation long before the formation of the Honduran state. Though this *mestizaje* includes Africans as contributors to the racial makeup of the population, the ideological place of "blackness" and "indianness" within this nationalist ideology is different because of hegemonic European notions of race, nation, and modernity.

From the period of colonization, Latin American elites saw Indians and Africans as embodying savagery and lack of civilization, living in a permanent state of backwardness as opposed to the supposedly rational, civilized, progressive European. These characteristics were believed to be connected to blood, inherited and unchangeable except through a miscegenation that would lead to the gradual whitening of the population (de la Cadena 2000; Skidmore 1995; Smith 1997; Wade 1993; Whitten and Torres 1998; Williams 1991). In the wake of debates about the effects of this racial diversity on national identity, Latin American elites initially called for white immigration to improve the nation with the blood of a people they accepted as naturally inclined toward modernity and progress. This blatant mimicry of Anglo ideologies of racial superiority was contested in a postcolonial era of nation formation (first half of the 20th century)based on the growing belief among Latin Americans (and other postcolonials) that to be legitimate, each nation-state should arise from a primordial cultural and racial identity that corresponded to the territory of the state (Chatterjee 1986; Smith 1986). As Wade has argued, the challenge for Latin American elites was how to be considered modern within a international hierarchy of nations that saw modernity as innately linked to European blood and culture and at the same time have an autocthonous identity that arose from the national territory itself. This modernist dilemma was resolved in many Latin American nations by promoting the idea of *mestizaje*—a racial and cultural identity that is uniquely Latin American. As Wade points out, although "blacks and especially Indians were romanticized as part of a more or less glorious past," this ideology held little promise for these two groups because "the future held . . . paternalistic guidance toward integration, which also ideally meant more race mixture and perhaps the eventual erasure of blackness and indianness from the nation" (Wade 1993, 11).

Wade also points out that even though both Africans and Indians are accorded a place in *mestizaje*, indigenous identity is usually privileged as the primary emblem of the roots of national identity. This is useful to nation-building because it unites the autocthony of the Indian (linking the nation to the national territory) with the culture of the European (linking the state to the culture of western civilization and modernity). Blacks were more problematic as national symbols because at the time (early part of 1900s) they were not seen to represent modernity or autocthony and they have no pre-Columbian civilization in the Americas to call upon as symbols of a glorious past. Latin American states often end up with a primarily "indo-hispanic" *mestizaje* that privileges the Indian as the roots of the nation and either minimizes blackness (as in Colombia; see Wade 1993) or erases it completely (as in Mexico; see Knight 1990).[2]

Dario Euraque (1998) argues that in Honduras, government efforts to present the population as a homogenous mestizo nation with little racial and cultural diversity began in the late 1920s and early 1930s in the context of the growing economic and political power of the Anglo-dominated multinational fruit companies. He shows that the 1910 national census included a wide range of racialized categories. According to this census, the Honduran population consisted of 61.1 percent ladinos (originally understood as anyone of any racial mixture who was acculturated to Spanish language and culture), 16.2 percent *indios* (indigenous peoples), 9.6 percent *mestizos* (those with indigenous and Spanish progenitors), 5.0 percent *blancos* (those with white and Spanish progenitors), 3.4 percent *negros* (blacks), 3.3 percent *mulatos* (those with black and white progenitors), and 1.3 percent *amarillos* (Asians). This list reflects both the racial diversity inherited from the colonial period and the growing number of immigrants attracted to the North Coast by employment and entrepreneurial opportunities in the enclaves of the fruit companies (Euraque 1998). In the 1920s this racial diversity became an issue of national debate. Both ladino workers and the ladino and white elite called for restrictions on the further immigration of blacks, "coolies," and even Arab Palestinians. The demands were made in the name of an emergent nationalism that conflated mestizo racial and cultural identity with the national identity and the national "body" whose purity was being threatened by nonmestizo (especially black) immigrants (Argueta 1992; Posas 1981b). As evidence of the fact that mestizo nationalism was also being promoted by the state, Euraque shows that the 1930 census was "sanitized" by removing the mixed categories of ladino and *mulato* and collapsing them into the category of mestizo. This achieved the goal of making mestizos the majority of the population and justifying the characterization of Honduras as a primarily mestizo nation. Since mestizos were still understood to be the products of indigenous and Spanish descent, that identity created the cultural space for the disavowal of blackness as an element of the newly declared mestizo population.[3] The category *indígena* remained in the 1930 census as the main signifier of racial difference and the symbol of the national past, and all other races were either ignored or minimized.

This "indo-hispanic *mestizaje*" (Euraque 1998) was clearly expressed by Dr. Jesus Aguilar Paz—a member of the National Congress during the 1920s and an important intellectual of nation-building. In the following quote he represents indigenous peoples and Spaniards as the two columns of Honduran national identity, leaving no space for the African element.

> In primitive history there are hidden mental treasures, that today we should seek like diamonds lost among the lethargic debris of such an illustrious ancestry. Such an indigenous element, that is encompassed within an interrogation as yet not answered by ethnologists, is the *predominant element of the constitution of the Honduran fatherland* [original emphasis]. On the other hand, the Spanish blood, valiant and generous, that has written immortal, glorious, and inimitable pages in world culture *constitutes the other column* [original emphasis] on which rests, in Honduras and in the majority of Hispanic-American countries, the structure of the nation. (quoted in Lang 1951, 210)

Other formulations of *mestizaje* include Africans in the racial makeup of the population. These comments written by a historian of the Honduran nation are typical of this brand of *mestizaje*:

> The Honduran is, ethnically, the result of a total and complete fusion of the three races: Spanish, autocthonous, and African, who have populated the territory of Honduras, which has contributed to giving the Honduran a great racial and spiritual homogeneity, and, as a consequence, has favored national integration, without there being, as in other iberoamerican countries, an "Indian problem," that is to say, the assimilation of the autocthonous race. [The results of *mestizaje* have been] that race has stopped being a differential factor not only in the political arena, but also in the economic arena and also in the social arena such that the pigmentation of the skin as a means of differentiation is something totally alien to the Honduran mentality. (Otero 1963, 21–22)

In this instance, the term mestizo can simply mean "mixed," a racial category that may or may not include blacks. The implication is that no matter what the particular mix, race is not an issue in Honduras because everyone is mestizo. Though this may seem to be evidence of racial democracy because it accepts the confluence of all races, it actually reinforces intolerance of cultural and racial difference by implying that the existence of "pure" ethnic groups would "naturally" lead to conflict. In this ideology, unity of the nation can be achieved only through homogeneity (see Barahona 1991, 64). The important point is that the inclusion of blacks in Honduran national identity generally refers to those who assimilated to the ladino population during the colonial period, not to those who continue to identify with blackness. African blood may be recognized as flowing in the veins of Hondurans, but blackness (as in black culture, black music, and affinity with Africa) has not been celebrated as part of the national identity.

Being Black, Ethnic, and Autocthonous

The primary representation of Honduras as an indo-hispanic nation has had consequences for the current mobilization of indigenous and black organizations. Any cultural and racial difference from the mestizo national subject (that is, any ethnic group) has come to be conflated with the notion of autocthony (that is, a people naturally rooted in Honduras). In other words, ethnicity is hegemonically understood as more than racial, cultural, and linguistic difference from the mestizo national subject; it also carries the connotations of a population that has a primordial link to the territory of the nation, occupying land "ancestrally" (that is, continuously from the precolonial era to the present). The terms "pueblos autóctonos" (autocthonous peoples) and "pueblos étnicos" (ethnic peoples) are used synonymously in Honduras (cf. Wade 1995 on similarities in Colombia). Within this hegemonic construction of ethnicity, the Garifuna are legally and anthropologically defined as a pueblo autóctono, though their blackness is generally noted as making them an exceptional kind of pueblo autóctono who can claim indigenous heritage but simultaneously identify as black (Cruz 1984; Rivas 1993).

The ability of Garifuna to claim autochthonous status has important implications in the current era of ethnic mobilization, when Latin American states are being pushed from above and below to confer special rights on indigenous peoples with primordial ties to the national territory and cultural and racial difference that seriously challenge assimilationist models of mestizaje (Escobar and Alvarez 1992; Varese 1994). These recent mobilizations are different from previous peasant and urban movements because instead of legitimating their claims to these rights as citizens of the state, they legitimate their claims through their difference from the nation-state. In other words, indigenous and ethnic peoples claim their rights to land through their "primordial" ties to that territory prior to the existence of the state; they claim their rights to cultural sovereignty and bilingual education due to their cultural difference from the national subject; and they claim their rights to economic sufficiency, health care, and other social benefits as universal human rights rather than simply as the rights of citizens of a particular nation-state. These ethnic movements challenge the assumption that the nation-state should serve as the primary locus of identity and rights and promote alternative forms of community within states and across national borders (see Hale 1994b; Sawyer 2004; Stavenhagen 1992; Warren 1998).

This recognition of "ethnic rights" has been legitimized in the international arena through NGOs, international organizations, and international accords that are pressuring nation-states to protect the territory and human rights of indigenous and ethnic populations (Mato 1996; Rogers 1996). Though these movements have formed in the name of *lo indígena, negro, y popular*, indigenous identity has had the most political salience thus far because of the primordial link of indigenous peoples to the Americas as an autocthonous population.

For example, the beneficiaries of the ILO's Convention (No. 169) Concerning Indigenous and Tribal Peoples are "tribal peoples" and "peoples regarded as indigenous on account of their descent from the populations which inhabited the country. . . at the time of the conquest or colonisation or the establishment of present state boundaries and who . . . retain some or all of their own social, economic, cultural, and political institutions" and self-identify "as indigenous or tribal" (ILO 1996, 325). Here cultural conservation and consciousness of cultural difference are criteria for special rights, coupled with the notion that this difference is linked to geographical separation in a territory occupied ancestrally or before colonization. This formulation of the cultural difference and autonomous rights of indigenous peoples challenges state ideologies that assume an undifferentiated citizenship and homogeneous nation within state borders. At the same time, the convention uses the same Euro-modern discourse of the "nation" in defining who counts as indigenous and tribal—peoples with discrete bounded cultures that are rooted to the land. In the ideologies of both state nationalism and autocthony, culture, people, and land are presented as one inherently connected unit (cf. Malkki 1992).

This image of autocthony is especially salient in debates concerning land. Article 13 of ILO Convention 169 states that indigenous and tribal lands must be understood as territories, a notion that taps into an acceptance of the collective spiritual relationship of a people to its land, a contrast to individualist capitalist models of land ownership and production.

> 1. In applying the provisions of this Part of the Convention governments shall respect the special importance for the cultures and spiritual values of the peoples concerned of their relationship with the lands or

territories, or both as applicable, which they occupy or otherwise use, and in particular the collective aspects of this relationship.

2. The use of the term "lands" in Articles 15 and 16 shall include the concept of territories, which covers the total environment of the areas which the peoples concerned occupy or otherwise use.

Article 14

1. The rights of ownership and possession of the peoples concerned over lands which they traditionally occupy shall be recognized. In addition, measures shall be taken in appropriate cases to safeguard the right of the peoples concerned to use lands not exclusively occupied by them, but to which they have traditionally had access for their subsistence and traditional activities. Particular attention shall be paid to the situation of nomadic peoples and shifting cultivators in this respect.

2. Governments shall take steps as necessary to identify the lands which the peoples concerned traditionally occupy, and to guarantee effective protection of their rights of ownership and possession.

3. Adequate procedures shall be established within the national legal system to resolve land claims by the peoples concerned. (ILO 1996, 328)

This philosophy of the relationship of ethnic peoples to the land is supported by programs such as Rescate Cultural Ecológico that represent indigenous and ethnic peoples as naturally rooted to the land and as natural conservators of the local resources. Here is that group's expression of its identity in a public letter to the president of Honduras that was signed by thirty-six Garifuna leaders in 1995:

Throughout many centuries, we ethnic autocthonous peoples have lived in our communities in permanent harmony with each other, with those who visit us, and with nature; maintaining the ecological equilibrium that our mother nature wisely gave us, and for which our natural resources have awakened the greed of cattle ranchers, the military, and economically powerful people, who, using all kinds of deceit are trying to remove us from the lands that historically and legally belong to us.

Throughout the 1990s, Garifuna grassroots organizations in Honduras stressed this trope of the autocthonous, timeless culture and primordial link to the land, consciously counterpoising this identity to the image of the culturally and racially mixed, mobile, and *desarraigado* (rootless) ladino population that had been settling around Garifuna villages:

The problem with ladinos is that you can't trust them, because they don't love the land, they don't have any roots. They sell their own land and then they come here to the North Coast and take our land and sell it to just anybody. If you ask a ladino where they're from, they can't even tell you because they move around so much. They are rootless so they don't care about *la madre tierra* [mother earth]. (Vice President of Iseri Lidawamari at a seminar in Tegucigalpa on indigenous rights violations sponsored by CAHDEA, October 1993)

Though Garifuna organizations often present themselves using the language of autocthony and claim rights that are similar to those claimed by indigenous peoples, Garifuna organizations rarely claim to be indigenous, even though their history could allow them that claim. For example, on October 12, 1993, the Organización de Desarrollo Etnico Comunitario (ODECO) organized a protest march in La Ceiba to unite Garifuna, indigenous, and popular groups to demand that ILO Convention 169 be ratified and protest the celebration of the Quincentenary. A flyer that lists the demands of the march reveals the multiple ways ethnic terminology is used to connote both political affiliation and racial difference between indigenous peoples and blacks on the one hand and racial affiliation and cultural difference between Garifuna and other blacks on the other. Note that when it refers to primordial rights to land, the flyer specifies Garifuna; however, when it refers to multicultural education, it uses the more inclusive word "*negros.*"

After five centuries we continue without social, political, or economic justice. October 12, 1492–October 12, 1993. The injustice continues . . . and the struggle continues.

In the International Year of Indigenous Peoples. To the government of the republic we demand:

1) The ratification and implementation of the *Convention 169* of the ILO, for the rights of indigenous peoples [*indígenas*] and tribal peoples [*tribales*].
2) The return of all the lands that have been plundered from the Indians [*indios*] and Garifunas of Honduras, because they are the legitimate owners.
3) The effective reform of Article 6 of the Constitution of the Republic, so that the languages of the ethnic groups (*pueblos étnicos*) be considered official languages.

4) Our participatory representation in the different powers of the state.

5) That the human, cultural, historical, and linguistic values of the Indians (*indios*) and blacks (*negros*) be inserted into the plans of national education.

6) Modification of the economic measures that sharpen the poverty of the popular sectors.

The national-level campaign on the part of Garifuna and indigenous organizations did lead to the ratification of ILO Convention 169 as well as the implementation of such programs as Nuestras Raíces, which channel international funding into ethnic communities for small development projects. These efforts have reinforced the political salience of being "indigenous" or "tribal" or "autocthonous" as defined in Convention 169. For example, in the opening address of a 1996 ceremony to celebrate the accomplishments of Nuestras Raíces attended by leaders from all of the ethnic groups and President Reina, the administrator of the program, Manuel Zelaya, justified it in the following way:

> Here we encounter many indigenous groups, Miskitu, Garifuna, English-speaking Natives[4]—the autocthonous peoples of Honduras. Here we are gathered for the first time in history with precise instructions from this administration because we know that you represent the most genuine and authentic element of our nationality because your communities and your ancestors were the first inhabitants of this continent. The highest levels of illiteracy, lack of income, lack of access to markets and production are all common factors facing the autocthonous peoples. These peoples by right of possession are historically the owners of the best of the nation, yet today they are the poorest peoples in the country. If any people have rights in this country, here they are this morning. (Manuel Zelaya 1996)

Though Zelaya referred to Garifuna as part of "our roots" in his speech, the efforts to fit them within this indigenous/autocthonous discourse has sometimes been contested. Garifuna claims to territory have been challenged because they are not actually indigenous to Honduras. In response to such challenges, the definition of indigenous has been expanded to include populations that were present before the founding of an independent state. But this logic gives the Garifuna claims that they are equal to the ladinos and does not give them the status of a people that existed on the land prior to colonization. As Attorney General of Ethnic Peoples Eduardo Villanueva told me in an interview:

> It doesn't seem just to me to say that blacks are not indigenous because their primordial antecedents are in Africa. Indigenous is that which is

original to this country, and the origins of this country are when it gained independence and set up its actual borders. So the Convention 169 favors those peoples who were already here before the formation of the state. In 1821 the Garifuna had already been here for many years. They came against their will, uprooted from their original country. This is a historical fact, and we cannot change that. But when I say indigenous I mean to include the Garifuna in the concept because they were here when the state was organized. So even the Garifuna and black Creoles are just as Honduran as any ladino. (1996, my translation)

This kind of explanation reflects how "ethnic" (understood as people who are culturally and racially different from ladinos) and "indigenous" (understood as people who were the original inhabitants of the Americas) are conflated. But having existed on the margins of mestizo society" and having "conserved their own social, economic, cultural, and political institutions, or part of them" (as outlined in Convention 169) is also the basis for a set of special rights. Both representatives of the state (Villanueva and Zelaya) are simultaneously claiming the rights of ethnic peoples based on their sameness with other Hondurans (because they are citizens and part of the Honduran national identity) and based on their difference from other Hondurans (as an ethnic group that is marginalized by ladino society). This newer vision of Honduran national identity that the state refers to as multicultural recognizes difference but contains this difference within the bounds of Honduran nationalism. Garifuna, and even black creoles, are recognized in this new state discourse of multiculturalism as autocthonous based on their ties to the land and territory of Honduras, not on a racial or cultural identity in St. Vincent or Africa. Blacks are recognized as a part of the national society, but blackness itself is still seen as emanating from elsewhere. The state does not celebrate blackness as part of the national identity unless it can be subsumed under the category of mestizo (*todos somos mestizos* [we are all mixed], *todos tenemos un poco de sangre africana* [we all have a little African blood]) or the category of autocthonous.

In the 1990s, Garifuna organizations in Honduras used the language of autoctony and allied themselves with indigenous groups, but an identification with blackness has also always been part of their culture. In daily practice, the Garifuna mainly self-identify as blacks and have adopted a self-conscious African American aesthetic in their style of dress and music, challenging common assumptions in Honduras about what an autocthonous population that is conserving its native culture should look like. In fact the seeds of Garifuna activism in Honduras can be found as early as 1958, when a group of Garifuna workers active in the North Coast unions founded La Sociedad Cultural Abraham Lincoln in La Ceiba to defend the rights of students and workers who felt they had been the victims of racial discrimination. Some of the prominent members of La Sociedad Lincoln, including Dr. Alfonso Lacayo, founded La Organización Fraternal Negra Hondureña (OFRANEH) in the 1970s, an organization that is still active in urban and rural Garifuna communities. Both La Sociedad Lincoln and OFRANEH articulated Garifuna identity in terms of being black and were influenced by the U.S. civil rights movement and later African American struggle (Centeno Garcia 1997). This is probably because many Garifuna merchant marines in the 1950s and 1960s were based in U.S. southern ports such as New Orleans and Mobile, Alabama, where they experienced segregation and the milieu of the civil rights movement. Later, many of these Garifuna settled in Harlem in the 1970s during the time of Malcolm X and the Black Panthers. Most of the older Limoneño migrants and merchant marines I interviewed said they never were directly involved in these struggles, but information about the racism of the United States and the African American struggle spread to Honduras.

This political and cultural identification with blackness has come to the fore recently with the formation of the Central American Black Organization (CABO), founded in 1995 to unite Garifuna and English-speaking blacks throughout Central America, and the Coordinadora Nacional de Organizaciones Negras en Honduras (National Coordinator of Black Organizations in Honduras), founded in 1996 to unite Garifuna and black creole organizations in Honduras. These organizations foreground their identity with the larger African diaspora and the racial identity of blackness and emphasize the historical and ideological particularities of Afro Central Americans living in mestizo nation-states, where they have either been "statistically invisible" or seen as outside the "nation" (cf. Conniff 1985; Gordon 1998; Purcell 1993). In the Declaration of Dangriga, the founders of CABO stated their reasons for forming the organization:

First: We Central American blacks have a history whose origins are based on common circumstances.

Second: We confront similar political, socioeconomic, and cultural problems.

Third: Territorial borders have impeded permanent communication and relations between the black Communities of the Central American region.

Fourth: The lack of organization has limited the development and representative participation of the black community in the different countries of Central America.

Fifth: After 500 years, it is necessary to put the process of unification and organization of the Central American black community into action with the purpose of instigating its integral development on the road to justice and participatory democracy. (August 27, 1995 in author's possession)

This declaration was written after a meeting held by Central American Black leaders on August 25–27 in Dangriga, Belize. Addressed to the presidents of Panama, Nicaragua, Honduras, Costa Rica, and Belize, it announced the founding and goals of the organization. As of this writing, the organization still exists and holds annual meetings in one of these Central American countries each year.

Though these organizations privilege blackness as their main racial and political affiliation, the meaning of blackness and its relation to the national society is not the same in each country. Gordon and Hooker's (2004) survey of black Central American organizations found that the kinds of demands different organizations make is the result of the particular historical formation of the group, the way it articulates its identity vis-à-vis the national society, and whether it is recognized as having collective rights parallel to those of indigenous groups. There are essentially three types of black Central Americans—those who are the descendents of former slaves brought to the colonies, the descendents of West Indians brought to Central America to work on the banana plantations and the Panama Canal, and people such as the Garifuna who can be classified as maroons. The first group tends to be heavily integrated into mestizo society and has little in the way of a collective identity. The second group tends to be geographically concentrated, speak English, and consider themselves to be racially and culturally distinct from the mestizo, but their organizations tend to frame their struggle in terms of increasing rights to participation and integration into national society as individual citizens, not as collectivities.

What Gordon and Hooker find interesting is that it is mainly the last category of black Central Americans, maroons, who have attempted to use legislation such as the ILO Convention 169 to claim rights to land and cultural autonomy as a people. Garifuna are often distinguished from other blacks as being "authentic," as having maintained an "autocthonous culture" (in the sense of being unassimilated) as opposed to having an "acquired culture" (that is, assimilated to a European culture). They have been uprooted from Africa and displaced from St. Vincent, but they have still conserved an "ancestral culture" in ways other blacks have not. For example, the director of the Ballet Folklorico Nacional Garifuna (also known as the Grupo Afro Hondureño) explained that the dance troupe has been internationally recognized as representing the only authentic African culture in the Americas: "In many countries we have been told that in all of Latin America, among all other blacks, only the Garifuna have maintained their own language; and we have been told that we are good because we have maintained our own culture" (quoted in Lopez Garcia 1993). Even in Belize, a country that has predominantly seen itself as black and identifies with the English-speaking Caribbean (more than with Central America), the Garifuna differentiate themselves from the black Creole majority as an autocthonous group and are allied with Mayan organizations in the Belizean National Indigenous Peoples Council (BENIC) in struggles over land and bilingual education vis-à-vis the Belizean state.[5] In Central America, the careful use of the term "autocthonous" as opposed to the term "indigenous"—with its connotations of biological sameness—allows Garifuna to make primordial claims parallel to indigenous groups while maintaining a racial distinction as black. The use of the term "autocthonous" also allows Garifuna to simultaneously show racial affiliation with and cultural difference from other blacks. This framing of identities has both bolstered and been bolstered by legislation that recognizes blacks as having the same set of collective rights as indigenous peoples in countries where Garifuna are found, namely Honduras, Guatemala, and Nicaragua. Panama, Costa Rica, and El Salvador do not have similar legislation (Gordon and Hooker 2004).

CONTRADICTIONS OF BEING AFRO HISPANIC IN NEW YORK CITY

We are sitting in a circle in the home of the president of Unificación Cultural Garifuna (UNCUGA; Garifuna Cultural Unification), an organization founded in 1991 in New York City with the goal of uniting Garifuna of all nation-states to preserve the culture and language through educational seminars, conferences, and the building of cultural centers. Even though it is snowing outside, it feels very warm with all the people crowded into the small living room of this South Bronx apartment. A man in the corner is getting the video camera ready, while the smells of *hudutu* (coconut milk–fish soup) waft in from the kitchen. We are here to meet with representatives from the World Council of Indigenous People, a pan-American indigenous organization, who have driven down from their main office in Toronto, Canada.

The session officially begins with a discussion of the links the Garifuna have with indigenous peoples by virtue of their formation on St. Vincent to their present struggles for land and cultural respect in their respective nation-states. There is a long discussion of the commonalties of their problems, the strategies they have used, the utility of the United Nations in pressuring national governments to respect international accords on the rights of indigenous peoples, and the links these two organizations could make in the future. One of the representatives of the World Council says that it is important to get information about Garifuna out to the public because when he mentions them people often say, "Oh, they're just blacks."

*   *   *

In this meeting, "getting the information out about Garifuna" meant that participants needed to emphasize their links to indigenous peoples through their history on St. Vincent in order to claim the same category of rights on the international level that indigenous peoples do. Otherwise, they could be construed as having no roots in the Americas, no primordial ties to the land, and no culture that has been conserved. In other words, they would be seen as interlopers on the continent just like the Europeans and their acculturated descendants, thereby disqualifying them from special legislation such as ILO Convention 169.

Later, the president of UNCUGA told me that he was uncomfortable with this characterization of them as indigenous. He said that he could recognize a common context of struggle, but indigenous was not their identity—they are black. Indeed, in New York City, the Garifuna encounter a different set of racial categories and the discourse of indigenous/autocthonous identity used by some Garifuna grassroots organizations in Central America has little resonance. In New York City, they experience the inner-city environment of the Bronx and Harlem, where they live in housing projects and large apartment buildings, work as porters and home attendants, and send their children to inner-city schools with their primarily African American, West Indian, Puerto Rican, and Dominican neighbors. This is not the experience of an isolated rural population close to *la madre tierra* but rather an urban culture of the working poor in a global city. Here Garifuna are a small group that few New Yorkers had even heard of until they made the news with such events as Hurricane Mitch or the Happy Land tragedy, a 1990 fire in a South Bronx social club that killed eighty-seven people, the majority of whom were Honduran Garifuna (Magnuson 1990). Garifuna have found themselves propelled into larger categories that are already familiar in the New York City ethnic mosaic: African American, Hispanic, or West Indian. While Garifuna in New York are still in dialogue with Honduran ideologies of race and nation, they also have the added complexity of being in dialogue with U.S. notions of race and nation. Whereas in Honduras they slip in and out of the categories of black and autocthonous, in the United States they negotiate between the categories of black and Hispanic.

Race and Ethnicity in the United States

Garifuna migration to the United States after 1965 forms part of a larger trend of increased migration from Latin America, the Caribbean, and Asia that began when the national origins quota system ended. This new wave of nonwhite immigrants in many ways contributed to changing conceptions of race, ethnicity, and nationalism in the United States. Before 1965, it was generally assumed that immigrants to the United States had followed a linear movement from one country to another, that they would eventually integrate into the host society, and that they would convert their national identity into an "ethnic" identity that is merely one of the many flavors in the U.S. multicultural "melting pot." Beginning in the 1960s, some researchers began to argue that this narrative of assimilation is not constant for all immigrant groups (Dominguez 1975; Fitzpatrick 1971; Glazer and Moynihan 1963; Laguerre 1984; Watson 1977). Caribbean, Hispanic, and Asian immigrants were not assimilating as the European immigrants had before them. Irish, Italian, Jewish and Eastern European immigrants to the United States had gone through phases of being racialized as nonwhite (or "white but not quite"), but they were eventually converted into "white ethnicities" and then into the much more diluted notion of being racially white but with some other national "heritage" (Brodkin 2000; Reimers 1987). For immigrants such as Afro Cubans, West Indians, and Haitians, on the other hand, assimilating into the U.S. race system means being assimilated as Hispanics or African Americans, racial categories with less status than that of white (Dominguez 1975). In other words, though immigrants can certainly assimilate to U.S. society, they assimilate to a peculiarly North American racialized hierarchy. Black West Indian and African immigrants especially resist assimilation on racial terms by continuing to identify with their "national" identity in order to be considered "ethnic" blacks, a step up from being African American (Kasinitz 1992; Vickerman 1999; Waters 1999).

At the same time, however, many black immigrants realize that no matter what their culturally defined "ethnicity" is, in the United States they are still racialized as black. Coming from Latin American and Caribbean race systems where racial categories are much more fluid and complexly articulated with class, many of these immigrants are shocked to find themselves racialized as nonwhite regardless of their skin color, class, or self-identification in the home country. This often leads to transformations in their own understandings of race and consciousness of racism that they carry back to the home country, contributing to changing conceptions of race there (Sutton and Makiesky-Barrow 1987). Although black immigrants may identify with a nation-based ethnicity, many also identify with the global racial category of blackness and the African diaspora, even if this identification is more on the level of politics, aesthetics, and music and less on the level of day-to-day interaction with African Americans.

For Spanish-speaking Latin Americans, this experience of racialization is slightly different from that of West Indians since the category "Hispanic" is based more on language and culture than on race. Because Hispanics can be of any "race" (understood as color), the ways they are integrated into U.S. society vary, and some are eventually "whitened" while others are "blackened" (Rodriguez 2000). These terms reflect not just skin pigmentation but also evaluations of what Ong calls "cultural citizenship," which she defines as "the cultural practices and beliefs produced out of negotiating the often ambivalent and contested relations with the state and hegemonic forms that establish belonging within a national population and territory" (Ong 1996, 738). In the United States, she argues, cultural citizenship is based on an evaluation of how closely a population approximates the white ideal of personhood. So, for example, although Puerto Ricans range in skin color (or "race"), they tend to be "blackened" in New York due to their general poverty and reputation for depending on welfare and involvement in drug dealing (Bourgois 1995). In contrast, Cubans in Miami tend to be "whitened" due to their more established position within the ranks of businessowners, bankers, and so forth (Stepick 1993). Like *mestizaje*, U.S. racial categories slip between notions of biology (expressed in terms of skin color) and notions of culture (expressed in terms of national origin or ethnic group).

Being Black, Hispanic, and Garifuna

The ambiguity of how Garifuna fit themselves into the "big five" pre-established U.S. racial/ethnic categories became apparent to me when I conducted surveys among Limeños in New York City. Forty-one percent said that they mark the category "Afro American/black" on official forms, while 38 percent said they mark "Hispanic." Sixteen percent said that they mark "Other" and write in "Garifuna," and 5 percent said they mark "Other" and write in "Afro Hispanic." Their uncertainty whether to classify themselves as Afro American or Hispanic seemed to revolve around the slipperiness of U.S. notions of race versus ethnicity. Those who identified themselves as African American often articulated it in the language of race—"We are black no matter what language we speak." Those who claimed Hispanic identity justified the choice as a matter of language, culture, and national origin—"African American is just for those blacks who are from here; we are from Honduras, so we are Hispanic." Those who wrote in "Garifuna" also justified it as a matter of language, culture, and origin but pointed to a Garifuna ethnic nationalist identity instead of a country of origin.

What is certain is that even those who like to think of themselves as Hispanics know that on the streets they are identified as blacks. Many Limoneños said that as long as they do not say anything, everyone assumes that they are African Americans. One woman, for example, said that when she walks into a store the white workers tense up just as they would for an African American. It is only when people hear them speaking Spanish or Garifuna that they take another look; in many cases, when they see that they are not "just blacks," they treat them with much more respect. A common refrain I heard was that whites discriminate against the Garifuna for being black, not for being Garifuna (*por ser negro, no por ser Garifuna*).

As is the case in Honduras, Garifuna organizations in New York City identify strongly with the African American political struggle against discrimination and poverty. The president of UNCUGA told me that when he arrived in New York City in 1973, he knew nothing about black history, black leaders, or black political movements. He grew up in a Honduran city, where he had been taught nothing about the African diaspora or even Garifuna history. He came to a consciousness of all of that in New York City, where he was inspired by African American leaders and authors. Like many other longtime Garifuna New York residents I interviewed who were educated professionals who speak fluent English, this man said his growing consciousness of the African American struggle provided both a basis of identification with the racial identity of blackness and a consciousness of racial discrimination in Honduras, where the ideology of *mestizaje* had taught him that such discrimination did not exist.

Yet even as Garifuna aesthetically and politically identify with "blackness," racial affiliation and cultural difference collide to create an uneasy relationship between Garifuna and African Americans. Many of those who told me that they consider themselves racially "black" simultaneously told me that they have little relations with African Americans because they are dangerous and have a bad influence on the youth.

> Franky and Roy were here today recounting all the run-ins they've had with African Americans since they've been living here in Harlem. It seems Franky was mugged on his way home from work today by two African Americans, but he didn't have any money on him so they just let him go. They both agree that African Americans are "the worst blacks in the world." So I asked them why they chose to live in Harlem. They said they feel more comfortable here than in other ethnic neighborhoods. (Field notes January 6, 1996)

> We had another meeting today with Leminigui Limun and Garifuna Kids (a *punta* band) and it turned into another forum on the problem of

the Garifuna youth in the United States. They continue to stress that the problem with the youth is that they assimilate to African American or Jamaican culture here and that leads to problems with their parents, who can no longer control them. Franco stood up and gave a mini-speech on the difference between the Garifuna and African Americans. He said that since African Americans had the experience of being slaves, they have no self-confidence and just blame all their problems on the system. The group agreed that the Garifuna youth are now adopting this attitude rather than maintaining the immigrant work ethic of their parents. (Field notes February 25, 1996)

Like other black immigrants, Garifuna often seek to avoid the low status that assimilating to African American culture carries (Kasinitz 1992; Waters 1999). I was often told that one of the main problems Garifuna face in the United States is that the youth come to associate with and identify as African Americans, from whom they are "poorly educated" in street culture. The proliferation of organizations whose goal is to conserve Garifuna culture and language among young people can be seen as an attempt to differentiate Garifuna from other blacks by emphasizing their ethnic identity. At meetings of youth groups, members often contrast the goals of Garifuna young people with the stereotype of the lazy African American who lives off welfare and crime and blames all his or her problems on the system. This characterization emphasizes individualist explanations of personal success and failure, mimicking the hegemonic ideology of the United States as a country of opportunity where failure is due to a lack of initiative, perseverance, and self-control instead of the result of systemic racism.

Another longtime New York resident who immigrated in the early 1970s explained why Garifuna could not really identify as African American despite the racial ideology in the United States that discriminated against African Americans and Garifuna in many of the same ways:

Whereas before Garifuna tended to identify with Black Americans, they now identify more as Hispanic or simply as Garifuna. I knew people who went to City College and were into the Black Panther movement, but I told them "This is for the Americans, it is not for us. The Black American does not identify with you; in fact they make fun of you when you speak Spanish. We might be the same color, but we have a different culture."

Culturally, the Honduran Garifuna have much in common with their Puerto Rican and Dominican neighbors, sharing favorite foods, musical styles, and the Spanish language. Surveys reveal that for Garifuna who speak little English, Puerto Ricans and Dominicans are their primary social circle (as neighbors,

Figure 6.2. Garifuna men at Vamos a la Peña del Bronx. Notice the painting of Emiliano Zapata on the wall. (Photo by author)

friends, and co-workers) outside the Garifuna community. Most stated that they have little contact with Honduran ladinos (except at soccer tournaments), West Indians, or white Americans (except as employers and patients). One interviewee affirmed, "We are here [in the South Bronx] like all other Latinos without good jobs, not speaking English, and living in decaying neighborhoods." For this man, the experience of being non-English-speaking immigrants makes the Honduran Garifuna part of the Hispanic community. Indeed, one of the strongest organizational supports the Garifuna had during my stay in New York City was Vamos a La Peña del Bronx, a community center established and run by a Chilean couple to cater to the social needs and cultural events of the South Bronx Hispanic community. Here Garifuna dance troupes joined with Dominican, Puerto Rican, and Ecuadorian groups in street fairs and parades organized to represent the Hispanic cultural mosaic of the South Bronx. Garifuna organizations met with South Bronx Hispanic politicians, mainly Puerto Rican and Dominican, to discuss ways they could be included in government and community-based programs for documented and undocumented immigrants.

However, their physical blackness intrudes on this cultural affinity, marking them as "*negritos*" and "*morenos*" within a Caribbean Hispanic population that has historically had ambivalent feelings about their Afro Hispanic history and identity (Grosfoguel and Georas 1996; Martinez-Alier 1974). It seems that when Garifuna drop Hispanic ethnic markers such as listening to Latino music and speaking Spanish, other Latinos identify them more with blackness. Indeed, Belizean Garifuna do not identify as Hispanic even though they come from Central America; instead, they identify more with the West Indian community. So while dance troupes of Honduran Garifuna participate in Hispanic culture parades, Belizean dance troupes participate in the West Indian Carnival parade (see Kasinitz and Friedenberg-Herbstein 1987). Both Garifuna groups participate in celebrations of the African diaspora.

The experience of one Limoneño reveals the contradictions of straddling all of these identities in New York City. Chato was brought to live in the Bronx in 1965 when he was 10 years old, attended high school there, entered the U.S. military, and later got a job with the U.S. postal service. His father worked in maintenance and his mother worked in a factory and then as a home attendant. They are all U.S. citizens and are called *merigana* (American) in Limón, but Chato says that he does not like this and insists that he is Honduran regardless of his citizenship.

> I had a hard time in junior high and high school [in the Bronx] because I was considered an outsider as a Spanish speaker. In school I was usually identified as Hispanic by the teachers because of my Hispanic surname. I always had to convince my African American friends that I was the same as them, maybe we have different histories but we are one people, one race. But on the other hand, whenever I was perceived as being an African American is when I received discrimination from Whites and Hispanics. There were many times that Hispanics assumed I was African American and would refer to me as "that black" and say negative things, thinking I could not understand. But I even had this experience with two Garifuna women on the subway who thought I was African American. One told the other to hold onto her purse because "here comes a black." She said this in Garifuna so I responded to them in Garifuna and they were very apologetic. I guess being Garifuna made me less dangerous.

Experiences like these are leading more and more Garifuna to mark the box "other" on census forms and write in "Garifuna" or "Afro Hispanic." As is the case in Honduras, there has been a move within Garifuna organizations to identify with the African diaspora as a racial affiliation. Yet they also point to the unique circumstances of Afro Hispanics in the Americas. In 1994, Garifuna became active in a hemispheric network of black organizations initiated by the Organization of Africans in the Americas (OAA) based in Washington, D.C., in collaboration with Mundo Afro, based in Uruguay, and Cimarron, based in Columbia (see Wade 1995 for a description of Cimarron). All three organizations

were founded to meet the needs of Afro Hispanics in the United States and
Latin America who have suffered a "hidden racial discrimination condoned by
Latin American society and stemming from colonial practices" (from an OAA
document). One of the first goals of these organizations is to make the hemispheric public aware that Afro Hispanics do exist and are a sizable community,
though they have been statistically invisible in official documents. This network
was instrumental in encouraging Garifuna in Central America to form CABO
and played a significant role in the organization of the Bicentennial celebration
in La Ceiba. In both Central America and the United States, this network has
created a space where Hispanic and black are not seen as mutually exclusive categories. This allows Honduran Garifuna who identify with the Hispanic New
York community and Belizean Garifuna who identify with the West Indian
New York Community to unify under a racial black identity and with their
connection to Central America, even if for Belizeans the latter is more a matter
of geography than cultural affinity.

"To identify as Honduran in New York City you have to Garifunize yourself"

It was a beautiful sunny day and many people had turned out for the festivities in
the park. I had placed myself strategically behind the table displaying Garifuna
arts and crafts and next to Mimi's "kitchen," where she was selling *hudutu, tapado*, rice and beans, and *pan de coco*. A few Dominicans stopped to look at the
paintings of scenes from Garifuna village life and to test the food, surprised that
the scenes and food from Honduras would look and taste so similar to what they
knew from "back home." I was pointed to as the resident anthropologist whose
task it was to explain who the Garifuna are and why their culture looks similar to
that of the Caribbean despite their location in Central America. Many Garifuna
also stopped to look at the table and admire the paintings, commenting on how
they were reminded of the good old days when they would go to the bush with
their mothers to plant cassava and to the sea with their fathers to fish, obtaining
the ingredients for *hudutu* that today Mimi buys in a Dominican *bodega*.

As I sat listening to these nostalgic exchanges, I noticed that more and more
people were moving toward the stage set up under the shade of the trees, framed
by the bulk of several tall housing projects in the distance. On the stage the musicians were setting up electric guitars, amplifiers, and mahogany-and-calfskin
drums. A crowd had already gathered in the few chairs set up in front of the
stage and a horde of video cameras was aimed at the MC, who was announc-
ing the opening of the Segunda Festival de Punta y Cultura Garifuna with the

Figure 6.3. A dance troupe called San Jose 5 Estrellas, dressed in the colors of the Honduran flag, performs at the Segunda Festival de Punta. (Photo by author)

Figure 6.4. The winner of the Miss Garifuna contest at the Segunda Festival de Punta. She is holding a *ruguma* used to squeeze the water out of cassava pulp in the process of making cassava bread. Each contestant was required to know facts about Garifuna culture and history and to recite something in Garifuna. (Photo by author).

singing of the Honduran national anthem. This was followed by a short speech from the Honduran consulate, who congratulated FEDOHNY for organizing the event, which brought together the Honduran population of New York in a South Bronx park to celebrate an important element of their national culture.

Despite the nationalist tone of the opening ceremony, the festival clearly transcended the boundaries of Honduran nationalism. Though most of the bands were Garifuna groups that played some version of *punta* (now considered to be the national musical style of Honduras) the members of the bands were just as likely to be from Belize and Guatemala as from Honduras. Also, with the exception of one Honduran dance group made up of ladinos performing the national folk dance (the *sique*) and a dance group of Garifuna children dressed in the colors of the Honduran flag (light blue and white), all of the performances were in some way identified with the African diaspora—from rasta to New York hip-hop to the Garifuna version of what their African ancestors arriving in St. Vincent would have looked like. In addition, FEDOHNY had invited the president-in-exile of Equatorial Guinea (the only Spanish-speaking African country) to address the crowd. But the clearest evidence that this was not merely a celebration of Honduran culture and national identity was the speeches by Garifuna community activists pointing out the necessity for Garifuna to join the struggles in their home communities against land invasion, racial discrimination, political marginalization, and the spread of the tourist industry. The always-present but never-stated enemy was the Honduran state because of its embrace of neoliberal economics and its prejudices toward Afro Hondurans.

Like other transmigrants in the United States, Garifuna have multiple overlapping identities that simultaneously include national, ethnic, racial, and even regional referents. All Garifuna have the experience of being racialized in the United States as black, thereby placing them in the same racial category as other members of the African diaspora. Yet they are also understood as being a particular kind of black with a particular culture, which gives them an ethnic identity as Garifuna. Though these identities are distinct, they do not contradict one another because Garifuna ethnic identity is merely a more specific form of black racial identity. However, Garifuna also have an identity that stems from their nation of origin—that is, they are also considered and consider themselves to be Guatemalans, Hondurans, and Belizeans. In this case, unlike many other transmigrants for whom racial identity and national identity are merely overlapping layers (for example, black Jamaicans or even black Belizeans), there is not always a neat correspondence between race and nation for the Honduran Garifuna. That is, identification with the politics of a black racial identity and an affiliation with the politics of a Honduran national identity are not necessarily coterminous.

The kinds of contradictions this creates for the relationship of Hondu-ran Garifuna transmigrants to the Honduran "deterritorialized nation-state" (Basch, Glick Schiller, and Szanton Blanc 1994) was symbolized in the mixed messages of the festival described above. On one hand, the festival was nomi-nally a Honduran event, as evidenced by the presence of the consul, the singing of the national anthem, and the performance of the *sique*. Garifuna music and culture were used to symbolize the unique elements of Honduran culture among Central American countries. This is not surprising as Garifuna are the majority of Hondurans in New York City, constituting perhaps 70 percent of Hondurans residing in the city (in contrast to Honduras, where Garifuna make up less than 5 percent of the population). They have a long history of strong community ties, voluntary associations, cultural organizations, and musical groups in the city. This has kept the community united and made it more visible in cultural events than ladinos, who tend to melt into the general Hispanic population and lack cultural particularities to distinguish them from other Central Americans, as many of them lament. Events that display Honduran culture tend to spotlight Garifuna and *punta*.

On the other hand, the fact that many of the performers at the Segunda Festival de Punta were Garifuna from other Central American countries shows that for most Garifuna the primary identification of Garifuna culture and music is with the Garifuna diaspora rather than with a particular national identity. Garifuna see themselves as having more in common with Garifuna from Belize and Guatemala than with ladinos from Honduras. This was evidenced by the political messages of the activists, who articulated both an identification with the Honduran deterritorialized nation-state (in the sense that they urged trans-migrants to participate in the politics of Honduras from abroad) and a suspicion of Honduran nationalism (in the sense that they discussed the existence of racist state policies back home). Even as Garifuna are becoming symbols of Honduran national culture, because of their experiences of racism and political and eco-nomic marginalization in Honduras, many Garifuna continue to be suspicious of Honduran ladinos and tend to keep apart socially. Even though they identify themselves as citizens of Honduras or children of citizens of Honduras, their relationship to Honduran nationalism is ambivalent.

I found evidence of this separation between Garifuna and ladinos in the kinship data I gathered from Limoneño transmigrants. In the lists of domestic partnerships,[6] there are very few partnerships between Garifuna and ladinos, either in New York or in Honduras. Only 3 of 105 relationships documented among transmigrants were with Honduran ladinos. Eighty-six domestic part-nerships were with other Garifuna (60 of whom were Limoneños). The most common non-Garifuna domestic partner mentioned by interviewees was African American (7). There were also 5 Latin American mestizos (3 Hondurans, a Peruvian, and a Cuban), 4 Afro Latinos (2 Costa Ricans, a Dominican, and a Panamanian), one Ethiopian, and two American whites. This data reveals a strong tendency toward endogamy within the village first, the Garifuna ethnic group second, and the "race" (black) third.

Further evidence of the tight-knit nature of the Garifuna community in New York City comes from the structure of its grassroots organizations. Until the 1990s, Garifuna organizations in New York City tended to be very village oriented. Garifuna maintain a strong connection to their village of origin and see New York as merely an extension of that community. Even longtime New York residents have run for mayor and serve as members of the Patronato. However, this concern with development and political participation has long been aimed at village rather than national affairs. Garifuna in New York City certainly identify as Hondurans more than as Americans, regardless of citizenship, but their identity as Honduran is not so much with a deterritorialized state as it is with a deterritorialized village that happens to be located within the state of Honduras.

This primary orientation toward village affairs is changing, though, as more leaders of village-level voluntary associations call for unity among the Honduran Garifuna organizations to promote increased political participation and representation of Garifuna in the Honduran state and increased economic participation of migrants in the development of the North Coast. They argue that though Garifuna remittances have helped family members survive, they have ultimately enriched Honduran banks and ladino shop owners. These activists argue that the solution is to form economic blocs in New York City to invest in projects that will generate employment instead of just donating infrastructure and to campaign for a stronger political presence of Garifuna in the Honduran Congress in order to be better positioned to protect their land from state-projected tourism. These New York–based organizations are linking forces with those in Honduras such as OFRANEH and ODECO through e-mail communication and the drafting of documents to be presented to the United Nations and the Honduran government regarding economic development projects, bilingual education programs, and the titling of land to Garifuna villages. Garifuna organizations are claiming citizenship rights *within the state* as Honduran citizens and nationals (even if they live abroad), but at the same time they are also claiming human rights through international institutions such as the United Nations as an ethnic group that deserves special protection *from the state* of Honduras.

Consequently, just as Garifuna migrants are engaging more with the Honduran state from abroad, their national loyalties are being questioned because of their ethnic nationalist orientation. In an interview, the Honduran consul in New York (a ladino) told me he felt the Garifuna are really clannish and do not want to mix much with other Hondurans. "You know they really just take care of themselves, as though they weren't even part of the Honduran community." This same clash between Honduran nationalism and Garifuna ethnic nationalism has been apparent in the history of FEDOHNY, one of the few organizations that has tried to represent and unite the Honduran New York community as a whole.

FEDOHNY was established in 1990 after the Happy Land tragedy with the goal of assisting Hondurans with issues of immigration, job training, English, and other social services. During the time of my field work, the members of the board were all Garifuna, most of the member organizations were Garifuna, and few ladinos participated in the organization or its programs. In meetings it was obvious that for Garifuna organizations in New York City, being Honduran implies being Garifuna.

> Meeting at FEDOHNY. Once again the room is filled mainly with Garifuna, only two ladinos showed up. This became a hot topic, why FEDOHNY has the reputation among the ladinos of being just for the Garifuna. A Ladina says its because her people are racist and "don't want to be around a bunch of blacks." A Garifuna says no, it's because his people are clannish and they exclude the ladinos; they don't think of themselves as Hondurans first but rather as Garifuna. Just because the ladinos discriminate against them is no reason for them to discriminate against the ladinos. "All Hondurans are not black," he said. They all agree that the federation has to make more efforts to integrate all the Honduran organizations to truly represent the Honduran community. (Field notes November 25, 1995)

Another controversy within FEDOHNY arose around a previous Honduran consul and the current Honduran representative to the United Nations, who are both Garifuna. Disputes centered on whether Honduran officials who are Garifuna should represent Garifuna interests or those of the Honduran state, which are often in conflict. Many ladinos find the prominence of Garifuna organizations and their ethnic nationalist rhetoric threatening and anti-Honduran. Despite the increasing importance of Garifuna culture as a Honduran national symbol, there is still an underlying assumption among ladinos that Garifuna ethnicity and Honduran nationalism cannot coexist unproblematically.

THE GARIFUNA NATION IN DIASPORA

Garifuna do not find an easy fit in the racial categories of the United States or in Honduras. They do not easily identify with the indigenous categories of Central America or with the racial categories of African American and Hispanic in the United States. Nor do they completely identify with their nation-states of origin. Some Garifuna organizations have postulated another identity, the Garifuna Nation in diaspora. Citing the lack of unity among the Garifuna due to national differences, proponents of the Garifuna Nation argue that the geographical dispersal and fragmented citizenships created by the Garifuna diaspora should not hamper the unification of the Garifuna people under the banner of a common language, culture, and homeland in St. Vincent. Though the discourse of these organizations uses the language of territory and nation (that is, St. Vincent as the homeland and source of ethnic nationalist identity), references to St. Vincent are primarily symbolic. Proponents of the Garifuna Nation do not make calls for a return to inhabit St. Vincent but rather promote recognition of the island as their historical point of origin and the cradle of their cultural distinctiveness—much like the ideological place Africa has within the African diaspora. They use St. Vincent as a symbol of nationhood to rally support around projects focused on where Garifuna actually reside—Central America and the United States. Rather than focus only on the needs of a particular village or a particular nation of origin, proponents of the Garifuna Nation argue that all Garifuna should recognize their common history and realize their common destiny through political activism that would benefit all Garifuna everywhere. The idea of a "nation in diaspora" challenges the categories of race and nationality within which Garifuna have been placed by others (as primarily Hispanic, Honduran, Guatemalan, and so forth) and challenges the notion that an ethnic nation should be geographically bounded by one particular territory. But at the same time, the discourse of the nation in diaspora continues to use the language and symbolic power of "territory" and "nation" within a global political arena in which race and place are still the ideological bases around which rights are negotiated and conferred.

In 1998, Garifuna activists from Belize, Guatemala, and Honduras who had served on the Comité Pro-Bicentenario (the committee that helped organize the bicentennial celebration from New York) formed an organization called the Garifuna Nation. Members of the organization (which has an equal number of men and women) are mainly Garifuna transmigrants from Honduras, Belize, and Guatemala who have lived in the United States for twenty years or more and who are professionals working in the fields of health care, social services, education, real estate, union organizing, and others. Most are involved in both hometown voluntary associations and Garifuna organizations that focus on the integration of Garifuna into New York City through the multiculturalist model—that is, through education and upward mobility combined with maintaining an ethnic identity and culture.[7] They conceive of the Garifuna Nation (now called the Garifuna Coalition) as the paramount organization in New York that would "bring together all Garinagu organizations to work together on unifying issues and begin to forge a common progressive vision for the next millennium" (Garifuna Nation Retreat Resolutions, May 7, 1998). They see themselves as the intermediaries between the Garifuna people and larger political bodies such as the Central American states, the U.S. government, the city of New York, and the UN. As such they draft letters on behalf of the community and regularly attend meetings of UN committees concerned with indigenous peoples and blacks. They also have strong ties to the Afro Hispanic organizations such as Mundo Afro and the OAA and to national-level Garifuna organizations in Central America such as OFRANEH and ODECO in Honduras, the National Garifuna Council of Belize, and the Organización Negro de Guatemala. A great deal of their communication with these various organizations is done using the Internet. Much of the material for this section comes from the Garifunas Link mailing list and the Garifuna World Web site,[8] where there are frequent references to the activities of the Garifuna Coalition as an organization and the Garifuna Nation as an ideal of cultural unity.

The initial impetus for the idea of a Garifuna nation in diaspora can be seen in the Garifuna Council of New York, a pan-Garifuna organization with members from Belize, Guatemala, and Honduras that was formed in the early 1990s. In 1993, the Council drafted a document to the United Nations to petition for reparations from the British for having exiled them from St. Vincent in 1797. In the document the authors explicitly compare the Garifuna to pre-1948 Jews as a nation-in-exile without a recognized homeland:

> What is extremely important is that not withstanding our varied political and national peculiarities, we remain one people, the Garifuna Diaspora, descendants of that common stock of about 2,000 survivors that were dumped for extermination in Honduras. We were all shipped from St. Vincent to be exterminated. The conqueror wanted to wipe us out. Therefore whether we individually are citizens of Honduras, Belize, Nicaragua, Guatemala, or the United States, our origin is those survivors of the massacre. That common ancestry makes us one people, Garifuna, and the accident of our individual birthplace matters none at all. We are brothers and sisters, Garifuna all. Although we survived the massacre, the expulsion from our home country deprived us of our power base, our achievements

were disrupted, our dignity was crushed and we were left completely destitute of political, social and other rights.

Here it is implied that the Garifuna need to recreate links to St. Vincent in order to have psychological and cultural stability, to suture the fragmentation of language and national identity the diasporic experience has created. Though these speakers use a language of diaspora, it is still based on the assumptions that each race should form a united nation with a given homeland. Being torn from one's roots is seen as disrupting the natural connection of people (race) to territory (place), which leads to loss of identity, rights, and unity. As Malkki has argued, "in the national order of things, the rooting of peoples is not only normal, it is also perceived as a moral and spiritual need" (1992, 30).

Other visions of the Garifuna Nation are not so explicitly linked to territory. The designers of the Garifuna World Web site and the Garifunas Link mailing list (twin brothers from Honduras who are professionals in real estate and computer programming) explain that the Garifuna diaspora places them squarely within the current moment of globalization, giving them the advantages of a bifocal or trifocal culture, transnational mobility, and access to multinational markets. They envision cyberspace as a tool that will unite the Garifuna across geographical borders, preserve Garifuna culture through technology, and promote the creation of what they call a "Global Garifuna Village" or a "Global Garifuna Nation":

> As we enter our 200 year anniversary our culture will become part of the cyber community that has been established by this great information highway and provide us the opportunity to break all barriers that have kept us separated as a nation. For the first time the Garifuna Nation has the opportunity to unite our voice and our efforts as one nation, regardless of each physical location. The Internet and our presence in Central America and the United States provides us the ability to become true participants in the economic development of the region as well as in the global economy. Through the Garifuna World and the Garifunas List we hope to provide the foundation for our borderless home away from home. ("Garifuna's Path to the Next Millennium," on the Garifuna World Web site)

At the Bicentennial celebration in La Ceiba, this view was echoed on the panel entitled "Economic Challenges Facing the Garifuna People and the North American Influence." Presenters on the panel included the twin brothers, the finance minister of Belize, a member of the Washington, D.C.–based NGO Appropriate Technologies, one of the founders of Garifuna Enterprises (which markets *punta* rock and other Garifuna products in the United States), and a Cornell University graduate in agronomy (all of them Garifuna). In general, they argued that instead of seeing transnational migration as the source of the disintegration of the Garifuna culture and economy (a viewpoint expressed by such organizations as Iseri Lidawamari), Garifuna should take advantage of their position on both sides of the border to become transnational capitalists themselves. They said that the position of the Garifuna in both the Central American and U.S. economies is a strength, not a weakness. With capital accumulated in the United States and access to the land and resources of the Atlantic coast, the Garifuna are in fact in a strategic position to invest in the burgeoning tourist trade. The most articulate proponent of this (the co-founder of the Garifuna-World Web site and Gavilan Inc., an Internet marketer of Garifuna products) argued that a convergence of three factors has placed the Garifuna in the right place at the right time to economically empower themselves: the growing tourist industry in Honduras on the Atlantic coast, the fact that U.S.-bound migration has situated them in a place that favors the accumulation of capital, and the emergence of new communications technology that makes commerce without frontiers possible in a global economy.

Yet even while celebrating globalization as the path to the next millennium for the Garifuna people, this presenter encouraged all who could do so to become U.S. citizens to take advantage of opportunities neoliberal trade agreements such as the North American Free Trade Agreement (NAFTA) and the Central American Free Trade Agreement (CAFTA) have opened up. Even the most ardent supporters of the communications revolution and the global economy as a source of empowerment recognize that while identities and national loyalties may be shifting and fluid, place and citizenship are not irrelevant to access to economic power. This position emphasizes the disjunctures between the idea of a nation in diaspora and the real differentials of power, identity, and sense of belonging within that nation.

Despite the peculiarities of national differences that affect local struggles within the Garifuna Nation, as a whole the Bicentennial was a unifying ethnic nationalist event. The reflections of a Belizean Garifuna activist from the Internet mailing list are indicative of the role of the Bicentennial and the Internet network in furthering the concept of the diasporic nation.

> The experience in Honduras [the Bicentennial] was not only awesome but a spiritual one too. Seeing Garifuna representation from Yurumein [St. Vincent], Belize, Honduras, Guatemala and Nicaragua created part of the circle that once was and created the image of one nation under one umbrella with one language, one culture: Garifuna. . . .

We need first to create an international body, such as an International Garifuna Council, which would become the government in exile of the Garifuna nation. This would be a body that would articulate the Garifuna agenda and policies and would be our legal and rightful representative of the Garifuna nation. This council, which is in essence a government, should be made up of representatives from Honduras, Belize, Guatemala, Nicaragua, Yurumein, and the United States and a petition should be made to the United Nations for its recognition. There is enough evidence written to substantiate that we were exiled as a nation, so I think it is time to create the right vehicle that can carry these ideas to fruition. (1997)

Though this proposal of converting identification with a deterritorialized ethnic nation to a real political entity has not yet been carried out, it would be an interesting strategy. By having their own political body, Garifuna would avoid the trap of having to negotiate for rights as small minorities within historically racist nation-states and would challenge the attempts of these nation-states to reinscribe Garifuna into their nationalist projects. It also creates a narrative of nation in which shared culture and identity is more relevant than shared territory. This claim to political sovereignty is not the same as that of nation-states because it is not attached to a particular territory, but it does go beyond merely claiming a cultural identification in diaspora to claiming the rights to political representation as a nation among others. Interestingly, this political representation was not used to make claims vis-à-vis the actual "homeland" that establishes and serves as the historical basis for their claims to nationhood (St. Vincent). Instead, it was used to make claims in the five other nation-states of which Garifuna are citizens and residents (Belize, Guatemala, Honduras, Nicaragua, and the United States). The idea of the Garifuna Nation remains a primarily symbolic and rhetorical evocation that serves several purposes: it provides a unified focus for an imagined Garifuna community that is geographically dispersed and it serves as a way to establish their status as an ethnic nation within the world community of nations who have rights above and beyond those of individual nation-state citizenship (much like the Kurds, who are also dispersed among several nation-states).

Conclusion

The Garifuna experience of existing in the interstices of hegemonic racial and nationalist categories throughout their places of residence in the diaspora has led to a complex articulation of identities. They are challenging the nation-states in which they were born, in which they reside, and of which they are citizens. They have created transnational migration circuits in which their home communities and transmigrant communities transcend national borders to create one fluid social system, and more recent interactions between these communities have generated the beginnings of a consciousness of a scattered people as one Garifuna nation, where country of birth and citizenship are less relevant than a sense of shared history, language, culture, and homeland.

The multiplicity of Garifuna identities is certainly a prime example of how racial, ethnic, and national identities are constructed and negotiated, proving once again that "identities are not things, they are matters of social dispute. This constructed character is not asserted as opposed to anything that may be considered more 'real.' From this point of view, the dilemmas 'real vs. imagined,' 'authentic vs. false' and 'genuine vs. spurious' are simply not pertinent" (Mato 1996, 64). Identities always shift and are negotiated both from above and below, and there is no original moment when they were fixed and bounded (Gupta and Ferguson 1992). Showing the multiple and shifting nature of Garifuna identity does not discredit the real experiences they entail or debunk the claims to rights Garifuna organizations are making through these identities. Rather, it reveals the "politics of location" (Frankenberg and Mani 1996) within which these identities are constructed, negotiated, and contested, particularly the current and historic configurations of power that make some more politically relevant than others. Garifuna actively form racial and ethnic identities even as they are constrained by U.S. and Central American ideologies of race, ethnicity, and nation as well as those of international organizations that often mediate between people and nation-states in the negotiation of rights.

It may seem odd that just at the time when globalization is being recognized in the media, in the international political arena, and in academic discourse as a force that is rupturing formerly hegemonic notions of territorial boundedness and cultural stability, modernist notions of race and place continue to be important for people's sense of identity, belonging, and political struggles in much of the world. Many have argued that this is a logical reaction to the profoundly uneven processes of globalization (Castells 1997; Featherstone 1990; Hall 1991a; Hannerz 1996; Watts 1992a). While economic and political power have become more decentralized and less attached to physical space because of the reorganization of capital into post-Fordist flexible regimes of accumulation (Jameson 1984; Lash and Urry 1987; Miyoshi 1993; Sklair 1995), the formation of supranational political entities (Soysal 1994), and the communications revolution (Castells 1997), this does not mean that power is spread more evenly throughout the globe. In fact, power is still concentrated at certain points throughout the network. Decentralization, fragmentation, and flexibility have actually strengthened those nodes of power while simultaneously marginalizing other sectors of the globe (Castells 1993; Sassen 1994). The global system is still a site of multiple axes of domination where some sectors benefit from globalization more than others (Mahler 1998; Ong 1999). As Rouse (1995) and Dirlik (1994) have argued, postmodern celebrations of the hybrid and the transnational as challenges to modernist structures of power—which are similar to transnational corporate claims that the revolution in communications technology will make borders, racial hierarchies, and differential access to the means of production obsolete—have mainly been articulated by those who benefit from the processes of globalization and have ignored or obscured the continuing power differentials global capitalism has created.

For others differentially placed in relation to the international division of labor, globalization is disintegrating the social fabric of local communities, where former mechanisms of social control and community identity are competing with a global sphere of ideologies and power relations that are less accountable to local conditions. In the face of this deterritorialization of power, both states and ethnic groups have reacted to fortify identities, notions of communities, and physical localities as sites of struggle (Castells 1997; Hall 1991b). In contradistinction to the transnational corporate parlance of the global village or the international ecology and human rights slogan "we are the world," fundamentalist nationalist and ethnic nationalist movements are predicated on the reessentialization of identity, the ideological construction of territorially bounded communities, and the claim to internal homogeneity. The deterritorialization of power has led to the reterritorialization of identity whereby some peoples in the world retreat to the local in the face of what they perceive to be an oppressive global economy and sweeping global culture (see Escobar 1997; Varese 1994; Watts 1992b). The fact that even people who are "chronically mobile and routinely displaced . . . invent homelands in the absence of territorial, national basis—not in situ, but through memories of, and claims on, places that they can or will no longer corporeally inhabit" (Malkki 1992, 24) is proof of the resilience of territorialized forms of identity, especially in the realm of political struggles.

Populations in diaspora and/or exile are always in dialogue with territorialized conceptions of both the nation-state and the indigenous/autocthonous. Malkki attributes this to the way the connection between people and place has been naturalized in nationalist discourses, making uprootedness and displacement from one's homeland seem pathological. This is especially true for indigenous peoples and tribes who are seen as connected to the land so intimately that they are literally talked about as part of flora and fauna. This idea of autocthony has enabled indigenous peoples to claim first nation status with rights as the original inhabitants, but it has also perpetuated the ideology that they are "incarcerated or confined to those places," where they are reproducing an authentic culture. When they move outside this space, this authenticity and often the rights that go along with it are questioned. This is often the dilemma of immigrants and refugees who are seen as displaced residents of somewhere else, from where they "naturally" belong. They do not fully belong within the nation-states in which they reside, sometimes even as citizens, nor are they on their "native soil." They continue to define their locus of identity and community elsewhere in order to be able to claim integrity as a group with "true roots" somewhere.

Gilroy (1993a) argues that for members of the African diaspora, this search for roots has taken place within the experience of being both inside and outside the west. Like other members of the African diaspora, the Garifuna are considered inside the west in the sense that the history of the diaspora population is intimately tied to that of the west via the spread of global capitalism, the formation of nation-states, and international migration. Yet they are simultaneously seen as outside the west through discourses of race and nation that place them on the margins of national identities and at the bottom of national and global economies. This experience of being a part of modernity yet ideologically constructed as existing on its margins leads Garifuna to posit authentic roots in Africa, where all localities and cultural forms of the diaspora, despite their different histories, are presented as originating from an essential racial identity. Furthermore, the experience of being racialized by racist, nationalist, and ethnic absolutist discourses wherever they travel within the diaspora reinforces Garifuna articulations of blackness as a global racial identity. For people such as the Garifuna, however, identification with the African diaspora has limited political force in the struggle for rights in the Americas. Despite efforts of organizations such as the OAA and CABO to argue for the intimate connection of blacks to the history of Latin America, groups that identify with blackness still run the risk of being located outside the national identities of Central America. Similarly, membership within the African diaspora is not connected with a set of political rights because it is not linked to a particular nation-state or territory within which members are seen as autocthonous.

Unlike most other members of the African diaspora, however, the Garifuna *can* make claims to rights as autocthonous peoples because of their indigenous heritage and the construction of ethnicity in Central America that conflates ethnic difference with autocthony. This affords them rights to particular territories in Central America to which they claim to have roots, reinforced by the current international political arena in which indigenous peoples are considered to be nations within nations who have rights almost identical to those of the nation-state. However, this image of autochthony and first nation status rests on the perpetuation of an ideology that autochthonous peoples necessarily live in bounded communities and have internal racial and cultural homogeneity and little class differentiation. Garifuna history, especially their long-standing participation in wage labor and migration, shows that this is not an accurate reflection of their reality and brings us to question how to reconcile indigenous rights with diasporic populations.

In contrast to the way autochthony continues to be linked to territory, national identity and citizenship is increasingly deterritorialized as nation-states attempt to integrate migrants abroad into their nationalist projects through dual citizenship and rights to political participation (Basch, Glick Schiller, and Szanton Blanc 1994). For the Garifuna, engagement with the Honduran state is a logistical necessity for negotiating rights to land in their home communities and for some measure of protection from their vulnerable legal status vis-à-vis the U.S. state. Unlike members of other deterritorialized nation-states, however, the Garifuna do not necessarily see themselves as having Honduran national identity because of that nation's history of marginalization and racism. Like Mixtec migrants in California who find themselves doubly discriminated against by the racism of U.S. society and that of their fellow Mexican transmigrants (Kearney and Nagengast 1990), Garifuna are in the double bind of being constructed outside U.S. nationalism (and therefore they focus on their country of origin) and yet being divided by absolutist notions of race and ethnicity among Hondurans. In this double bind, Garifuna, like the Mixtec, have developed a political consciousness around an ethnic rather than a national identity. Unlike the Mixtec, however, this political consciousness must engage with not two but five different nation-states and nationalisms.

The articulation of the Garifuna Nation in diaspora resolves many of these contradictions. Placing the Garifuna homeland in St. Vincent is a much more precise, unique, and territorialized claim to roots than that of the African diaspora. It places Garifuna history squarely within the history of the Americas, substantiating claims to being autochthonous. At the same time, the racial and cultural hybridization of Garifuna "ethnogenesis" on St. Vincent allows them to identify with both autochthony and blackness. And finally, it transcends nation-states, nationalisms, and citizenships, unifying Garifuna as one nation instead of as minorities within other nations. Whether this kind of nation without territory will ever be recognized as politically equal to territorialized indigenous nations or nation-states remains to be seen. Until that time, Garifuna will continue to need to negotiate their rights and identity in relation to other nation-states and the international bodies that mediate between them.

Conclusion

In May 1996, after much pressure from OFRANEH, ODECO, Iseri Lidawamari, and other Black Honduran organizations, the Honduran government declared April 12 the Dia de la Etnia Negra Hondureña (Day of the Black Honduran Ethnic Group). This date was chosen to commemorate the day the Garifuna first arrived in Central America in 1797 after being exiled from St. Vincent by the British. Every year since then, Garifuna organizations have celebrated the anniversary of this arrival with cultural and political events, kicking it off with the Bicentnennial Celebration of 1997.

In October 2002, the Honduran government went further with the declaration that the whole month of April would be the Mes de la Herencia Africana (Month of African Heritage) with the purpose of "organizing cultural events of many types in order to make known the riches of the African culture and its contribution to the development of Honduran culture and society." The legislative decree states that this is necessary because "the African presence and culture in Honduras goes back to the first decades of the 16th century and yet its contributions to Honduran society and our culture have been recognized only in a very limited way" (*La Gaceta* December 24, 2002).

In some ways, these legislative decrees can be seen as a real step forward; they constitute the first official recognition of the importance of blackness to Honduran national society. They present blackness not as something that was simply submerged by and merged into *mestizaje* but as something that has its own unique set of contributions that are worth recognizing and preserving. It is a step toward the multicultural model of citizenship that recognizes the value and contribution of all the ethnic groups that make up Honduran society and challenges the dominant ideology of *mestizaje* as the only legitimate national identity. And yet Garifuna organizations recognize that such decrees are only a small step forward and in fact are the easy ones for the Honduran government to take because they still frame Garifuna culture and blackness within Honduran national identity and in the relatively apolitical realm of "cultural heritage." Unless radical meaning is given to the celebrations of this African heritage, Garifuna organizations run the risk of simply falling back into the folkloric model of Garifuna culture as singing, dancing, and selling *pan de coco*, an image presented by tourist agencies and on many postcards.[1] As Juliet Hooker (2005) has argued, framing of ethnic rights in a way that is primarily based on cultural difference has allowed some states to ignore race-based structural inequalities that affect all blacks and indigenous peoples even though such groups claim status as an autocthonous people who have contributed to the roots of the national identity.

In order to avoid this version of black identity that does not hold the government accountable for much more than allowing Garifuna to have public celebrations of cultural heritage, Garifuna organizations, in league with indigenous organizations, pushed for the passage of a decree to form the Comisión Nacional Contra la Discriminación Racial, el Racismo, la Xenofobia, y Formas Conexas de Intolerancia en Honduras (National Commission against Racial Discrimination, Racism, Xenophobia, and Connected Forms of Intolerance in Honduras). This decree, which was passed in 2004, creates campaigns to sensitize the public about overt and covert forms of racism and brings those who commit acts of racial discrimination to court. It is too early to tell how successful this commission will be in taking concrete measures to address and eradicate forms of racism. A report written in the same year by the Inter-American Commission on Human Rights declares that despite such gestures on the part of the government to recognize the importance of Afro Honduran culture, racism is alive and well in Honduras. According to the report, Honduran society exhibits the following traits, which are characteristics of "profound racial discrimination": "1) A disturbing correspondence between the map of poverty and the geographic distribution of indigenous and afro-descent communities, 2) the marginal participation of the representatives of these populations in the structures of power (government, parliament, judiciary) and their scarce presence in the structures of power of the media, 3) the folkloric image of them that is projected by the means of [information] diffusion" (Diène 2004, 2). The special rapporteur who wrote the report found especially troubling the fact that many of the Honduran officials with whom he spoke maintained the idea that "Honduras is not a country with fertile ground for racial discrimination given the degree and variety of mixture in the country" (11). His report states that racism in Honduras continues to exist as much by acts of commission (as can be seen in the clear relationship between race and poverty) as by acts of omission, in the sense that Honduran officials either deny its existence or merely pay lip service to its eradication but take no concrete action.

This is not an unfamiliar story in Latin America, where indigenous, black, and popular social movements have arguably made great strides in forcing their concerns into the national consciousness and onto the national agenda but getting their demands met in a substantial way is still a huge struggle. Marches of indigenous peoples in Ecuador, truth and reconciliation tribunals in Guatemala, roadblocks in Bolivia, international conventions in the jungles of Chiapas, and tours with rock stars in Brazil are some of the strategies that have brought international attention to the plight of indigenous peoples in Latin America and have worked in tandem with a host of international conventions and declarations to force governments to enact legislation and other programs to protect their rights (Brysk 2000). Peoples of African descent in the Americas have not been as visible, but in Central America they have used some of these strategies to bring attention to their situation and, in the case of the Garifuna and the peoples of the Pacific Coast of Colombia, have taken advantage of some of this legislation to make claims to land, cultural autonomy, bilingual education, and the like (Hooker 2005). And yet, as can be seen with this brief description of the strides ethnic communities have made in Honduras, it is apparent that national governments are entering into this process reluctantly, signing legislative decrees and articles of the constitution on paper without making much of a commitment to the ideologies that are behind them because they challenge understandings of race and class that have shaped Latin American society for 500 years. So while we can say that "new" social movements have opened the door to a new way of doing politics that is more democratic and participatory because it includes a variety of actors (state officials, NGOs, grassroots activists, international aid institutions, transmigrants) from a variety of locations (local, national, and transnational), many of the same discursive and structural contradictions still remain. They are simply being played on a wider field. The Honduran state, Garifuna organizations, and international aid organizations are all fighting to define the terms of struggle regarding race, nationalism, and ethnic rights. Whereas in the past minority groups such as the Garifuna were not even part of the dialogue, they are now at least active players in the game, and sometimes they have powerful allies. But with so many different sectors of the national and global community involved there are always contradictions, both in terms of ideologies that talk past one another and in terms of policies that seem to cancel each other out. Garifuna are located at the crossroads of these many discursive and political contradictions, a location that shapes the contours of their struggle as they negotiate economic constraints, dominant ideologies, and political maneuvering.

This complex location of Garifuna is true not only for the politics of race but also for the politics of development. After Hurricane Mitch there was much hope that the dominant development model of agribusiness, tourism, and maquiladoras would be severely challenged and a space would open for more sustainable and equitable methods of economic development. Unfortunately, this did not happen and the first investments of loans and aid were given to rebuild the infrastructure multinational corporations needed to recreate the same economic strategies as before (Russell 1999). This could be and has been attributed to structural constraints the IMF continues to place on Central American countries (even after much of their debt was cancelled in 2005) that require governments to fully adhere to the neoliberal economic and political agenda if they want to receive aid and loans. There is some evidence that the Reina administration (1994–1997) tried to resist this model but was defeated by the combined interests of the international lending agencies and the Honduran elite, which stands to benefit most from foreign investment. The administrations of Carlos Flores Facussé (Miguel Facussé's nephew) and Ricardo Maduro have done little to deviate from the neoliberal model (Robinson 1998).

Garifuna have a tenuous place within this development model. They are useful as tourist attractions, tourism service workers (because so many speak English after having worked on cruise ships), and cheap labor in the maquiladoras, but they are also seen as a pesky obstacle because they stubbornly refuse to have their beaches taken over by resorts and their agricultural lands taken over by agribusiness without a fight. As of this writing, Garifuna organizations had managed to prevent the reform of Article 107 of the Honduran Constitution that prohibits the sale of land to foreigners along Honduran national borders (which would include the beach). Both the Flores and Maduro administrations tried to reform this article to stimulate the development of the tourism industry along the Caribbean coast precisely where Garifuna villages are located. Though the article has yet to be reformed, the Maduro administration has tried to find other avenues of achieving the same goal with the new Ley de Propriedad, which promotes the alienation of all forms of collective landholdings, ostensibly to stimulate the creation of new enterprises. In addition, Maduro signed on to CAFTA, which is expected to have much the same results in Central America as NAFTA had in Mexico.

Despite all the mobilization by Garifuna and indigenous organizations to make the public aware of how such neoliberal policies harm their communities, Garifuna and indigenous claims to communal land continue to be seen as a direct challenge and obstacle to this vision of progress. And yet because Honduras has signed documents such as Convention 169 of the ILO, the International Convention concerning the Elimination of All Forms of Racial Discrimination, and the Universal Declaration of Human Rights, the Honduran state is obliged to protect the rights of Garifuna and indigenous peoples to territory and economic and cultural autonomy to some degree. In a gesture toward such protection, from 1998 to 2001 the Honduran government gave out titles to *tierras comunitarias* (communal lands) to many Garifuna and indigenous communities. As with the law against racism, these titles can be seen as a step forward because they provide a degree of protection from land loss because they are collective and therefore cannot be sold to *terceros* (third parties; that is, non-Garifuna). While the communal titles provide an extra safeguard against the invasion, expropriation, and private sale of land where Garifuna actually live and where they are cultivating, the area covered by these titles is rarely enough to provide for the needs of the whole community. In 1998 Limón received title to 503 hectares of *tierra communitaria* in La Barra, Malajuaz, and Salado. This was national land that Garifuna were cultivating, and now it is protected and managed by the *patronato*. According to my estimation of the number of households in Limón (500), this comes out to only about one hectare for each household, which is clearly insufficient. (The *jefe de catastro* in Limón estimated that the average Garifuna household needs about ten hectares of land just for basic subsistence agriculture.)

This situation has led to calls to increase the amount of the communal lands to meet the needs of future growth and regularize the land (that is, remove people with illegally obtained documents from the land, mainly *colonos*). In 2001, another legislative decree was established that set aside money for the creation of the Comisión Intersectorial de Titulación, Ampliación, Saneamiento, y Protección de las Tierras de las Comunidades Misquitas y Garifunas de Honduras whose job it is, as can be seen from its name, to title, amplify, protect, and regularize land in Miskito and Garifuna communities. The goals of this commission sound good on paper, but the process itself has been extremely slow and complicated because it takes years to determine the actual boundaries of municipal, national, communal, and private landholdings (each type is under a different jurisdiction) and trace the histories of who owns what and how they got their titles in order to even begin the process of regularizing and amplifying lands in Garifuna communities. For example, the *jefe de catastro* told me that ladino and isleño cattle ranchers in Malajuaz and Salado who came in the 1960s are not being removed because they have dominio pleno (private title) from the INA. This excludes them from expropriation even though Limoneños argue that their mode of acquiring that land was illegitimate. In addition to this legal loophole, the community will have to pay them the value of the land and any improvements that have been made if they want to add those parcels to the *tierra comunitaria*. So while the communal titles may provide protection for future invasions, they do nothing to redress the invasions of the past and do not provide for future growth of the community.

It is exactly this scenario that prompted the formation of Iseri Lidawamari in 1990. Lombardo, Horacio, Bernardo, Teofilo and others saw that Limón, like most Garifuna communities, was being squeezed, losing land and with it the possibility of its residents being anything but dependent remittance recipients and workers. And yet despite the enthusiasm of the community and the hard work of many Limoneños, Iseri Lidawamari has suffered greatly from the contradictions between gestures toward the protection of Garifuna communities and the neoliberal economic policies of the state. On the positive side, in 1998, the cooperative finally ended an eight-year battle to get *dominio pleno* of the *empresas asociativas*. Despite the clear legal right of activists to form this cooperative, the INA was slow to measure the land and process the paperwork because of the looming presence and interests of Miguel Facussé in the area. As a legally recognized cooperative, Iseri Lidawamari was able to get government loans to plant rice and other crops. It supplemented this with donations from foreign embassies, development funds, and other international organizations that continued to support their efforts to create sustainable development and community empowerment. Some of this money was given specifically to build houses in Vallecito, where a good number of Limoneño families relocated. But then Lombardo's house, the Centro de Capacitación, and some crops were destroyed by fire. (Most suspect that this was done by people working for Facussé, but there was never any investigation so it is not known for certain.) Later that year Hurricane Mitch destroyed what crops were left, leaving the cooperative with a huge debt. Despite these setbacks, the cooperative experienced one major success when it won a suit against Miguel Facussé in the supreme court after he illegally invaded and planted African palm on the land of one of the *empresas*. Because the cooperative could prove that it has *dominio pleno*, it was able to both remove him from the land and claim the palm, which they now own and manage. However, real tragedy struck the cooperative in 2001 when Lombardo, the founder of Iseri Lidawamari and the true backbone of the organization, died of a sudden brain hemorrhage. The families living in Vallecito continued to work and administer the palm until 2004, when one member was found hacked to death with a machete. Since then, Limoneños have been reluctant to work in Vallecito directly, preferring instead to hire ladinos to clear the weeds and harvest the palm for them. Thus, despite all the support the cooperative has received from NGOs, churches, international organizations, and even the Honduran state as an exemplar of community development, these forms of harassment (arson and murder) have gone unpunished, sending the clear message that a cooperative that is too successful and too radical in its critique of the dominant development model will receive only so much support from the state.

As with the politics of race, then, Garifuna receive conflicting messages from the Honduran state and international agencies, who praise them on the one hand as the conservators of forms of sustainable development and simultaneously enact policies that make these sustainable practices (mainly in agriculture and fishing) increasingly difficult to maintain. It is no wonder that many Garifuna continue to see migration, whether to Honduran cities or the United States, as the only real mode of upward mobility and community development. But to what degree has migration enabled Garifuna to achieve these goals? Garifuna have different opinions on this question, stemming from the complexity of their position within two systems of inequality where race and class interact somewhat differently. For those who side more with the interpretation of the Pro-Electrification Committee, the fact that Limón did finally get the long-sought electricity in 1999 is a sign of progress. Today all households in Limón have electric light and most have televisions and fans; a few businesses even have air conditioning. This is seen as a dramatic improvement in the standard of living in the village in the sense that it more closely approximates that of the Honduran middle class. Through family remittances and hometown associations, transmigrants have been able to invest in the housing and education of their family members in Honduras, some of the elements of upward mobility. The presence of electricity has also spurred greater investment by migrants in businesses such as restaurants, hotels, and even two Internet cafes. And yet, as proponents of Iseri Lidawamari had predicted, electricity has mainly served to provide these "comforts" without significantly affecting the employment situation in the community. The road is still not paved, so Limón is still pretty much off the beaten track for tourists, and no new industries have entered the community to bring new jobs. More and more Limoneños continue to migrate every day, some joining the masses of Hondurans taking the increasingly dangerous and costly land route through Mexico, others taking advantage of family reunification made possible by the long-term presence of Garifuna in the United States. People in the community continue to travel to Tocoa and La Ceiba to buy food and household goods with remittances sent by those abroad, and ladinos continue to enter the community to sell *guineo* and plantain. Migration has thus not abated and remittance dependency has not decreased as the result of the entrance of electricity into the community. This continued reliance on migration is a function both of the continued structural constraints that have made Honduras one of the poorest countries in the Americas and the continuing belief among the majority of Garifuna that migration is the fastest route to resolving their position within those structures.

As most of the literature has shown, remittances do have many positive effects; they contribute to household expenses so other funds can be invested in human capital (such as education) and make it possible to open business-es, both of which ultimately benefit the community. But without significant sources of employment in the community, these business generally have few multiplier effects. Restaurants in Limón, for example, buy much of their food outside the community and employ mainly family labor. Garifuna activists ar-gue that using remittances for collective enterprises would be the most direct route to community development, but there are few examples of this strategy on the ground (Cantor, Schoenharl, and Valerio 2004). This may be due to the fact that migrant resources are already so stretched with family obligations that there is little left for community projects. It may also be related to the fact that while Garifuna have a long history of hometown associations and other forms of communal organizing, membership in them is not obligatory and there is no real social sanction against not joining them. For example, one study of Mixtec communities in Oaxaca shows that communities whose members are strictly required to contribute to collective projects through *tequio* have made good use of remittances for communal projects and management of communal re-sources (Vanwey, Tucker, and McConnell 2005). There have been some efforts by organizations such as Iseri Lidawamari and ODECO to generate this more collective use of remittances, but these goals are difficult to attain because mi-grants mainly concentrate on their own families. Just as many of my Limoneño informants had told me, migration continues to be a double-edged sword. It helps families survive but at the same time subsidizes a national economy that does little to provide for the basic needs of its people. According to an ODECO document, Garifuna communities were not included in the most recent map of poverty in Honduras because so many households receive remittances and so many transmigrants have invested in infrastructure that Garifuna communities do not exhibit the dire poverty that is seen in many indigenous communities. This way of measuring poverty does not take into account the sacrifices that Garifuna transmigrants make when they split up families, work double shifts, and risk deportation in order to send those remittances. For organizations such as ODECO, then, the strong propensity for Garifuna to migrate is a sign of the failure of the Honduran state to provide adequate employment, not a long-term solution to structural poverty.

Ironically, what has generated some new employment and infusion of cash into some Garifuna (and Miskito) communities is a transnational enterprise that relies on the combination of geographic isolation, minimal infrastructure, and transnational networks Limón has to offer: drug trafficking. According to the U.S. government, 60 percent of the cocaine that entered the United States in 2000 passed through Central America, a threefold increase since 1993, leading to what analysts are calling the "Colombianization of Central America" (Arana 2001). In Guatemala and El Salvador, former military personnel are some of the main participants in this industry, while in Honduras it is largely the transnational gangs made up of Hondurans deported from the U.S.[2] The drugs come by boat from Colombia, are unloaded in Garifuna and Miskito villages from Limón eastward to the Mosquitia (see Burnett 2004 on effects of cocaine trade on Nicaragua's Mosquito Coast), and are then carried by land through Guatemala to Mexico. Though there were rumors of boats laden with arms occasionally washing up on shore and people landing on the beach in the middle of the night with mysterious cargo when I was there in the 1990s, these have now become regular occurrences. The presence of the drug traffickers, all of whom are ladinos from other parts of Honduras, is palpable in Limón, where they sit in the restaurants every day drinking beer, brazenly flash their pistols and assault rifles in the newest hotel, and drive through town in SUVs with tinted windows. Some Limoneños have begun working for them in different capacities, and everyone else makes a point of staying quiet.

Drug trafficking represents the latest in a long line of threats to the integrity and autonomy of Garifuna communities. Like the multinational fruit companies, the tourism industry, and the maquiladoras, the drug trade is both somewhere and nowhere, relying on a specific combination of human resources (cheap labor and cooperative elites), geography (good weather, beautiful beaches, and relative isolation), and social structures (a poor population with no political voice and extreme socioeconomic inequality) but at the same time quite capable of and willing to pick up and move operations somewhere else when any one of these conditions deteriorates. The industries are all transnational in the sense that the networks of capital, contacts, shared ideologies, and markets are really what constitute them, not the particular place where they happen to be located at any one time or even the particular actors involved. As many scholars have argued, this is the evil twin of transnational migration and transnational social movements. Drug trafficking and transnational migration and social movements all challenge the power of the nation-state to regulate all processes within its borders, they all create opportunities by taking advantage of different economic and social conditions in multiple nation-states, and they all rely on alternative constructions of community that fall outside as well as within national borders. Yet transnational migration and transnational social movements can be seen as attempts by normally disenfranchised populations to level the playing field somewhat, to take advantage of currency differentials, conflicts between states and international organizations, and the mutual support of community members in multiple locations to improve their position within the larger structures of inequality. Transnational capital (both legal and illegal), on the other hand, continues to profit from and therefore perpetuate those same inequalities as they are constituted in the gendered and racialized international division of labor.

Garifuna, like other peoples who have strong traditions of immigration, are caught up in these processes, trying to improve their lives through immigration, return migration, hometown associations, grassroots organizations, and other creative forms of "movement." As Garifuna, money, goods, ideas, and forms of organization move back and forth between these national contexts, they create lives, families, and communities that are truly bi-national, dependent on the contradictions of the international division of labor but also making creative choices about how to negotiate those contradictions. I do not want this book to read like one of those documentaries about peoples losing their way of life and their culture as the machinery of modernization steamrolls over them. Garifuna have never been isolated from the processes of globalization, colonization, and nation-building—all the hallmarks of modernity—but were born as a people within the very center of these processes in the Caribbean. For earlier anthropologists, this historically traceable ethnogenesis led to claims that they were "neoteric"—that is, having shallow roots—and therefore doomed to disappear through the processes of assimilation and integration all ethnic groups face (Gonzalez 1988). While it is true that Garifuna villages are under intense pressure from both external and internal sources, changing their way of making a living, consumption habits, musical styles, language choices, and so forth, their society and culture are far from disappearing. As with the transnational corporations, the real backbone of Garifuna society lies in the networks of families and community activists, the shared ethnic and racial identities, the rituals of community solidarity, and the common experience of being Garifuna, regardless of whether that takes place in Honduras or New York City, Belize or Los Angeles. This not to say that the Garifuna experience is homogeneous; they encounter different conditions and opportunities in the many places where they reside. As with any category of people, the continuity in principles of community, identity, and culture are also fractured by race, class, gender, place of residence, and other axes of difference. Thus there is both continuity and variation within the Garifuna diaspora, creating contradictions that lead to differing organizing goals and strategies but also providing an impetus and source of support for continued struggle.

Notes

Chapter 1. Transnational Movements, Racialized Space

1. *Indigenismo* refers to the valorization of the indigenous roots of society, whether they are cultural or racial. I explain this in more detail in Chapter 6.

2. In Honduras, the Caribbean coastline is on the northern side of the country. Hondurans refer to the North Coast as a region that includes the departments of Cortes, Atlántida, Yoro, Colón, and Gracias a Dios. This region is distinguished not only by its location in the northern part of the country but also by a particular historical connection to the multinational fruit companies. Therefore when I am referring to Honduras in particular I will use the term "North Coast" to refer to this region. However, when I am referring to Central America as a whole I will refer to the coastline as the "Caribbean coast."

3. Suazo (1996) cites a total figure of 70,000 and the Summer Institute of Linguistics cites 98,000 based on Rivas (1993, 257). The 2001 Honduran census gives a figure of 49,952, which most Garifuna activists consider to be a gross undercount. The CIA World Factbook on Honduras states that blacks (which would include Garifuna and English-speaking blacks) make up 2 percent of a population of 6.9 million. This would put the black population as a whole at about 139,000 (www.odci.gov/cia/publications/factbook/geos/ho.html#People).

4 The Summer Institute of Linguistics cites the 1991 census figure as 12,274 (www.ethnologue.com/show_language.asp?code=cab). The 2005 CIA World Factbook cites the Garifuna population as 17,046, or 6.1 percent of the population (www.odci.gov/cia/publications/factbook/geos/bh.html#People).

5. The Summer Institute of Linguistics estimates 16,700 for Guatemala, but that seems to me to be a very high figure.

6. There are still some "Black Carib" communities in St. Vincent, but they have only recently made contact with Central American Garifuna through organizations and the Internet (see the Caribbean Amerindian Centrelink Web site at www.centrelink.org). It is unclear whether the "Black Caribs" of St. Vincent consider themselves to be Garifuna in the same way that Central Americans do. Salvador Suazo (1996, 10) includes them in his count of the total Garifuna population, saying there are 7,500 in six villages in St. Vincent.

7. "Ladino" is currently used to refer to peoples of mixed Spanish and indigenous origin, the same as mestizo in other parts of Latin America.

8. Current population estimates for these groups are: Lenca 300,594; Miskitus 55,500; Tolupanes 10,343; Chortis 37,052; Pech 4,138; Tawakas 2,649; and Negro Ingles 13,303. These estimates are from the 2001 Honduran census (www.hondurasinfo.hn/eng/pub/Censo_2001.pdf).

9. The main exception to this is *Tráfico de esclavos negros a Honduras* by Rafael Leiva Vivas (1982).

10. The issue of when an indigenous person becomes a ladino is an interesting problematic that has been written about extensively in recent years. For a long time anthropologists followed the ideological foundations of *mestizaje* that indigenous people inevitably acculturate by losing their language and customs and marrying into the ladino population. For example, in his survey of the Central American population, Adams (1957) uses the terms "Indians" to refer to those who are racially and culturally distinct from ladinos, "ladinoized Indians" for those who are racially but not culturally distinct, and "ladinos" for those who are both racially mixed and "assimilated." He states that often the distinction between indigenous people and ladinos is mainly attributable to poverty and self-designation rather than race or culture (see also Chavez Borjas 1983). Based on fluidity of categories, anthropologists have long argued that "ladino" is less a racial designation than a cultural one and therefore it is easy for an indigenous person to simply acculturate and become a ladino. In more recent work, scholars have questioned this characterization of the ladino as a cultural category and pointed out the ways that it is still quite racialized (Gould 1998; C. Smith 1999). Many have also questioned the extent to which *mestizaje* or acculturation is a "natural" process (de la Cadena 2000; C. Smith 1990, 1997; J. Warren 2001).

11. According to linguists, Garifuna is a mixture of the grammars of Island Carib, Island Arawak, and African languages. Garifuna also has many loan words from English, Spanish, and French (Bertilson 1989; Suazo 1994).

12. A municipality in Honduras is not exactly the same as one in the United States because it not only encompasses an urban area but also a great number of rural settlements. It is more akin to a county.

13. This figure is based both on Limoneño estimates and my own count of the number of houses in Limón (roughly 500) multiplied by the average household size of 6.5. I rounded up to 4,000 to take into consideration the large numbers of Limoneños who work outside the village temporarily.

14. I define Limoneños as those born in Limón or born to Limoneño parents outside Limón.

Chapter 2. From Indigenous Blacks to Hispanic Immigrants: A History of Garifuna Movement and Labor Migration from the 1600s to the 1990s

1. Some versions of Garifuna history place their "ethnogenesis" in the 1300s as the result of the migration of Africans across the Atlantic of their own accord (Van Sertima

1976). I have chosen, nonetheless, to use the version that places this historical moment of "ethnogenesis" in the 1600s because it is more clearly documented by written sources. I recognize that this does not mean that archeology may not prove the validity of the other version in the future.

2. The following quotes from Thomas Young, a British envoy who resided on the Mosquito shore in the 1840s, are exemplary:

The West Indian productions, coffee, tobacco, sea-island cotton, etc. when cultivated in proper situations, might be grown with advantage; but I much fear no positive dependence could be placed on the Mosquitians for labourers, for although they will in general hire themselves for a month or two, in exchange for goods, yet perhaps, when the planter required his crops to be housed, they might refuse to work; and extensive plantations would take more men than could always be obtained. A Mosquitian will hire for six to eight dollars per lunar month, besides rations. The province of Victoria has however, the decided advantage of having within itself, and adjacent thereto, numbers of that well-ordered people, the Caribs, who are at all time willing to work for from eight to ten dollars per calendar month, and rations; one moiety in cash, and another in goods; but even with these people the expenses would be great, as their wages for agricultural purposes I consider too high (Young 1847, 108).

The influx of the Caribs has had a decided influence in benefiting the country; and, in my opinion, another 50 years will be attended with important advantages, and that the Caribs will become a very numerous people, friendly to the English, but jealous of their rights "(159).

3. Gonzalez (1988) claims the Garifuna were "company men" and did not get involved in the strike, but I talked to many Garifuna men who were involved as activists and in the unions. In fact, some fled to New York as a result of the repression of union leaders following the strike. See Euraque 2004 for a more detailed discussion of this era.

4. This data was never published. I was able to obtain it from Pierre Beaucage himself, who has graciously agreed to let me use it in this book.

5. Beaucage chose interviewees who were "heads of household." The absence of women in the sample of heads of household is certainly not a reflection of the actual number of female heads of household. Beaucage himself recognized female-headed households as one of the major forms in his book. It is unclear why he largely omitted them from his survey.

6. "White, non-Hispanic" decreased from 34 percent of the Bronx population to 23 percent. "Hispanics" increased from 34 percent of the population to 43 percent.

7. The categories that are employed in Bailey and Waldinger's (1991) analysis are "native blacks," "immigrant Hispanics," "immigrant Asians," and "immigrant blacks." Though many Garifuna could be considered to be immigrant blacks, the data is taken from the U.S. population census, which classifies peoples as Hispanic/non-Hispanic

first, and by race second. I believe that Honduran Garifuna would have been most likely counted among the sample of immigrant Hispanics. Belizeans, on the other hand, were most likely counted as "immigrant blacks," since Belize is classified as a "non-Hispanic" Central American country.

8. Though a large number of Salvadorans were migrating to New York, even larger numbers were migrating to Los Angeles, Washington, D.C., San Francisco, and Houston.

9. Of about 59,000 Hondurans who entered the United States legally from 1990 to 1999, about 52,000 came through family reunification (New York City Department of City Planning 2000).

10. This is actually a composite of the three primary migration families in Limón. I have given this composite family the pseudonym Ramirez.

11. This usually amounted to the military getting on a crowded bus and dragging off all men that appeared to be of appropriate age for immediate conscription. This practice was finally banned during the presidency of Carlos Roberto Reina (1994–1997), thanks to the work of the Committee for Human Rights in Honduras (CODEH) and other civil society organizations.

Chapter 3. Families in Space: The Transnationalization of Matrifocal Kinship

1. This movie was made by director Ali Allié, with his wife, a Garifuna woman from Honduras, as the leading actress. It came out in 1999.

2. Garifuna men refer to their domestic partners as *esposa*, *mujer*, or *compañera* whether or not they are legally married.

3. I include grandmothers here as mothers because they raised their grandchildren in the absence or death of the mother. This also includes a woman who was raised by her aunt.

4. These last two categories may appear to be similar but in fact they are quite different. Women who are receiving remittances as wives, legal or common-law, may or may not be the mother of the sender's children. Remittances are sent to the woman for her needs and to maintain a household the man considers to be his other home. A man who has children with a woman he no longer considers to be his wife or whom he never considered to be his wife will still send money to her for his children. Men often have to defend accusations that this implies they still want to maintain some kind of relationship with that woman. To deflect these accusations, they argue that the money is meant solely for the maintenance of the children.

5. These are not mythical distant ancestors but rather real relatives who died within the living memory of the person who falls ill, often a grandparent or great-grandparent.

6. Since Garifuna families are large and all extended kin are expected to contribute, this could have included more than 100 individuals.

Chapter 4. "Los Pobres Allá Somos Los Ricos Acá en Honduras": Navigating the Contradictions of the International Division of Labor

1. The Garifuna village directly to the west of Limón, Aguan, was nearly washed away. Its story was featured in the *New York Times* (McKinley 1999).

2. An *empresa asociativa* is similar to a cooperative in that all members contribute to the labor of production and share the profits of the sale of goods produced, be it agricultural produce or livestock. There is a legal maximum of fifty members.

3. Much of the data used in the study came from the research of anthropologist Pierre Beaucage (personal communication, Pierre Beaucage; Instituto de Investigaciones Económicas y Sociales, Facultad de Ciencias Económicas 1965, 9), yet the conclusions different authors drew from the same information reveal different assumptions about the nature of economic rationality and development. For the authors of the socio-economic study of Limon, Garifuna economic activities seem to be mired in traditional subsistence attitudes that prevent rational profit-maximization behavior. For Beaucage, all humans exhibit "economizing behavior" but this behavior is embedded in a set of social relations governed by values and norms of behavior that have their own logic. Beaucage argues that in the case of the Garifuna, such notions as reciprocal exchange, mutual help among kin, and food abundance for all govern the rules of production, distribution, and exchange within which Garifuna make rational decisions.

4. According to Limoneño informants, until the 1960s, Laude was cultivated by Limoneños as occupied land; that is, no one had legal title over it. It is a particularly fertile area and sustained a wide variety of crops. In the 1970s, several wealthy *capitalino* families arrived and put cattle on the land, thereby destroying the crops of the Garifuna (they were not accustomed to fencing in their property). Those who refused to leave even after their crops were destroyed were threatened, and eventually all Limoneños abandoned the area. The wealthy families, who had connections to the government and the INA, easily gained legal title to the land and now have large ranches.

5. For the purposes of understanding economic strategies in Limón, I use the term household in the sense of a co-residential unit. However, as in Chapter 4, I recognize that economic input and decision-making can be transnational, so I include all sources of income whether "local" or not, including remittances, U.S. retirement checks, and the like.

6. I did not collect information on the exact extension of land-holdings as this was a touchy subject due to the atmosphere of land conflict. However, the municipal *jefe de catastro* (head of the land register) told me that the average size of the landholdings of "*foraneos*" (foreigners; that is, non-Garifuna) in Laude and Limóncito is 600 manzanas

(about 1,020 acres), whereas the average Garifuna landholding is 20 manzanas (about 34 acres). This seems correct; the few people who did specify the size of their landholdings cited anything from one-half a manzana for a *yucal* (cassava plot) to 80 manzanas for cattle.

7. The *ruguma* (or *culebra* in Spanish) is a long tube woven of reeds that is suspended from the ceiling of a kitchen and used to squeeze the liquid out of the grated cassava pulp. Once the cassava pulp is dry, it is sifted through a round flat woven seive called a *hibisi*. These two implements can also be found in use among Carib in some areas of the Caribbean and northern South America and in some Amazonian tribes of Brazil (see, for example, Murphy and Murphy 1985).

8. Garifuna have become quite savvy about calculating the cost of doing business. For example, some men now fish with outboard motors and try to include the cost of gas in the price of the fish.

9. There are also many Puerto Ricans, but they are not considered to be immigrants by the INS and so are not counted as such by the New York City Planning Department in *The Newest New Yorkers*.

10. This changed in 1996 with the passage of the Illegal Immigrant Reform and Immigrant Responsibility Act and welfare reform, both of which tried to limit the amount of social services both legal and illegal residents could receive.

Chapter 5. ¿Superando o Desintegrando? Disparate Discourses of Development in Transnational Grassroots Organizations

1. Union Corazaleña, Pro-Kindergarden Sambo Creek, Illuminación Triunfeño, Pro-Mejoramiento de San Antonio, Pro-Mejoramiento de Masca, Comité Union Cristaleña, Mejoramiento Travesia, Iriona, Santa Rosa de Aguan, and Guadelupe.

2. The money raised by the committee amounted to about 10 percent of the cost of the project, with the state providing the other 90 percent.

3. In the quotes I intentionally keep the word *pueblo* in Spanish, maintaining the ambiguity as to whether they are referring to the "village" or the Garifuna "people." This ambiguity of *pueblo* reveals the way in which territory and peoplehood are often conflated in Garifuna discourse.

4. The Brooks and Goff families are both white Isleños.

5. Escobar makes a distinction between the types of sustainable development proposed by indigenous and ethnic organizations and by the World Bank. Escobar argues that the World Bank version maintains the same basic assumption of development economics, that the environment and nature are commodities to be exploited in the name of industrialization and economic growth. What is ultimately to be sustained then is economic growth, via a more careful and rational use of the earth's resources so that they can be renewed. This then simply reinforces the belief that western technology is the answer to the world's problems and can be rationally implemented to exploit

nature as a commodity, denying again the value of local belief systems with alternative attitudes towards nature (1993:192–99).

6. At the time of this writing, Limoneños had still not been successful in annulling the sale because of Facussé's economic and political power.

7. This corresponds to the findings of many of the early studies of the links between migration and development in which authors argued that in many communities remittances are simply used for consumption and the creation of "redundant businesses" (i.e., everyone has a restaurant) and therefore remain reliant on remittances (Ballard 1987, Gmelch 1980, Kearney 1986).

Chapter 6. Black, Indigenous, and Latino: The Politics of Racial and Ethnic Identity in the Garifuna Diaspora

1. In practice, the distinction is more ambiguous. For example, diasporic populations formed through exile or other processes that diminish the hope of return may later establish more immediate relations with the homeland as political situations change, taking on characteristics more akin to transnational migrants and the deterritorialized nation-state. Likewise, many transmigrant populations migrate to multiple nation-states and maintain networks that unite them in these various locales, thus taking on some of the characteristics of a diaspora.

2. The main exceptions to this are Brazil and Cuba, where there has been more glorification of African ancestry and integration of blackness into national identity in a manner parallel to *indigenismo* in other Latin American countries. But even in these two countries blackness has been valued very unevenly and racism is still prevalent in societies characterized by structural racism (Skidmore 1995; Telles 2004; Winndance-Twine 2000).

3. Though the word mestizo appears on the census and in academic texts, ladino is still the main word used in popular speech to refer to the mestizo population. Ladino now carries the same connotations of a mixture of indigenous and Spanish ancestry.

4. English-speaking Natives (*Nativos de habla inglesa*) was the term used to refer to the black creoles at this meeting. This was the first time I had ever seen them referred to in this way. The use of the term "*nativos*" for a population that has no claim to indigenous heritage is further proof of the ideological conflation of ethnicity with autocthony.

5. Though Belizean Garifuna consider themselves to be ethnic minorities who have suffered discrimination, their relation to the Belizean state is not so antagonistic. According to Macklin (1985) this is because Belizean nationalism embraces ethnic pluralism, as opposed to the homogenizing nationalism of *mestizaje* in Honduras. Therefore Garifuna identity and music have come to be accepted as part of Belizean national identity. Settlement Day, which celebrates the day the Garifuna arrived in Belize, was declared a national holiday in 1977 and is celebrated throughout the nation (Macklin

1985). The Garifuna movement in Belize can be characterized as ethnic nationalist, because they still differentiate themselves as an ethnic group, but that is not necessarily seen as threatening to the state (Wright 1995).

6. In this category I include any relationship that produced children, whether the couple lived together or were married.

7. For example, many of the women who are members of the Garifuna Nation are also members of Mujeres Garifuna en Marcha (MUGAMA), an organization of professional women who raise money for student scholarships to New York high schools and colleges and sponsor Miss Garifuna contests and other cultural events. Others are members of UNCUGA, which sponsors classes in the Garifuna language in New York.

8. This Web site no longer exists. Currently the main site for Garifuna news and organizations is http://garinet.com.

Conclusion

1. An article by Traci Carl for the Associated Press reveals this sentiment in the words of Sunni Bergess, manager of a resort near a Garifuna community, when she said "Pretty much they just make bread and dance. That's pretty much the extent of their talents" (Carl 2002).

2. As I mentioned in Chapter 2, there does not seem to be much evidence that Honduran Garifuna are involved in these gangs. Pictures of Central American gang members that have appeared in the Honduran and U.S. newspapers are always of heavily tattooed ladinos. In addition, I encountered very few Garifuna who had been deported and heard no stories of Garifuna gang members from Limoneños. On the other hand, an article by Linda Miller Mathai and David Smith (1998) does mention Belizean Garifuna joining the Bloods and the Crips in Los Angeles and taking those forms of gang activity back to Belize.

Bibliography

Adams, Richard. 1957. *Cultural Surveys of Panama, Nicaragua, Guatemala, El Salvador, Honduras*. Pan American Sanitary Bureau, World Health Organization.

———. 1975. "Nationalization." In *Handbook of Middle American Indians*, ed. Manning Nash. Austin: University of Texas Press.

Alvarado Garcia, Ernesto. 1958. *Legislación Indígenista de Honduras*. Mexico City: Instituto Indígenista Iberoamericano.

Anderson, Benedict. 1983. *Imagined Communities*. London: Verso.

Anderson, Mark. 1997. "The Significance of Blackness: Representations of Garifuna in St. Vincent and Central America, 1700–1900." *Transforming Anthropology: Journal of the Association of Black Anthropologists* 6 (nos. 1–2): 22–35.

———. 2000. "Garifuna Kids: Blackness, Modernity, and Tradition in Honduras." Ph.D. diss. University of Texas, Austin.

Andrade-Eekhoff, Katherine, and Claudia Marina Silva-Avalos. 2003. "Globalization of the Periphery: The Challenges of Transnational Migration for Local Development in Central America." Working Document. April 2003. Facultad Latinoamericana de Ciencias Sociales. San Salvador, El Salvador.

Andreas, Peter. 1999. "Borderless Economy, Barricaded Border." *NACLA* 33 (no. 3).

———. 2001. "The Transformation of Migrant Smuggling across the U.S./Mexico Border." In *Global Human Smuggling in Comparative Perspective*, ed. David Kyle and Rey Koslowski. Baltimore: Johns Hopkins University Press.

Anzaldua, Gloria. 1987. *Borderlands/La Frontera: The New Mestiza*. San Francisco: Spinsters/Aunt Lute Books.

Appadurai, Arjun. 1996. *Modernity at Large: Cultural Dimensions of Globalization*. Minneapolis: University of Minnesota Press.

Arana, Ana. 2001. "The New Battle for Central America." *Foreign Affairs* 8 (no. 6): 88–101.

———. 2005. "How the Street Gangs Took Central America." *Foreign Affairs* 84 (no. 3).

Arancibia, Juan. 1984. *Honduras: Un Estado Nacional?* Tegucigalpa: Editorial Guaymuras.

Argueta, Mario. 1992. *Historia de los sin Historia*. Tegucigalpa: Editorial Guaymuras.

Back, Les, and John Solomos, eds. 2000. *Theories of Race and Racism*. London: Routledge.

Bailey, Thomas, and Roger Waldinger. 1991. "Changing Ethnic/Racial Division of Labor." In *Dual City: Restructuring New York*, ed. John Mollenkopf and Manuel Castells, 25–42. New York: Russell Sage Foundation.

Baker-Cristales, Beth. 2004. *Salvadoran Migration to Southern California: Redefining el Hermano Lejano*. Gainesville: University Press of Florida.

Balibar, Etienne. 1991. "Racism and Nationalism." In *Race, Nation, Class: Ambiguous Identities*, ed. Etienne Balibar and Immanuel Wallerstein, 37–67. New York: Verso.

Ballard, Roger. 1987. "The Political Economy of Migration: Pakistan, Britain, and the Middle East" In *Migrants, Workers, and the Social Order*, ed. Jeremy Eades, 17–41. London: Tavistock.

Banton, Michael. 1977. *The Idea of Race*. London: Tavistock.

Barahona, Marvin. 1991. *Evolución Histórica de la Identidad Nacional*. Tegucigalpa: Editorial Guaymuras.

Basch, Linda, Nina Glick Schiller, and Cristina Szanton Blanc. 1994. *Nations Unbound: Transnational Projects, Postcolonial Predicaments, and Deterritorialized Nation-States*. New York: Gordon and Breach.

Beaucage, Pierre. 1970. "Economic Anthropology of the Black Carib (Garifuna) of Honduras." Ph.D. diss., London School of Economics.

———. 1989. "La Dynamique Autocthone et L'Etat: L'Exemple des Garifonas du Honduras." In *L'Etat et les Autocthones en Amérique Latine et au Canada*, ed. M. Lapointe. Quebec City: Université Laval.

Behar, Ruth. 1993. *Translated Woman: Crossing the Border with Esperanza's Story*. Boston: Beacon Press.

Bello, Walden. 1994. *Dark Victory: The United States, Structural Adjustment, and Global Poverty*. London: Pluto Press.

Benedict, Ruth. 1943. *Race and Racism*. London: Routledge.

Bertilson, Kathryn. 1989. *Introducción al Idioma Garifuna*. Tequeigalpa: Cuerpo de Paz de Honduras.

Bhabha, Homi. 1990. "The Third Space: Interview with Homi Bhabha." In *Identity: Community, Culture, Difference*, ed. J. Rutherford, 207–221. London: Lawrence and Wishart.

Bibler Coutin, Susan. 2005. "Being En Route." *American Anthropologist* 107 (no. 2): 195–206.

Bolland, Nigel. 1977. *The Formation of a Colonial Society: Belize, from Conquest to Crown Colony*. Baltimore: Johns Hopkins University Press.

Bourgois, Philippe. 1989. *Ethnicity at Work: Divided Labor on a Central American Banana Plantation*. Baltimore: Johns Hopkins University Press.

———. 1995. *In Search of Respect: Selling Crack in El Barrio*. Cambridge, England: Cambridge University Press.

Boyer, Jeffrey, and Aaron Pell. 1999. "Mitch in Honduras: A Disaster Waiting to Happen." *NACLA* 33 (no. 2).

Breslin, Pat. 1995. "On the Sidewalks of New York, the Sun Is Shining Again." *Smithsonian: Second Anniversary Issue* (April): 100–111.

Brodkin, Karen. 2000. *How Jews Became White Folk and What That Says about Race in America*. New Brunswick, N.J.: Rutgers University Press.

Brysk, Alison. 2000. *From Tribal Village to Global Village: Indian Rights and International Relations in Latin America*. Stanford, Calif.: Stanford University Press.

Burnett, John. 2004. "Cocaine's Influence on Nicaragua's Miskito Coast." *Morning Edition*, National Public Radio, October 22.

Burns, Allan. 1993. *Maya in Exile: Guatemalans in Florida*. Philadelphia, Pa.: Temple University Press.

Calix Suazo, Miguel, and Zonia Vindel de Calix. 1991. *Política Económica antes y despues de 1989*. Tegucigalpa, Honduras: Litografia Lopez.

Cantor, Eric, Julia Schoenharl, and Teofila Valeria. 2004. "Remittances and Development: Lessons from the Garifuna Transnational Community." Research report prepared for Deutscher Entwicklungsdienst Cooperación Técnica Alemana.

Carl, Traci. 2002. "Honduras Looks to Develop Northern Coast; Garifuna Fight to Keep Beaches." Associated Press, January 2. Available online at http://forests.org/articles/.

Castells, Manuel. 1993. The Informational Economy and the New International Division of Labor." In *The New Global Economy in the Information Age*, ed. Martin Carnoy, 15–43. University Park, Pa.: Pennsylvania State University Press.

———. 1997. *The Power of Identity*. Oxford: Blackwell.

Castro Rubio, Angel Augusto. 1994. *Un Plan de Desarrollo Regional: El Bajo Aguan en Honduras*. Mexico City: Universidad Iberoamericana.

Centeno Garcia, Santos. 1997. *Historia del Movimiento Negro Hondureño*. La Ceiba, Honduras: Jose Hipólito Centeno Garcia.

Chapman, Ann. 1992. *Masters of Animals: Oral Traditions of the Tolupan Indians, Honduras*. Philadelphia: Gordon and Breach.

Charles, Cecil. 1890. *Honduras: The Land of Great Depths*. New York: Rand McNally.

Chatterjee, Partha. 1986. *Nationalist Thought and the Colonial World: A Derivative Discourse?* London: Zed Books.

Chavez, Leo. 1991. "Outside the Imagined Community: Undocumented Settlers and Experiences of Incorporation." *American Ethnologist* 18 (no. 2): 257–278.

———. 1998. *Shadowed Lives: Undocumented Immigration in American Society*. Orlando: Harcourt Brace College Publishers.

Chavez Borjas, Manuel. 1983. "Para comprender la cuestión étnica en Honduras." *Alcaraván* 19: 18–21.

———. 1984. "La cultura Jicaque y el proyecto de desarrollo indígena en Yoro." *América Indígena* 44 (no. 3): 587–612.

Clifford, James. 1997. *Routes: Travel and Translation in the Late 20th Century*. Cambridge, Mass.: Harvard University Press.

Coehlo, Ruy Galvão de Andrade. 1995. *Los Negros Caribes de Honduras*. Published version of 1955 dissertation in English. Tegucigalpa: Editorial Guaymuras.

Comité para la Defensa de los Derechos Humanos en Honduras (CODEH). 1991. "Modernización y Desarrollo Agrícola: El final de más de 30 años de lucha campesina." *Boletín del Comité para la Defensa de los Derechos Humanos en Honduras* 9 (no. 82).

Conniff, Michael. 1985. *Black Labor on a White Canal*. Pittsburgh: University of Pittsburgh Press.

CONPAH. 1993. "Comunicado." *Diario El Tiempo* (San Pedro Sula), July 14, 29.

Cruz Sandoval, Fernando. 1984. "Los indios de Honduras y la situación de sus recursos naturales." *América Indígena* 44 (no. 3): 423–445.

Davidson, William. 1974. *Historical Geography of the Bay Islands, Honduras: Anglo-Hispanic Conflict in the Western Caribbean*. Birmingham, Alabama: Southern University Press.

———. 1976. "Black Carib (Garifuna) Habitats in Central America." In *Fronteir Adaptations in Lower Central America*, ed. Mary Helms and F. Loveland, 85–94. Philadelphia: Institute for the Study of Human Issues.

———. 1980. "The Garifuna of Pearl Lagoon: Ethnohistory of an Afro-American Enclave in Nicaragua." *Ethnohistory* 27 (no. 1): 31–47.

de la Cadena, Marisol. 2000. *Indigenous Mestizos: Politics of Race and Culture in Cuzco, Peru, 1919–1991*. Durham, N.C.: Duke University Press.

Diène, Doudou. 2004. "El Racismo, La Discrimiánción Racial, La Xenofobia y Todas Las Formas de Discriminación: Informe del Sr. Doudou Diene, Relator Especial sobre las formas contemporáneas de racismo, discriminación racial, xenophobia, y formas conexas de intolerancia. Mision a Honduras." Inter-American Commission on Human Rights, Washington, D.C.

Dirlik, Arif. 1994. "The Postcolonial Aura: Third World Criticism in the Age of Global Capitalism." *Critical Inquiry* 20 (no. 2): 328–356.

Dominguez, Virginia. 1975. *From Neighbor to Stranger: The Dilemma of Caribbean Peoples in the United States*. New Haven, Conn.: Yale University Press.

Drennan, Mathew. 1991. "The Decline and Rise of the New York Economy." In *Dual City: Restructuring New York*, ed. John Mollenkopf and Manuel Castells, 25–42. New York: Russell Sage Foundation.

Dunkerly, James. 1988. *Power in the Isthmus: A Political History of Modern Central America*. London: Verso.

Durham, William. 1979. *Scarcity and Survival in Central America: The Ecological Origins of the Soccer War*. Stanford, Calif.: Stanford University Press.

Echeverri-Gent, Elisavinda. 1992. "Forgotten Workers: British West Indians and the Early Days of the Banana Industry in Costa Rica and Honduras." *Journal of Latin American Studies* 24 (May): 275–308.

Enloe, Cynthia. 1989. *Bananas, Beaches, and Bases: Making Feminist Sense of International Politics*. Berkeley: University of California Press.

Escobar, Arturo. 1995. *Encountering Development: The Making and Unmaking of the Third World*. Princeton, N.J.: Princeton University Press.

———. 1997. "Cultural Politics and Biological Diversity: State, Capital, and Social Movements in the Pacific Coast of Colombia." In *The Politics of Culture in the Shadow of Capital*, ed. Lisa Lowe and David Lloyd, 201–226. Durham, N.C.: Duke University Press.

Escobar, Arturo, and Sonia Alvarez. 1992. *The Making of Social Movements in Latin America: Identity, Strategy and Democracy*. Boulder, Colo.: Westview Press.

Euraque, Darío. 1996a. *Estado, Poder, Nacionalidad y Raza en la Historia de Honduras*. Choluteca, Honduras: Ediciones Subirana.

———. 1996b. *Reinterpreting the Banana Republic: Region and State in Honduras, 1870–1972*. Chapel Hill: University of North Carolina Press.

———. 1998. "The Banana Enclave, Nationalism and Mestizaje in Honduras, 1910s–1930s." In *Identity and Struggle at the Margins of the Nation-State*, ed. Aviva Chomsky and Aldo Luaria-Santiago, 151–168. Durham, N.C.: Duke University Press.

———. 2004. "Negritud garifuna y coyunturas políticas en la costa norte hondurena, 1940–1970." In *Memorias del Mestizaje: Cultura política en Centroamerica de 1920 al Presente*, ed. Darío Euraque, Jeffery Gould, and Charles Hale, 295–324. Antigua Guatemala: Centro de Invertigaciones Regionales de Mesoamerica.

Featherstone, Mike. 1990. "Global Culture: An Introduction." In *Global Culture*, ed. Mike Featherstone, 1–14. London: Sage.

Fisher, Julie. 1993. *The Road from Rio*. Westport, Conn.: Praeger.

Fitzpatrick, Joseph P. 1971. *Puerto Rican Americans: The Meaning of Migration to the Mainland*. Englewood Cliffs, N.J.: Prentice Hall.

Floyd, Troy. 1967. *The Anglo-Spanish Struggle for Mosquitia*. Albuquerque: University of New Mexico Press.

Foner, Nancy. 1986. "Sex Roles and Sensibilities: Jamaican Women in New York and London." In *International Migration: The Female Experience*, ed. Rita Jane Simon and Caroline Brettell, 133–151. Totowa, N.J.: Rowman and Allanheld.

———, ed. 2001. *Islands in the City: West Indian Migration to New York*. Berkeley: University of California Press.

Franke, Richard, and Barbara Chasin. 1992. *Seeds of Famine: Ecological Destruction and the Development Dilemma in the West African Sahel*. Lanham, Md.: Rowman and Littlefield.

Frankenberg, Ruth, and Lata Mani. 1996. "Crosscurrents, Crosstalk: Race, 'Postcoloniality,' and the Politics of Location." In *Displacement, Diaspora, and Geographies of Identity*, ed. Smadar Lavie and Ted Swedenberg, 273–293. Durham, N.C.: Duke University Press.

Frantz, Douglas. 1999. "For Cruise Ships' Workers, Much Toil, Little Protection." *New York Times*, December 24, 1.

La Gaceta: Diario Oficial de la República de Honduras. 2002. Decreto No. 33–2002. December 24. Tegucigalpa.

Georges, Eugenia. 1990. *The Making of a Transnational Community: Migration, Develop-*

ment, and Cultural Change in the Dominican Republic. New York: Columbia University Press.

———. 1992. "Gender, Class, and Migration in the Dominican Republic: Women's Experiences in a Transnational Community." In *Towards a Transnational Perspective on Migration: Race, Class, Ethnicity, and Nationalism Reconsidered*, ed. Nina Glick Schiller, Linda Basch, and Cristina Blanc Szanton, 81–99. New York: New York Acadamy of Sciences.

Gilroy, Paul. 1993a. *The Black Atlantic: Modernity and Double Consciousness.* Cambridge, Mass.: Harvard University Press.

———. 1993b. *There Ain't No Black in the Union Jack: The Cultural Politics of Race and Nation.* Chicago: University of Chicago Press.

Glazer, Nathan, and Daniel Moynihan. 1963. *Beyond the Melting Pot.* Cambridge, Mass.: MIT Press.

Glick Schiller, Nina, and Georges Fouron. 2001. *Georges Woke Up Laughing: Long-Distance Nationalism and the Search for Home.* Durham, N.C.: Duke University Press.

Gmelch, George. 1980. "Return Migration." *Annual Review of Anthropology* 9: 135–159.

Goldring, Luin. 1998. "The Power of Status in Transnational Social Fields." In *Transnationalism from Below*, ed. Michael Peter Smith and Luis Guarnizo, 165–195. New Brunswick, N.J.: Transaction Publishers.

Gonzalez, Nancie. 1969. *Black Carib Household Structure: A Study of Modernization and Migration.* Seattle: University of Washington Press.

———. 1987. "Garifuna Settlement in New York: A New Fronteir." In *Caribbean Life in New York City: Sociocultural Dimensions*, ed. Constance Sutton and Elsa Chaney, 150–159. New York: Center for Migration Studies of New York.

———. 1988. *Sojourners of the Caribbean.* Urbana: University of Illinois Press.

———. 1992. *Dollar, Dove, and Eagle: One Hundred Years of Palestinian Migration to Honduras.* Ann Arbor: University of Michigan Press.

Gordon, Edmund T. 1998. *Disparate Diasporas: Identity and Politics in an Afro-Nicaraguan Community.* Austin: University of Texas Press.

Gordon, Edmund, and Juliet Hooker. 2004. "The State of Black Land Rights in Central America." Paper presented to the Latin American Studies Association, Las Vegas, Nevada, October 7–9.

Gould, Jeffrey. 1998. *To Die in this Way: Nicaraguan Indians and the Myth of Mestizaje, 1880–1965.* Durham, N.C.: Duke University Press.

Gramsci, Antonio. 1971. *The Prison Notebooks.* New York: International Publishers.

Grasmuck, Sherri, and Patricia Pessar. 1991. *Between Two Islands: Dominican International Migration.* Berkeley: University of California Press.

Grosfoguel, Ramon, and Chloe Georas. 1996. "The Racialization of Latino Caribbean Migrants in the New York Metropolitan Area." *Centro* 8 (nos. 1–2): 190–201.

Guarnizo, Luis. 1994. "Los Dominicanyorks: The Making of a Binational Society." *Annals of the American Academy of Political and Social Science* 533 (May): 70–86.

———. 1997. "'Going Home': Class, Gender, and Household Transformation among Dominican Returned Migrants." In *Caribbean Circuits: New Directions in the Study of Caribbean Migration*, ed. Patricia Pessar, 13–60. New York: Center for Migration Studies.

Guarnizo, Luis, and Michael Peter Smith. 1998. "The Locations of Transnationalism." In *Transnationalism from Below*, ed. Michael Peter Smith and Luis Guarnizo, 3–34. New Brunswick, N.J.: Transaction Publishers.

Guha, Ramachandra. 1989. *The Unquiet Woods: Ecological Change and Peasant Resistance in the Himalaya*. Oxford: Oxford University Press.

Gullick, C. J. M. R. 1976. *Exiled from St. Vincent*. Malta: Progress Press.

Gupta, Akhil, and James Ferguson. 1992. "Beyond 'Culture': Space, Identity, and the Politics of Difference." *Cultural Anthropology* 7 (no. 1): 6–23.

Hagan, Jacqueline Maria. 1994. *Deciding to be Legal: A Maya Community in Houston*. Philadelphia: Temple University Press.

Hale, Charles. 1994a. "Between Che Guevara and the Pachamama: Mestizos, Indians and Identity Politics in the Anti-Quincentenary Campaign." *Critique of Anthropology* 14 (no. 1): 9–39.

———. 1994b. *Resistance and Contradiction: Miskitu Indians and the Nicaraguan State, 1894–1987*. Stanford, Calif.: Stanford University Press.

Hall, Stuart. 1991a. "The Local and the Global: Globalization and Ethnicity." In *Culture, Globalization, and the World System*, ed. Anthony King, 19–39. London: McMillan.

———. 1991b. "Old and New Identities, Old and New Ethnicities." In *Culture, Globalization, and the World System*, ed. Anthony King, 41–38. London: McMillan.

Hamilton, N., and N. Stolz Chinchilla. 1991. "Central American Migration: A Framework for Analysis." *Latin American Research Review* 26 (no. 1): 75–110.

———. 2001. *Seeking Community in a Global City: Guatemalans and Salvadorans in Los Angeles*. Philadelphia: Temple University Press.

Hannerz, Ulf. 1996. *Transnational Connections: Culture, People, Places*. New York: Routledge.

Hecht, Susanna, and Alexander Cockburn. 1990. *The Fate of the Forest: Developers, Destroyers, and Defenders of the Amazon*. New York: Harper.

Helms, Mary. 1971. *Asang: Adaptations to Culture Contact in a Miskito Community*. Gainesville: University of Florida Press.

———. 1977. "Negro or Indian? The Changing Identity of a Frontier Population." In *Old Roots in New Lands: Historical and Anthropological Perspectives on Black Experiences in the Americas*, ed. Ann Pescatello. London: Greenwood Press.

———. 1981. "Black Carib Domestic Organization in Historical Perspective: Traditional Origins of Contemporary Patterns." *Ethnology* 20 (no. 1): 77–86.

Herlihy, Peter, and Andrew Leake. 1990. "The Twahka Sumu: A Delicate Balance in the Mosquitia." *Cultural Survival Quarterly* 14 (no. 4): 13–16.

Ho, Christine. 1993. "The Internationalization of Kinship and the Feminization of Caribbean Migration: The Case of Afro-Trinidadian Immigrants in Los Angeles." *Human Organization* 52 (no. 1): 32–40.

Hondagneu-Sotelo, Pierrette. 1994a. *Gendered Transitions: Mexican Experiences of Migration*. Berkeley: University of California Press.

———. 1994b. "Regulating the Unregulated? Domestic Workers' Social Networks." *Social Problems* 41 (no. 1): 50–64.

Hondagneu-Sotelo, Pierrette, and Ernestine Avila. 1997. "'I'm Here but I'm There': The Meanings of Latina Transnational Motherhood." *Gender and Society* 11 (no. 5), pp. 548-571.

Hooker, Juliet. 2005. "Indigenous Inclusion/Black Exclusion: Race, Ethnicity, and Multicultural Citizenship in Contemporary Latin America." *Journal of Latin American Studies* 37 (no. 2): 285–310.

Howe, James. 1998. *A People Who Would Not Kneel: Panama, the United States, and the San Blas Kuna*. Washington, D.C.: Smithsonian Institution.

Hulme, Peter. 1986. *Colonial Encounters: Europe and the Native Caribbean, 1492–1797*. London: Methuen.

Hulme, Peter, and Neil Whitehead, eds. 1992. *Wild Majesty: Encounters with Caribs from Columbus to the Present Day*. New York: Oxford University Press.

Instituto de Investigaciones Económicas y Sociales, Facultad de Ciencias Económicas. 1965. *Estudio Socio-Economico del Municipio de Limón*. Tegucigalpa: Universidad Nacional Autónoma de Honduras.

International Labour Organization. 1996. *International Labour Conventions and Recommendations, 1977–1995*. Geneva: International Labour Office.

Irish, George. 1997. "Revisiting the Garifuna Bicentennial." *Diaspora: A Global Black Magazine August* 18 (no. 5): 29–32.

Jameson, Frederic. 1984. "Postmodernism, or the Cultural Logic of Late Capital." *New Left Review* 146: 53–92.

Jeffrey, Paul. 1999. "Rhetoric and Reconstruction in Post-Mitch Honduras." *NACLA* 33 (no. 2).

John-Sandy, Rene. 1997. "The Garifuna Bicentennial Commemoration, 1797–1997." *Black Diaspora: A Global Black Magazine* 18 (no. 5): 26–28.

Kasinitz, Philip. 1992. *Caribbean New York: Black Immigrants and the Politics of Race*. Ithaca, N.Y.: Cornell University Press.

Kasinitz, Philip, and Judith Freidenberg-Herbstein. 1987. "The Puerto Rican Parade and West Indian Carnival: Public Celebrations in New York City." In *Caribbean Life in New York City: Sociocultural Dimensions*, ed. Constance Sutton and Elsa Chaney, 327–350. New York: Center for Migration Studies of New York.

Kearney, Michael. 1986. "From the Invisible Hand to Invisible Feet: Anthropological Studies of Migration and Development." *Annual Review of Anthropology* 15: 331–361.

———. 1996. *Reconceptualizing the Peasantry*. Boulder, Colo.: Westview Press.

Kearney, Michael, and Carole Nagengast. 1989. *Anthropological Perspectives on Transnational Communities in Rural California*. Davis: California Institute for Rural Studies, University of California.

——. 1990. "Mixtec Ethnicity: Social Identity, Political Consciousness, and Political Activism." *Latin American Research Review* 25 (no. 2), pp. 61-91.

Kearney, Michael, and James Stuart. 1981. *Causes and Effects of Agricultural Labor Migration from the Mixteca of Oaxaca to California*. San Diego: University of California, San Diego.

Kerns, Virginia. 1982. "Structural Continuity in the Division of Men's and Women's Work among the Black Carib (Garifuna)." In *Sex Roles and Social Change in Native Lowland Central America*, ed. C. Loveland and F. Loveland, 23–43. Chicago: University of Illinois Press.

——. 1983. *Women and the Ancestors: Black Carib Kinship and Ritual*. Urbana: University of Illinois Press.

Knight, Alan. 1990. "Racism, Revolution, and Indigenismo: 1910–1940." In *The Idea of Race in Latin America, 1870–1940*, ed. Richard Graham, 71–113. Austin: University of Texas Press.

Koptiuch, Kristin. 1997. "Third-Worlding at Home." In *Culture, Power, Place: Explorations in Critical Anthropology*, ed. Akhil Gupta and James Ferguson, 234–248. Durham, N.C.: Duke University Press.

Kraul, Chris. 2004. "El Salvador Comes to Grips with Gangs." *Los Angeles Times*, December 13, A1, A9.

Kraul, Chris, Robert Lopez, and Rich Connell. 2005. "LA Violence Crosses the Line." *Los Angeles Times*, May 15, A1, A28-A29.

Kyle, David. 2000. *Transnational Peasants: Migration, Networks, and Ethnicity in the Ecuadorian Andes*. Baltimore: John Hopkins University Press.

Lacayo Sambula, Gloria Marina. 1998. *Bosquejo de la Vida del Primer Medico Garifuna de Honduras Dr. Alfonso Lacayo Sanchez*. New York: Prometra Society.

Laguerre, Michel. 1984. *American Odyssey: Haitians in New York*. Ithaca, N.Y.: Cornell University Press.

Lang, Julio. 1951. "Espectro Racial de Honduras." *América Indígena* 11 (no. 3): 209–217.

Lapper, Richard, and James Painter. 1985. *Honduras: State for Sale*. London: Latin American Bureau.

Lash, Scott, and John Urry. 1987. "Postmodern Culture and Disorganized Capitalism: Some Conclusions." In *The End of Organized Capital*, ed. Lash and Urry, 285–314. Cambridge, Mass.: Polity Press.

Leiva Vivas, Rafael. 1982. *Tráfico de Esclavos Negros a Honduras*. Tegucigalpa: Editorial Guaymuras.

Levine, Barry, ed. 1987. *The Caribbean Exodus*. New York: Praeger.

Levitt, Peggy. 2001. *The Transnational Villagers*. Berkeley: University of California Press.

Lewis, Oscar. 1965. *La Vida: A Puerto Rican Family in the Culture of Poverty—San Juan and New York.* New York: Vintage Books.

Lopez Garcia, Victor Virgilio. 1993. *Lamumehan Garifuna: Clamor Garifuna.* Tornabe, Tela, Honduras.

———. 1994. *La Bahia del Puerto del Sol y la masacre de los Garifunas de San Juan.* Tegucigalpa: Editorial Guaymuras.

Macklin, Catherine. 1985. "Crucibles of Identity: Ritual and Symbolic Dimensions of Garifuna Ethnicity." Ph.D. diss., University of California, Berkeley.

MacLeod, Murdo. 1973. *Spanish Central America: A Socio-Economic History, 1520–1720.* Berkeley: University of California Press.

Magnuson, Ed. 1990. "The Devil Made Him Do It." *Time Magazine*, April 9.

Mahler, Sarah. 1995. *American Dreaming: Immigrant Life on the Margins.* Princeton, N.J.: Princeton University Press.

———. 1998. "Theoretical and Empirical Contributions toward a Research Agenda for Transnationalism." In *Transnationalism from Below*, ed. Michael Peter and Luis Guarnizo Smith, 64–100. New Brunswick, N.J.: Transaction Publishers.

———. 1999. "Engendering Transnational Migration: A Case Study of Salvadorans." *American Behavorial Scientist* 42 (no. 4): 690–719.

———. 2001. "Transnational Relationships: The Struggle to Communicate across Borders." *Identities* 7 (no. 4), 588–619.

Malkki, Lisa. 1992. "National Geographic: The Rooting of Peoples and the Territorialization of National Identities among Scholars and Exiles." *Cultural Anthropology* 7 (no. 1): 24–44.

Marcus, George. 1998. *Ethnography through Thick and Thin.* Princeton, N.J.: Princeton University Press.

Marks, Jonathon. 2002. *What It Means to be 98% Chimpanzee: Apes, People and Their Genes.* Berkeley: University of California Press.

Martinez-Alier, Verena. 1974. *Marriage, Class, and Colour in Nineteenth Century Cuba: A Study of Racial Attitudes and Sexual Values in a Slave Society.* Ann Arbor: University of Michigan Press.

Massey, Doreen. 1994. *Space, Place, and Gender.* Minneapolis: University of Minnesota Press.

Massey, Douglas, Rafael Alarcon, Jorge Durand, and Humberto Gonzalez. 1990. *Return to Atzlan: The Social Process of International Migration from Western Mexico.* Berkeley: University of California Press.

Mato, Daniel. 1996. "On the Theory, Epistimology, and Politics of Social Construction of 'Social Identities' in the Age of Globalization: Introductory Remarks to Ongoing Debates." *Identities* 3(nos. 1–2): 61–72.

McKinley, James. 1999. "Still Locked in Storm's Terror, Hondurans Are Fearful of Future." *New York Times*, January 17.

Merrill, Tim, ed. 1993. *Honduras: A Country Study*. Washington, D.C.: Federal Research Division, Library of Congress.

Miles, Anne. 2004. *From Cuenca to Queens: An Anthropological Story of Transnational Migration*. Austin: University of Texas Press.

Miller, Linda. 1993. "Bridges: Garifuna Migration to Los Angeles." Ph.D. diss., University of California, Irvine.

Miller Mathai, Linda, and David Smith. 1998. "Belizean 'Boyz 'n the Hood'? Garifuna Labor Migration and Transnational Identity." In *Transnationalism from Below*, ed. Michael Peter and Luis Guarnizo Smith, 270–290. New Brunswick, N.J.: Transaction Publishers.

Mines, Richard. 1981. *Developing a Community Tradition of Migration: A Field Study in Rural Zacatecas, Mexico, and California Settlement Areas*. Program in United States–Mexican Studies (conference book; monographs in U.S.-Mexican studies). University of California, San Diego.

Miralda, Danira. 1992. "Iseri Lidawamari (Nuevo Amanecer)." *Diario El Tiempo* (San Pedro Sula), July 12, 18.

Miyoshi, Masao. 1993. "A Borderless World: From Colonialism to Transnationalism and the Decline of the Nation-State." *Critical Inquiry* 19 (no. 4): 726–751.

Mollenkopf, John, and Manuel Castells, eds. 1991. *Dual City: Restructuring New York*. New York: Russell Sage Foundation.

Montagu, Ashley. 1964. *The Concept of Race*. London: Collier Books.

Murphy, Robert, and Yolanda Murphy. 1985. *Women of the Forest*. New York: Columbia University Press.

NACLA. 1999. "Central America After Mitch." *NACLA Report of the Americas* 33 (no. 2).

Nash, June. 1993. *We Eat the Mines, the Mines Eat Us: Dependency and Exploitation in Bolivian Tin Mines*. New York: Columbia University Press.

Nash, June, and Helen Safa. 1986. *Women and Change in Latin America*. South Hadley, Mass.: Bergin and Garvey.

Naylor, Robert. 1986. *Penny Ante Imperialism: The Mosquito Shore and the Bay of Honduras, 1600–1914*. London: Associated University Presses.

Nazario, Sonia. 2002. "Enrique's Journey." *Los Angeles Times*, October 1–6.

Nelson, Diane. 1999. *A Finger in the Wound: Body Politics in Quincentennial Guatemala*. Durham, N.C.: Duke University Press.

New York City Department of City Planning. 1992a. *The Newest New Yorkers: An Analysis of Immigration into New York City During the 1980s*. New York: Department of City Planning. June.

———. 1992b. *The Newest New Yorkers: A Statistical Portrait*. New York: Department of City Planning, August.

———. 1993. *Socioeconomic Profiles: A Portrait of New York City's Community Districts from the 1980 and 1990 Censuses of Population and Housing.* New York: Department of City Planning, March.

———. 1994/1995. *Community District Needs: The Bronx, Fiscal Year 1996.* New York: Office of Management and Budget, Department of City Planning.

———. 2000. *The Newest New Yorkers, 2000.* New York: Department of City Planning.

Newson, Linda. 1986. *The Cost of Conquest: Indian Decline in Honduras under Spanish Rule.* Boulder, Colo.: Westview Press.

Nietschmann, Bernard. 1973. *Between Land and Water: The Subsistence Ecology of the Miskitu Indians, Eastern Nicaragua.* New York: Seminar Press.

O'Connor, Anne-Marie. 1998. "American Threat to a Proud Heritage." *Los Angeles Times,* April 4.

Ojito, Mirta. 1998. "Change in Laws Sets off Big Wave of Deportations." *New York Times,* December 15, 1.

Olien, Michael. 1985. "E. G. Squier and the Miskito: Anthropological Scholarship and Political Propaganda." *Ethnohistory* 32 (no. 2): 111–133.

Omi, Michael, and Howard Winant. 1994. *Racial Formation in the United States: From the 1960s to the 1990s.* London: Routledge.

Ong, Ahiwa. 1996. "Citizenship as Subject Making: New Immigrants Negotiate Racial and Ethnic Boundaries." *Current Anthropology* 37 (no. 5): 737–762.

———. 1999. *Flexible Citizenship: The Cultural Logics of Transnationality.* Durham, N.C.: Duke University Press.

Orozco, Manuel. 2002. "Globalization and Migration: The Impact of Family Remittances in Latin America." *Latin American Politics and Society* 44 (no. 2): 41–66.

Otero, Luis Mariñas. 1963. *Honduras.* Tegucigalpa: Editorial Universitaria.

Palmer, Ransford, ed. 1990. *In Search of a Better Life: Perspectives on Migration from the Caribbean.* New York: Praeger.

Parreñas, Rachel. 2002. "The Care Crisis in the Philippines: Children and Transnational Families in the New Global Economy." In *Global Woman: Nannies, Maids, and Sex Workers in the New Economy,* ed. Barbara Ehrenreich and Arlie Russell Hochschild, 39–54. New York: Metropolitan Books.

Pastor Fasquelle, Rodolfo. 1997. "Ser Garifuna." *Diario El Tiempo* (San Pedro Sula), April 14, 10.

Patterson, Orlando. 1987. "The Emerging West Atlantic System: Migration, Culture, and Underdevelopment in the United States and the Circum-Caribbean Region." In *Population in an Interacting World,* ed. W. Alonso. Cambridge, Mass.: Harvard University Press.

Perry, Pamela. 1990. "Subordinate to No One." M.A. thesis, University of Texas, Austin.

Pessar, Patricia. 1994. "Sweatshop Workers and Domestic Ideologies: Dominican Women in New York's Apparel Industry." *International Journal of Urban and Regional Research* 18 (no. 1): 127–142.

------. 1999. "The Role of Gender, Households, and Social Networks in the Migration Process: A Review and Appraisal." In *Handbook of International Migration: The American Experience*, ed. C. Hirschman, P. Kasinitz, and J. DeWind, 53-57. New York City: Russell Sage Foundation.

Popkin, Eric. 1999. "Guatemalan Mayan Migration to Los Angeles: Constructing Transnational Linkages in the Context of the Settlement Process." *Ethnic and Racial Studies* 22 (no. 2): 267-289.

Portes, Alejandro. 1995. "Transnational Communities: Their Emergence and Significance in the Contemporary World System." Paper presented at the conference "Political Economy of the World System: Latin America in the World Economy," North-South Center at the University of Miami, April 21, 1995.

Portes, Alejandro, and Ruben Rumbaut. 1990. *Immigrant America: A Portrait.* Berkeley: University of California Press.

Posas, Mario. 1981a. *El Movimiento Campesino Hondureño.* Tegucigalpa: Editorial Guaymuras.

------. 1981b. "El 'Problema Negro': Racismo y Explotación en las Bananeras." *Alcaraván* 9: 6-9.

Posas, Mario, and Rafael del Cid. 1983. *La Construcción del Sector Público y del Estado Nacional en Honduras 1876-1979.* Ciudad Universitaria RodrigoFacio, Costa Rica: Editorial Universitaria Centroamericana.

La Prensa. 1996. "Garifunas invaden capital exigiendo tierras." October 12.

Purcell, Trevor. 1993. *Banana Fallout: Class, Culture, and Color among West Indians in Costa Rica.* Los Angeles: University of California Press.

Reichman, Daniel. 2004. "A Case Study of Honduran Emigration to the United States and its Significance to Theories of Social Class." Paper presented to the Latin American Studies Association, Las Vegas, Nevada, October 7-10.

Reimers, David. 1987. "New York City and Its People: An Historical Perspective up to World War II." In *Caribbean Life in New York City: Sociocultural Dimensions*, ed. Constance Sutton and Elsa Chaney, 31-53. New York: Center for Migration Studies of New York.

Repak, Terry. 1995. *Waiting on Washington: Central American Workers in the Nation's Capital.* Philadelphia: Temple University Press.

Replogle, Jill. 2004. "Hunger on the Rise in Central America." *The Lancet* 363 (June 19), pp. 2056-57.

Richardson, B. C. 1992. *The Caribbean in the Wider World, 1492-1992.* Cambridge, England: Cambridge University Press.

Rivas, Ramon. 1993. *Pueblos Indígenas y Garifuna de Honduras.* Tegucigalpa: Editorial Guaymuras.

Robinson, William. 1998. "(Mal)development in Central America: Globalization and Social Change." *Development and Change* vol. 29: 467-497.

Rodriguez, Clara. 2000. *Changing Race: Latinos, the Census, and the History of the Ethnicity in the United States*. New York: New York University Press.

Rogers, Mark. 1996. "Beyond Authenticity: Conservation, Tourism, and the Politics of Representation in the Ecuadorian Amazon." *Identities* 3 (nos. 1–2): 73–125.

Rouse, Roger. 1991. "Mexican Migration and the Social Space of Postmodernism. *Diaspora* vol. 1 issue 1: 8–23."

———. 1992. "Making Sense of Settlement: Class Transformation, Cultural Struggle, and Transnationalism among Mexican Migrants in the United States." In *Towards a Transnational Perspective on Migration: Race, Class, Ethnicity, and Nationalism Reconsidered*, ed. Nina Glick Schiller, Linda Basch and Cristina Blanc Szanton, 25–52. New York: New York Academy of Sciences.

———. 1995. "Thinking through Transnationalism: Notes of the Cultural Politics of Class Relations in the Contemporary United States." *Public Culture* 7: 353–402.

Rubenstein, Hymie. 1983. "Remittances and Rural Underdevelopment in the English-Speaking Caribbean." *Human Organization* 42 (no. 4): 295–306.

Russell, Grahame. 1999. "Hurricane Mitch and Human Rights." Development in Practice 9 (no. 3): 322–325.

Sanderson, Steven. 1985 "The 'New' Internationalization of Agriculture in the Americas." In *The Americas in the New International Division of Labor*, ed. Steven Sanderson, 46–68. New York: Holmes and Meier.

Sassen, Saskia. 1994. *Cities in a World Economy*. London: Pine Forge Press.

Sassen-Koob, Saskia. 1984. "Notes on the Incorporation of Third World Women into Wage-Labor Through Immigration and Off-Shore Production." *International Migration Review* 28 (no. 4): 1144–1167.

———. 1985. "Capital Mobility and Labor Migration." In *The Americas in the New International Division of Labor*, ed. Steven Sanderson, 226–252. New York: Holmes and Meier.

Sawyer, Suzana. 2004. *Crude Chronicles: Indigenous Politics, Multinational Oil, and Neoliberalism in Ecuador*. Durham, N.C.: Duke University Press.

Selverston-Scher, Melina. 2001. *Ethnopolitics in Ecuador: Indigenous Rights and the Stengthening of Democracy*. Coral Gables: University of Miami North-South Center Press.

Silverblatt, Irene. 1987. *Moon, Sun, and Witches: Gender Ideologies and Class in Inca and Colonial Peru*. Princeton, N.J.: Princeton University Press.

Skidmore, Thomas. 1995 *Black into White: Race and Nationality in Brazilian Thought*. Durham, N.C.: Duke University Press.

Sklair, Leslie. 1995. *Sociology of the Global System*. Baltimore: John Hopkins University Press.

Smedley, Audrey. 1999. *Race in North America: Origin and Evolution of a Worldview*. Boulder, Colo.: Westview Press.

Smith, Anthony. 1986. "State-Making and Nation-Building." In *States in History*, ed. John Hall, 228–263. New York: Basil Blackwell.

Smith, Carol, ed. 1990. *Guatemalan Indians and the State: 1540–1988*. Austin: University of Texas Press.

———. 1995. "Race/Class/Gender Ideology in Guatemala: Modern and Anti-Modern Forms." *Comparative Studies in Society and History* vol. 37 issue 4: 723–749.

———. 1997. "The Symbolics of Blood: Mestizaje in the Americas." *Identities* vol. 3 issue 4: 483–509.

———. 1999. "Racismo en el análisis socio-histórico sobre Guatemala: una crítica ge-neológica." In *Identidades y Racismo en Guatemala? Abriendo el debate sobre un tema tabu*, ed. Clara Arenas Gustavo Palma and Charles Hale. Guatemala City, Guatemala: Facultad Latinoamericana de Ciencias Sociales.

Smith, Robert. 1998a. "Closing the Doors on Undocumented Workers." *NACLA* 31 (no. 4).

———. 1998b. "Transnational Localities: Community, Technology and the Politics of Membership within the Context of Mexico and U.S. Migration." In *Transnationalism from Below*, ed. Michael Peter and Luis Guarnizo Smith, 196–240. New Brunswick, N.J.: Transaction Publishers.

———. 2005. *Mexican New York: Transnational Lives of New Immigrants*. Berkeley: University of California Press.

Smith, Raymond T. 1973. "The Matrifocal Family." In *The Character of Kinship*, ed. Jack Goody, 121–144. Cambridge, England: Cambridge University Press.

Socolow, Susan Migden. 2000. *The Women of Colonial Latin America*. Cambridge, England: Cambridge University Press.

Soysal, Yasemin Nuhoglu. 1994. *Limits of Citizenship: Migrants and Postnational Membership in Europe*. Chicago: University of Chicago Press.

Squier, E. G. 1870/1970. *Honduras: Descriptive, Historical, Statistical*. New York: AMS Press.

Stack, Carol. 1974. *All Our Kin: Strategies for Survival in a Black Community*. New York: Harper Colophon.

Stavenhagen, Rodolfo. 1992. "Challenging the Nation-State in Latin America." *Journal of International Affairs* 45 (no. 2): 421–440.

Steiner Bendeck, Ricardo. 1993. Farallones, el ocaso de un parque nacional potencial. *Diario El Tiempo* (San Pedro Sula), July 15,.

Stephen, Lynn. 1991. *Zapotec Women*. Austin: University of Texas Press.

Stepick, Alex. 1993. "A Repeat Performance? The Nicaraguan Exodus." In *City on the Edge: The Transformation of Miami*, ed. Alejandro Portes and Alex Stepick. Berkeley: University of California Press.

Stiefel, Mathias, and Marshall Wolfe. 1994. *A Voice for the Excluded*. London and Atlantic Highlands, N.J.: Zed Books.

Stolcke, Verena. 1991. "Conquered Women." *NACLA* 24 (no. 5) pp. 23-9.

Stonich, Susan. 1993. *"I Am Destroying the Land!" The Political Ecology of Poverty and Environmental Destruction in Honduras.* Boulder, Colo.: Westview Press.

Suazo, Salvador. 1994. *Conversemos en Garifuna: Gramática y manuel de conversación.* Tegucigalpa: Editorial Guaymuras.

———. 1996. *La Sociedad Garifuna: Un vistazo sobre el estilo de vida garifuna.* Tegucigalpa: Centro de Desarrollo Comunitario.

Sutton, Constance, and Elsa Chaney. 1987. *Caribbean Life in New York City: Sociocultural Dimensions.* New York: Center for Migration Studies of New York.

Sutton, Constance, and Susan Makiesky-Barrow. 1987. "Migration and West Indian Racial and Ethnic Consciousness." In *Caribbean Life in New York City: Sociocultural Dimensions*, ed. Constance Sutton and Elsa Chaney, 92–116. New York: Center for Migration Studies of New York.

Taussig, Michael. 1980. *The Devil and Commodity Fetishism in South America.* Chapel Hill: University of North Carolina Press.

Taylor, D. M. 1951. *The Black Carib of British Honduras.* New York: Viking Fund Publications in Anthropology.

Telles, Edward. 2004. *Race in Another America: The Significance of Skin Color in Brazil.* Princeton, N.J.: Princeton University Press.

Thompson, Ginger. 1999. "Storm Victims Surge North, with U.S. as Goal." *New York Times*, January 18, 1.

Tsuda, Takeyuki. 2003. *Strangers in the Ethnic Homeland: Japanese-Brazilian Return Migration in Transnational Perspective.* New York: Columbia University Press.

"U.S. Citizen and Immigration Services Fact Sheet. Illegal Immigration and Immigrant Reform and Immigrant Responsibility Act of 1996." <http:uscis.gov/graphics/publicaffairs/factsheets/948.html>. U.S. Department of Justice, Immigration, and Naturalization Service, Washington, D.C.

Van Sertima, Ivan. 1976. *They Came Before Columbus: The African-American Presence in Ancient America.* New York: Random House.

Vanwey, Leah, Catherine Tucker, and Eileen Diaz McConnell. 2005. "Community Organization, Migration, and Remittances in Oaxaca." *Latin American Research Review* 40 (no. 1): 83–107.

Varese, Stefano. 1994. "Globalización de la Política Indígena en Latinoamerica." *Cuadernos Agrários* 4 (no. 10): 9–23.

Vickerman, Milton. 1999. *Crosscurrents: West Indian Immigrants and Race.* New York: Oxford University Press.

Villanueva, Eduardo. 1996. Interview by Sarah England. October 14. Tegucigalpa.

"Voz del Frente." 1978. *Voz Garifuna: Boletin Informativaa del Frente Limoreño*, vol. 2 (Garifuna pamphlet). September–October. New York.

Wade, Peter. 1993. *Blackness and Race Mixture: The Dynamics of Racial Identity in Colombia.* Baltimore: John Hopkins University Press.

———. 1995. "The Cultural Politics of Blackness in Colombia." *American Ethnologist* 22 (no. 2): 341–357.

Waldinger, Roger, and Mehdi Bozorgmehr, eds. 1996. *Ethnic Los Angeles*. New York: Russell Sage Foundation.

Warren, Jonathon. 2001. *Racial Revolutions: Antiracism and Indian Resurgence in Brazil*. Durham, N.C.: Duke University Press.

Warren, Kay. 1998. *Indigenous Movements and Their Critics: Pan-Maya Activism in Guatemala*. Princeton, N.J.: Princeton University Press.

Waters, Mary. 1999. *Black Identities: West Indian Immigrant Dreams and American Realities*. New York: Russell Sage Foundation.

Watkins-Owens, Irma. 2001. "Early 20th Century Caribbean Women: Migration and Social Networks in New York City." In *Islands in the City: West Indian Migration to New York*, ed. Nancy Foner. Berkeley: University of California Press.

Watson, James L., ed. 1977. *Between Two Cultures: Migrants and Minorities in Britain*. Oxford: Basil Blackwell.

Watts, Michael. 1992a. "Capitalism, Crisis, and Culture: Notes Towards a Totality of Fragments." In *Reworking Modernity: Capitalisms and Symbolic Discontent*, ed. Allan Pred and Michael Watts, 1–19. New Brunswick, N.J.: Rutgers University Press.

———. 1992b. "The Shock of Modernity: Petroleum, Protest, and Fast Capitalism in an Industrializing Society." In *Reworking Modernity: Capitalisms and Symbolic Discontent*, ed. Allan Pred and Michael Watts, 21–63. New Brunswick, N.J.: Rutgers University Press.

Weismantel, Mary. 2001. *Cholas and Pishtacos: Stories of Race and Sex in the Andes*. Chicago: University of Chicago Press.

Wellmeier, Nancy. 1998. *Ritual, Identity, and the Mayan Diaspora*. New York: Garland.

Whitten, Norman, and Arlene Torres, eds. 1998. *Blackness in Latin America and the Caribbean*. Bloomington: Indiana University Press.

Wilk, Richard. 1990. "Consumer Goods as Dialogue about Development." *Culture and History* 7: 79–100.

———. 1995. "Learning to be Local in Belize: Global Systems of Common Difference." In *Worlds Apart: Modernity through the Prism of the Local*, ed. Daniel Miller, 110–133. London: Routledge.

Williams, Brackette. 1989. "A Class Act: Anthropology and the Race to Nation across Ethnic Terrain." *Annual Reviews in Anthropology* vol. 8: 401–44.

———. 1991. *Stains on my Name, War in my Veins: Guyana and the Politics of Cultural Struggle*. Durham, N.C.: Duke University Press.

Williams, Robert. 1986. *Export Agriculture and the Crisis in Central America*. Chapel Hill: University of North Carolina Press.

Willis, Eliza, Christopher da C. B. Garman, and Stephan Haggard. 1999. "The Politics of Decentralization in Latin America." *Latin American Research Review* 34 (no. 1): 7–56.

Wilson, Samuel. 1993. "The Cultural Mosaic of the Prehistoric Caribbean." *The Meeting of Two Worlds: Europe and the Americas 1492–1650*. Warwizle Bray, ed. *Proceedings of the British Academy* 81: 37–66.

———. 1997. "Surviving European Conquest in the Caribbean." *Revista de Arqueología Americana* 12 Jan.–June.

Wilson, William Julius. 1996. *When Work Disappears: The World of the Urban Poor*. New York: Vintage Books.

Winndance-Twine, France. 2000. *Racism in a Racial Democracy: The Maintenance of White Supremacy in Brazil*. New Brunswick, N.J.: Rutgers University Press.

Wright, Pamela. 1995. "The Timely Significance of Supernatural Mothers or Exemplary Daughters: The Metonymy of Identity in History." In *Articulating Hidden Histories: Exploring the Influence of Eric R. Wolf*, ed. Jane Schneider and Rayna Rapp, 243–261. Berkeley: University of California Press.

Yearbook of Immigration Statistics: 2004. Table 3, "Immigrants Admitted by Region and Country of Birth: Fiscal Years 1989–2004." <uscis.gov/shared/statistics/yearbook/2004/table3.xls>. Office of Immigration Statistics, U.S. Department of Homeland Security, Washington, D.C.

Yearbook of Immigration Statistics: 2004. Table 36, "Deportable Aliens Located by Region and Country of Nationality: Fiscal Year 2004." <uscis.gov/graphics/shared/statistics/YrBk04En.htm>. Office of Immigration Statistics, U.S. Department of Homeland Security, Washington, D.C.

Young, Thomas. 1847. *Narrative of a Residence on the Mosquito Shore*. London: Smith, Elder.

Index

Page numbers in italics refer to figures.

gies of, 70, 73; matrifocality principle and, 71–73

Georges, Eugenia, 73

Gilroy, Paul, 225

Glick Schiller, Nina, 4, 185

Globalization, 220–24

Gonzalez, Nancie, 46, 69, 71; female networks and, 92; household types of, 73–74; polygyny studies by, 72

Gordon, Edmund, 203

Government, Honduras: decentralization of, 178; discrimination by, 4–5, 108–10, 135–36, 227–29

Government, United States: assistance programs by, 129, 134–36; immigration reform by, 50–51, 56–59, 64

Grassroots organizations. *See* Social movement(s)

Great Britain: Caribbean colonization by, 34–37; Central American colonization by, 38–39; Garifuna characterization by, 35–37, 41–42; Garifuna exile by, 1, 36–37

Guerrero, Bernardo, 22

Hale, Charles, 183

Happy Land tragedy, 205, 217

Harlem, New York, 60; ethnic composition of, 51, *52*; Garifuna migration to, 51–53; Garifuna neighborhood in, *62*; socioeconomic conditions of, 125–27, *126*

Helms, Mary, 41

Hervasio (case study), 61

Hometown associations, 153–56

Honduras: caste system within, 15–16; class mobility in, 131–46; discrimination within, 4–5, 26, 42–43, 108–10, 135–36, 141, 173–74, 227–29; economic development in, 23, 25, 31–33, 45–46, 48–49, 63–64, 89–92, 103, 107–20, 122, 150–86, 197–99, 201, 229–35, 242n5; education in, 135; ethnography on, 19–24; Garifuna decrees by, 227–28, 230–31; Garifuna population in, 13, 237n3; Garifuna social movements in, 5–6, 8–9, 23–24, 153, 156–66; hurricane's influence on, 57–58, 117, 229, 232; ladino

population in, 14, 194; land ownership in, 48–49, 110–12, 115–16; mestizo promotion by, 191–95; national identity of, 4, 7–8, 191–204; New York City migration from, 44, 49–56; racial/ethnic history of, 13–19. *See also* Class mobility; Discrimination; Economic development, Honduras; Identity, Garifuna; Limón, Honduras; Social movement(s)

Hooker, Juliet, 203, 227

Household case studies, 78; local and transnational affinal, 79–80; matrifocal extended kin network, 83–85; New York City affinal, 81–82; transnational affinal, 80–81; transnational female serial monogamy, 82–83; transnational polygyny, 85–87

Households, Garifuna: case studies on, 78–87; Limón, 73–76, *74, 75*, 78–87; New York City, 76–87; organization of, 69–76; socioeconomic standings of, 74–75; transnational, 78–87, *79*; types of, 73–87, *74, 75*

Hulme, Peter, 35

Hurricane: Fifi, 135–36; Mitch, 57–58, 105, 117, 229, 232

IDB. *See* Interamerican Development Bank

Identity, Garifuna: activism influenced by, 7–10, 20–21, 24, 187–92, 196–205, 216–26; African diaspora and, 206–7, 211, 214–15, 225; Afro-American identity v., 207–9; afro-indigenous contradictions and, 191–204; autocthony and, 196–204; Bicentennial celebration and, 188–91; black, 191–217; class, 7–9, 146–48, 151–52; cultural bifocality and, 7, 24, 188–91; cultural citizenship and, 207; ethnic, 7–9, 11, 12, 50–51, 196–204; extended community, 216; Garifuna diaspora and, 188–91, 218–22; gender, 7–9, 89–92, 144–45; globalization's influence on, 223–24; Hispanic identity v., 205, 209–12; Honduran identity v., 216–17; in Honduras, 191–204; ILO Convention 169's tie to, 197–201, 203; indigenismo, 191–204, 225–26; mestizaje, 191–96; national, 4, 7–8, 191–204; racial, 7–9,

Sponsorship, migration, 49, 53; case study reflecting, 60–63; requirements for legal, 64–65, 86, 101

Squier, E. G., 109

Standard Fruit Company, 42, 44

Stiefel, Mathias, 184

Stonich, Susan, 107

Sustainable development: agrarian sector, 159–62, 166, 184–86; NGO models of, 184–86, 242n5; transnational organizations' tie to, 159–62, 166

Tamo (case study), 81, 87

Tawaka people, 15

El Tiempo, 171, 191

Tino (case study), 139–40

Tolupanes people, 15

Tomás (case study), 79–80, 87

TORNASAL, 174

Transnationalism: aspects of, 4; household case studies regarding, 78–87, *79*; matrifocality's tie to, 68–69, 78–92; movement of, 6–10; socioeconomic status and, 89–92. *See also* Household case studies; Matrifocality principle

Transnational organization(s): African diaspora association with, 202; autonomy's relation to, 176–83; Comité de Damas, 97, 154–55; Comité Pro–Agua Potable, 149–50, 154–55; Comité Pro-Electrificación, 150, 152, 155, 165, 169, 181–82, 186; Consejo de Maestros, 153, 180–81; economic development through, 153–66; Frente Social Limoneño, 97, 154–55; funding for, 161; Garifuna diaspora and, 187; history of, 153–66; hometown associations as, 153–56; Iseri Lidawamari, 20–24, 141–42, 150, 152, 156–57, *163*, 163–66, 171–74, 176–81, 183, 185–86, 227, 231–32, 234; La Nueva Juventud Limoneña, 153; La Organización Fraternal Negra Hondureña, 23, 25, 161; Patronato Pro–Mejoramiento de Limón, 153; remittance criticisms and, 166–76; soccer clubs as, 154–55, 156; structure of, 216;

sustainable development through, 159–62, 166; Unificación Limoneña, 155. *See also* Economic development, Honduras; Remittances; *specific organizations*

Treaty of Paris, 36

Truxillo Railroad Company, 102

Unificación Cultural Garifuna (UNCUGA), 204–5, 208

Unificación Limoneña, 155

United Fruit Company, 57, 115; ladino migration for, 22; operation reduction by, 44, 60; preferred labor of, 42

United Nations, 178, 216; Garifuna Nation and, 219; Honduran representative to, 217; indigenous rights and, 205; rights seminars by, 23; social justice and, 159; sustainable development and, 164, 177

United Nations Research Institute for Social Development (UNRISD), 159–60

United States (U.S.): class mobility in, 124–46; discrimination in, 141–42, 146; ethnicity of, 50–51, 206–7; ethnography based in, 24–27; Garifuna activism within, 8, 24–25, 97, 149–56, 165, 169, 179, 181–82, 186, 216; Garifuna identity within, 204–17; Garifuna migration to, 44–47, 49–59; Garifuna racial landscapes in, 13, 18–19; immigration reform in, 50–51, 56–59; imperialism of, 108–9. *See also* Class mobility; Identity, Garifuna; Migration, Garifuna; Transnational organization(s)

Universal Declaration of Human Rights, 180, 230

Universidad Nacional Autónoma de Honduras, 153

Univision, 10, 150

UNRISD. *See* United Nations Research Institute for Social Development

U.S. *See* United States

Vallecito, Honduras, 157, 162, 178–79, 187

Vamos a La Peña del Bronx, 210; Garifuna men at, *210*

Sarah England is associate professor of anthropology at Soka University of America in Aliso Viejo, California.

Printed in the USA
CPSIA information can be obtained
at www.ICGtesting.com
CBHW020450170924
14433CB00003B/4